LESSONS IN EVIL

LESSONS FROM THE LIGHT

LESSONS IN EVIL

LESSONS FROM THE LIGHT

A True Story of Satanic Abuse and Spiritual Healing

GAIL CARR FELDMAN, PH.D.

Foreword and Afterword by Carl Raschke, Ph.D.

CROWN PUBLISHERS, INC. NEW YORK

Published by Crown Publishers, Inc., 201 East 50th Street, New York, New York 10022.
Member of the Crown Publishing Group.
Random House, Inc. New York, Toronto, London, Sydney, Auckland

CROWN is a trademark of Crown Publishers, Inc.

Manufactured in the United States of America

Book design by June Bennett-Tantillo

Library of Congress Cataloging-in-Publication Data
Feldman, Gail Carr.
Lessons from hell, lessons from the light : a true story of satanic abuse and spiritual healing / by Gail Carr Feldman.
— 1st ed.
p.   cm.
1. Satanism—Case studies.   2. Psychotherapy—Case studies.
3. Spiritual healing—Case studies.   4. Maddox, Barbara.
5. Feldman, Gail Carr.   I. Title.
BF1548.F45   1992
616.85'8—dc20   92–15466
CIP

ISBN 0-517-58877-3

10 9 8 7 6 5 4 3 2 1

First Edition

For all of the Barbaras of the world,
who suffer torture and find the strength
to do the work of healing.

C O N T E N T S

Note: All names and identifying information have been changed except for the author's name and the names of most professionals. Transcripts from hypnosis sessions are verbatim.

F O R E W O R D

BY CARL RASCHKE, Ph.D.,
PROFESSOR OF RELIGIOUS STUDIES,
UNIVERSITY OF DENVER

Gail Feldman's book is a straightforward retelling of how a young black woman named Barbara slowly remembers frightening incidents from her past that disclose a phenomenon that is the center of much current concern and controversy—satanic ritual abuse.

Her story is not all that different from narratives provided by many other so-called "survivors" of such abuse. There is the random, and seemingly gratuitous, sexual torture of a young girl in training to become a satanic "princess." There are disturbing flashbacks of bloody corpses and a dead baby. There are ceremonial invocations to the mysterious "power of darkness."

The pattern is familiar both to many psychological professionals and to those scholars of religion who have begun to grope their way through the dank, dimly lit labyrinth of archaic occultism. It is not some "hysterical" fantasy of horror insinuated into the subconscious of gullible and suggestible patients by devious therapists, as a growing number of shrill critics have contended.

The memories may not be focused; the precise details may be fogged at times by emotions associated with severe trauma. Yet what is known from other sources about the occult in general frequently buttresses the survivors' reports.

Although there is no way any academic inquiry can either validate or deny the specific circumstances of a case reconstructed by means of hypnotic regression, Barbara's story is at minimum possible, and at most plausible, for a number of key reasons.

First, the usual caricature of crimson-hooded, glassy-eyed cultists assembled on Halloween night before a smoky altar is absent from Feldman's account. If patients, as some scoffers have asserted, are merely providing subcortical reruns of books they have read or movies they have watched on television, one would expert Barbara's story to resemble an old Alfred Hitchcock or *Twilight Zone* thriller. Many of the more grotesque and notorious survivor histories have exactly this air to them. Barbara's does not.

Second, the painstaking clinical process through which Barbara's memories emerge is recorded with extreme vigilance and care, so that the reader can easily see that the present, fashionable accusation that survivors are simply telling tales in order to "please the therapist" has no grounding.

Third, the survivor herself, at the first inkling of the memories, reacts with skepticism—a trait not necessarily found among "dissociative" patients who would be simply confabulating about what went on previous times of their lives.

Fourth, the survivor recalls real places that are identifiable. That Feldman herself is a highly respected hypnotherapist who understands both the potentialities, and the limitations, of her art leaves far less doubt in the reader's mind about winnowing out what is fact from what is fiction.

But survivor stories, like single witness testimony in a courtroom, are not sufficient in themselves to build a case for or against the practice of "satanism." Whereas much of the present-day debate over the credibility of the survivors has focused on the reliability of hypnotic techniques and relatively flimsy hypotheses about unconscious "transference" between therapist and client, scant energy has been expended in the direction of correlating first-person observations with what has been known for generations and studied by anthropologists about so-called "blood cults," let alone the actual history of satanism. Even though these sorts of correlations are insufficient to "prove" any particular survivor's contentions, they do raise the confidence level of some accounts from "highly dubious" to "rather cogent."

What are some of the more telling linkages between the incidents in Barbara's saga and the body of interdisciplinary knowledge concerning the occult? One clue may lie in Barbara's recall of a goat-headed figure, the sign of the "Baphomet" associated with the ministrations of a certain Aleister Crowley.

In an essay entitled "De Lege Lebellum" the modern English spiritual showman and "satanist" Aleister Crowley (1875–1947), who called himself "The Beast 666" and was in turn designated by some of his contemporaries as "the wickedest man in the world," wrote:

> There be . . . many other modes of attaining the apprehension of true Life, and these two are of much value in breaking up the ice of your mortal error in the vision of

your being. And of these the first is the constant contemplation of the Identity of Love and Death, and the understanding of the dissolution of the body as an Act of Love done upon the Body of the Universe. . . .

Crowley has often been called the father of contemporary satanism, although his voluminous writings have inspired numerous fashions and forms of mystical and occult experimentation that run the gamut from *wicca,* or "white witchcraft," to certain strands of what is today called the New Age movement.

Whether Crowley himself was a "satanist" depends on the technical meaning of the word. Yet the long shadow he casts over the religious underworld of the twentieth century can be traced to his singular and strange view of reality, which as the "St. Paul" of contemporary occultism he strewed and seeded in secret communities throughout the Western world. As the self-declared "Great Beast," which Christian theology identifies with the satanic ruler of the endtimes, Crowley pronounced varying versions of a basic message intimated through the foregoing quotation.

The message, which has leaked out for decades into the public consciousness through Crowley's copious essays and hundreds of thousands of copies of his writings sold in so-called "occult" or "metaphysical" bookstores, breaks down as follows:

- There is no "god" but oneself, which magically wills all worlds and circumstances into existence. There is no "divine law" to restrain the will, which Crowley identified by the Greek word *thelema.* "Do what thou wilt shall be the whole of the law" was his motto.
- "Love is the law," Crowley proclaimed repeatedly. Crowley's "magick" was sexual magic, derived from a very ancient set of traditions and practices invented in India and

known as tantrism. Crowley thought that sexual energy and erotic love constituted the great unifying force of the entire cosmos. Spiritual liberation consisted of carnal union "in rapture with each and everything that is . . . [by] overstepping even the limiting laws of sex and species in their necessity to transcend normality."

■ The law of "union" through love, for Crowley, also meant the annihilation of the individual self and the overcoming of all opposites in the mind, including the distinction between desire and morality, between good and evil. Behavior unchained from what Crowley termed "base law"—religious doctrine such as the Ten Commandments, the ideals of civilization, the everyday rules of society—would lead to a kind of ultimate knowledge the average Christian in his or her superstitious fear of the Biblical Deity could never comprehend. Crowley indeed saw this kind of knowledge, which he called "gnostic" after the Greek term for "illuminated vision" (i.e., *gnosis*), as both a spiritual and a fleshly ecstasy. According to Crowley himself, the greatest ecstasy would be to die at the moment of orgasm. Crowley called this particular delight "eroto-comatose lucidity" and termed it "the most favorable death."

Crowley, however, was neither a sociopathic madman, as his Christian critics have tended to regard him, nor a master of true wisdom, as his growing number of occult devotees and admirers are used to characterizing him. In violent rebellion all his life against what he considered a sexually repressive, mean-spirited, and hypocritical Christian culture, he posed as a prophet of a new world society. Crowley scarcely "thought up" the religious ideas and practices of what he baptized "the new aeon," in which Christian morality would be trampled underfoot by the very dark, antediluvian gods who "spoke" to him on different occasions during his lifetime.

Crowley himself was a brilliant popularizer of religious

forms that had previously been kept concealed throughout the ages—ceremonies, symbols, and activities that were, and still are for the most part, regarded as bloody, brutal, and barbaric. Crowley's own fascination with blood and semen was notorious, and it was through the joining of the "bloody sacrifice" with the violent "life force" of human sexuality, he believed, that the world would be changed—dramatically!

There is much expert dispute nowadays over whether Crowley advocated, or actually practiced as part of his religious life-style, what we would call "ritual abuse." Crowley's ardent defenders, who routinely blame such charges on "Christian" bigotry and propaganda, demand that different passages in his works that seem to refer to the injury, or even death, of children as "metaphoric" or "symbolic." For example, one citation in his *Magick in Theory and Practice* that appears to prescribe taking the life of a child, his defenders argue, in fact signifies the killing of sperm.

Furthermore, certain groups that consider themselves the official torch-bearers of Crowley's legacy not only deny he encouraged or condoned child abuse, they claim not even to be satanists.

There is one theory, of course, that Crowley's apologists overlook. First, Crowley envisaged the quest of the genuine spiritual initiate as one of learning to experience, and at long last to tame, all the primal pleasures and horrors of human life. Second, he wandered all over the globe to discover and test the most exotic, sometimes violent, enduring examples of magical and earth-based religiosity. Third, it is typical for religious "reformers," even if they be as perverse in a relative sense as Crowley, to take what is common and crude and give it a new "spiritual" interpretation.

The problem, however, is that their adepts and imitators—and Crowley, it should be noted, has had too many of the latter even to estimate—rarely can distinguish the literal from the allegorical. Even if Crowley, not to mention certain contemporary satanists, had meant primarily to shock rather than to incite with their grisly, entrails-on-the-rocks rhetoric, the truth behind their "figures of speech" is quite authentic.

Satanic ritual abuse, or "SAR" as some psychologists have begun to call it, is not a new phenomenon. It is merely a making manifest, or "coming out of the closet," of what has been lurking behind the curtains for centuries. The history of satanism in the modern world, which I have outlined in my own book *Painted Black*, is too complex to outline in these few pages. Crowley made it respectable and seductive to many twentieth-century persons at the margins of society who, since the First World War especially, have felt a deep and unrelenting rage against the terrors and sufferings of the age, which they blame on two thousand years of Christianity and faith in its God.

But the "genteel satanism" that Crowley spread about was only borrowed from, and accredited by, those who were already within families with genealogies spanning centuries bent on "attaining the apprehension of true Life" by rituals that made painfully obvious to the participant "the Identity of Love and Death." The curious recollections of those rituals, which follow the logic of occult practices in general, comprise what has come to be recognized as ritual abuse.

In many respects, however, the current controversy over whether there truly is such a thing as violent, "ritual," or "satanic" abuse of children—which may or may not include deliberately exposing the young victim to scenes of gory mayhem as well as constant sexual molestation and torture—is misplaced. The large majority of constant naysayers, whom the eminent forensic psychologist George Greaves has termed "nihilists," tend either to be professional hacks, ideological zealots, or academic opportunists distinguished chiefly by their gross ignorance of the history and anthropology of religions.

The patterns of belief and behavior documented in many

ritual abuse cases correspond on the whole to well-known specimens of sanguinary initiation rites observed both by leaders of the early Christian Church, and their pagan and Jewish predecessors.

Child sacrifice was so common in ancient Middle Eastern society that it was routinely condemned by the Biblical writers as an "abomination." The Phoenicians even worshipped a terrifying deity named Moloch, who required the slaughter of countless infants. Ceremonial mutilation, including self-castration, was practiced by the priests of the ancient Anatolian mother goddess Cybele. And Roman soldiers routinely became members of an extremely secretive, reputedly violent, exclusively masculine cult called Mithraism, for which inductees were placed naked in a pit before being inundated with a gusher of blood from a live bull that had just been slain on a platform above. Tourists today can visit a reconstructed ceremonial chamber for this Mithraic rite at an archaeological park just outside the German city of Frankfurt.

From the religious vantage point, the prime function of so-called "ritual abuse" is to indoctrinate the child with the idea that rebellion or flight is exceptionally dangerous, as well as futile, and that the only thing he or she can count upon is the violence of the group—or in Barbara's case, the "clan"—itself.

The same psychology, of course, has welded criminal brotherhoods such as the Cosa Nostra together for centuries, and it is not surprising that many families of so-called "generational satanists" also are reported to be "crime families" as well. Several years ago the FBI actually recorded and played back for a jury a Mafia initiation ceremony, which bears striking similarities with what survivors of "satanist" families have recalled.

The basic law of criminal brotherhoods is "blood in, blood out." The initiate is pricked or injured so that his or her blood merges with the generational "blood" of the family, or clan. The mingling of blood in this sense was recalled by Barbara. At the same time, the initiate is made to understand that any betrayal of the interests or secrets of the group will result in a fearful, and vengeful, death.

Young women are often sexually abused as part of the "cult pedagogy" in order to bond them inexorably to the inner circle of the family and to frighten them away from any love for, or emotional attachment to, outsiders. The common practice of incest between father and daughter, brother and sister, or uncle and niece, is intended to foster an identification at a very tender age between sexuality and absolute family loyalty. As a type of religious "brainwashing," ritual abuse is both calculated and designed to keep the family, and its unspeakable confidences, intact over lengthy time periods.

Survivors of ritual abuse, therefore, are actually undergoing a harsh discipline and programming that aims at the preservation of the group in its combat with society at the total expense of the individual. The same is true of repressive state systems such as communism and fascism, and occult organizations often operate like totalitarian regimes with their carefully constructed terror apparatuses in miniature.

Yet there is a dimension of groups guilty of ritual abuse that is largely neglected by researchers and investigators. That is the collective thought processes of the "perpetrators" themselves and the belief system conducive to their deeds. In one respect the very notion of "satanic ritual abuse" is misleading, because it presupposes a virtually homogenous body of practitioners who are part of some "orthodox" tradition revering the conventional figure of satan.*

The popular image of "devil worshipers" carrying candles

---

*Please see Gail Feldman's footnote on page 55.

and wrapped in black robes contributes to this stereotype. In fact, a sizable percentage of the tales of ritual abuse, including victims I myself have interviewed extensively, entail secretive undertakings behind the visible cloak of mainline Christianity. Many of these purported "black covens" consist of persons who are outwardly Christians by day and technicians of the demonic forces by night. Some stories of abuse even take place in the basements of churches and, in Barbara's case, a synagogue.

This sort of data raises the tantalizing question of whether most satanists, as certain occultists and "white witches" have frequently charged, are little more than "fallen Christians." Certainly, the incidents of satanism in the late Middle Ages and as recently as the high Victorian era comport with this point of view. One of the notorious satanists of all time, a fifteenth-century French nobleman named Gilles de Rais who was executed for sadistic atrocities committed against children, had been an exceptionally pious Catholic earlier in his career. Even Crowley's excesses can be explained as a virulent reaction against the puritanical Protestantism in which he was reared.

But that particular explanation fails to account for the preoccupation of satanists throughout history with physical abuse and the shedding of blood. It is not merely a case, as conventional scholarship maintains, of "turning upside down" the rules of Christian morality. Satanist practices and ceremonies, as the religion's own "black pope" Anton La Vey has written, are highly "eclectic."

In other words, satanists consciously adapt and borrow from a welter of occult sources, in particular those that anthropologists have documented as "blood magic." Such magic is based on the primitive concept that the vital essence of a person is contained in the blood. When that person's blood is spilled, his or her power ebbs away.

To watch and partake in the suffering of another individual, by the same token, is to appropriate to oneself the life force. To drink the same person's blood and to actually consume the heart—something which Barbara herself recalled happening—is not a loathsome act of cannibalism as much as it is a "logical" attempt at incorporating his or her vital nature, thereby increasing one's own magical strength.

The Aztecs of Mexico, known to history for their ceremonial slaughter of hundreds upon thousands of human beings in a rite where blood-soaked priests would rip out the beating hearts of live victims and devour them, crafted an entire religion around this way of thinking. In a 1970s Western film called *Ulzana's Raid*, a bemused American cavalry officer listens to a defecting Apache warrior describe how the brutal butchery of white settlers by his counterparts could be explained as a means of gaining magical "power" by causing suffering.

This "metaphysics of violence" pervading satanist psychology creates an almost indelible impression in the cult member that the world is a horrible place, that no such thing as "goodness" can be attributed to life in the body, and that moral codes are meaningless. The victim slowly acquires the confused belief that sexual pleasure is tantamount to pain, that love is hate, that ugliness is beauty, and that black is white.

Among the ancient Gnostics, to whom Crowley claimed to be a successor, this deliberate inversion of all human values constituted a kind of basic training. Modern satanist observances hark back in certain details to old-style Gnosticism. Once the initiate grasps firsthand the perversity of life in the body, he or she will begin to obtain the kind of ice-cold illumination that goes along with becoming a godlike adept in the magical arts. One woman in her early twenties, who had been ritually abused, described how her parents had sought to teach her that the aim of life was "pure solace amid the pain."

The woman's version of events could easily have been Barbara's.

What differentiates Barbara's story from most survivor literature is the fact that she is black, and that the clan itself
allegedly was Afro-American. Blood magic among Afro-
Americans is usually connected to the practice of specific religions such as voodoo or *santería* and rarely to "satanism" per
se. Yet the revelation that Barbara's "clan" had its origins in
a mixed marriage between a black woman and an Irishman,
who supposedly was responsible for the practices in question,
sheds startling light on the fragmentary history of the group.
No psychotherapeutically kindled type of "make-believe"
could possibly lurk behind making such a subtle, and an-
thropologically sophisticated, mode of explanation.

    Lessons in Evil, Lessons from the Light is the first major
book for a general audience to lay bare a broad and intricate
context, into which is woven not only the life story of the
survivor, but the challenges and professional anxiety of the
therapist struggling to make sense out of what has been told.
The truth or falsity of survivor claims in general will not be
settled by this account. Only the accumulated weight of evidence over the years will suffice to that end. But Barbara's tale,
compelling and poignant as it is, should serve as an unprece-
dented "paradigm case" for the discussion.

INTRODUCTION

thought I couldn't be shocked. After working as a social worker and then a psychologist for twenty-five years, I thought if I hadn't seen everything, at least I'd heard it. I had also grown unafraid.

They say that small doses of fear teach mastery and the ability to cope with later frightening situations. Maybe that's what happened to me. Born in San Diego at the outbreak of World War II, I had lots of things to be afraid of. Mostly bombs. The American military thought the Japanese might invade our west coast, so we pulled black shades over the windows at night, and my father sat on the beach with other police officers, "just in case."

Following the war, my parents divorced. When my father moved out, I developed all sorts of fears. For several years I couldn't do sleepovers. I also stopped eating. When forced to eat vegetables, I would vomit. Feeling nauseated was normal. Now I know that these symptoms expressed unconscious fears of abandonment. If my father could leave, so could my mother. And then, what would become of me?

On the other hand, I learned independence and resourcefulness. I was alone much of the time, and since Mother worked long hours in an aircraft factory, I shopped, cooked, and pushed the laundry through the hand-operated wringer and hung it on the line. Time with my father was deep-sea fishing, target shooting, and trailing after him at the police department. I enjoyed fingerprinting and having a "mug shot" taken. I overcame my fear of the "lock-up" area and began to see those in jail as just other people, even though I couldn't comprehend the behaviors that brought them there.

I was the first person in my family to graduate from college. My father had escaped the poverty of a small mining town in West Virginia, and my mother had fled the boredom and heat of a desert farm town in the Imperial Valley of southern California. I wanted to flee from the working-class neighborhood in which I'd grown up. I saw no romance in factory work, low incomes, and rampant alcoholism. While most of my girlfriends were being told to find a husband, I was being told to get a solid career and learn to rely upon myself.

"Don't think you can depend on a man!" my grandmother always said. "Look what happened to your mother." Divorce had happened to Grandmother, too. While she was taking several years to recover from the influenza epidemic of 1918, my grandfather left her.

San Diego State University was among the first to offer a bachelor's degree in social work, so I chose that field of study. For my field placements, I worked at the courthouse and the mental health center learning about mental illness commitment proceedings, and then at the county hospital learning about discharge planning. Since social workers with BA degrees can only work for state social services, I was determined to get a scholarship to graduate school to get a master's degree. The University of Southern California was the perfect place. Located in the middle of a black section of Los Angeles, USC provided all the social work experiences one could imagine. I counseled rural farm workers in Ventura County, black gang groups in Watts, male prison parolees in a halfway house, and white hippies hooked on drugs and alcohol.

By the time I got my first full-time job at Harbor General Hospital, a UCLA teaching hospital, I thought I'd heard everything. Surprises come in strange places. During a routine family-therapy intake session involving two small boys, I asked the father to tell me about his parents. He answered blandly, "My father killed my mother and then shot and killed himself." The two boys' eyes bulged and they said, "What?" My jaw dropped at the inappropriate manner of the revelation, and I struggled to help the little boys process such a shocking family truth.

The biggest surprise that occurred when I worked at the Kennedy Child Study Center in Santa Monica was perpetrated by a shriveled little psychoanalyst during a family session. In the traditional mental-health-clinic arrangement, the social worker counseled parents and the psychiatrist did play therapy with the children. That's how Dr. Myers worked. She was trained in Europe and retained her Viennese accent. When she informed me that we must meet together with the family members we were both treating, I did the scheduling, arrived at the appointed time, and sat down smiling.

I expected to focus on the custody and visitation arrangements for the four children. About ten minutes into the meeting, Dr. Myers began pointing to each child and stating which parent that child must live with. I was stunned. The children began crying. The parents were becoming so furious I was afraid the father might physically attack the little doctor. Right at that point, Dr. Myers stood up and said in her thick accent, "And now I must go teach at UCLA," and left the room. I had to clean up the emotional mess she had made.

I fell in love with a medical intern in 1966 and married that same year. He was drafted into the Air Force and we found ourselves looking at a map to discover just where Alamogordo, New Mexico, was located. Holloman Air Force Base was our destination after his flight-surgeon training in Texas. It was in Alamogordo, near the Mescalero Apache Indian reservation, that I began to learn the story of the American Indians. I supervised child-welfare social workers on the reservation and later provided services to adolescents who were sent to the Albuquerque Indian School from reservations all over the Southwest.

The girls I worked with at the boarding school were bright, creative (many wrote beautiful poetry), and poignantly sad. They felt out of place in the city, they missed their homelands and their families, and they saw no future for themselves in the land of the white man. Following Christmas break at the school in 1973, the girls in our group were completely silent. It took many questions before I could get them to describe what had happened.

Much had gone wrong, one girl finally said. Another girl from Mescalero told that all the dances had been canceled. Too many people had died between Thanksgiving and Christmas. "What do you mean?" I asked. She told of a girl who had hung herself, a man who killed his wife and then killed himself, two others who had died on the highway, killed by cars as they staggered along drunk. Similar incidents had occurred on the other reservations. I was dumbfounded at this graphic depiction of the suicide rate of the American Indians, which I knew was ten times the rate of the rest of the population. At night I went through boxes of tissues while reading *Bury My Heart at Wounded Knee*, the story of the genocidal Indian Wars.

So I was used to shocking revelations and surprises. I was used to poverty and the effects of oppression. I was dispassionate about sexual perversions and nearly bored with the effects of divorce. I was completely unprepared for Barbara.

I had come to view my own childhood as normal. What unfolded in Barbara's psychotherapy was abnormal beyond understanding. Child abuse is one thing. Ritualistic torture as an aspect of religion and sadism as an integral part of child-rearing were incomprehensible to me. But this is her story. I had to be persuaded to write it. It will take courage to read it.

I was afraid that Barbara's story would seem sensationalistic and unbelievable on the one hand, or assault the reader on the other. Even worse was the thought that it might become a handbook, along with *The Satanic Bible,* for potential psychopathic perpetrators.

Of the people who urged me to tell the story, Barbara herself exerted the most influence. Barbara, like most survivors of torture, wanted the public to know what happened. She believes that if people realize that satanic abuse is more than a teen fantasy and is related to drug abuse, child pornography, prostitution, and murder, the awareness might galvanize measures to prevent other children from suffering as she did. If publishing her story is helpful in any way to society, she can feel that her suffering had some meaning.

My sense of outrage places final responsibility for the book on my shoulders. For most people, child abuse has little meaning. The term may conjure up thoughts of an occasional beating or, at worst, some type of single act of sexual molestation. The American public needs to know that acts of sadistic violence are perpetrated against children in this country on a daily basis. Somehow, we must stop it.

Gail Carr Feldman
July 1992

PART ONE

FALL
1988

S ailing,'' I said, trying to sound interested. ''You went sailing this summer?'' I was paying more attention to the elegant food before me than the words being spoken by Paul Perris, my dinner companion.

"Yes. I go sailing at least twice a year. It's my passion. What I love most is sailing in storms."

"Isn't that dangerous?" I said, taking another bite of pâté with watercress.

"I suppose so, but I've never been scared. This spring a friend and I left San Diego Harbor to get out in a storm when everyone else was coming in. I keep looking for *the* big storm. In college when I crewed, we got caught in a storm, and I was in the stern singing. My bowman was crying he was so scared."

I put down my fork and looked at Paul, my attention suddenly focused. His wife, Brenda, was out of town, as was my husband, Dan. We were at a fiftieth birthday party for a good friend, and all the celebrants were doctors and lawyers. I had expected a dull conversation about internal medicine, the only passion erupting when malpractice costs and managed medical care came up.

Instead, this mild-mannered Clark Kent–type physician, bespectacled and in his pin-striped suit, was telling me about peril at sea.

"Does Brenda ever go with you?"

"No, she's afraid of the ocean."

"Sounds halfway sensible to me. I grew up in San Diego and I love it. But I'd be scared out of my wits in a storm."

Paul went on to tell me how he loved the radar equipment and studying the technical skills necessary to be truly competent on the sea. His normally rather placid face reflected excitement and joy.

"I'll bet you were a sailor in a past life," I teased.

"Maybe so. All I know is, I live and work these days to get to the ocean."

In the past, I would have shrugged off his tales as male midlife-crisis counterphobic behavior. But now that I was approaching fifty myself, I was more respectful of other's actions and more curious about my own emotional lows.

I, too, loved adventure, so I couldn't dismiss Paul's attraction to it so easily. Dan and I were known among our friends as the couple who sought and found unusual things to do. We had rafted the Colorado River, camped on five islands in Hawaii, hiked in the Himalayas, skied most of the major North American downhill ski areas, and swum with dolphins in the middle of the Caribbean.

During these times, I felt free. At this transition point in my life, I thought, the goal must be to continue to feel alive, as opposed to the dull fear of degeneration and death. I could understand the excitement of being in the eye of a storm, where every aspect of knowledge and performance mattered. I could imagine the thrill of reliving the experience and feeling a sense of deep comfort at having survived.

What I could not imagine was Barbara.

Dan and I had never gotten over the Sunday-night blahs. It was a genuine puzzle to us that we both liked our work, but dreaded the last of the weekend knowing that with the Monday-morning alarm we were on a schedule that was so full it felt that we had temporarily lost control of our lives. Dan and his partner ran an internal medicine practice and also taught at the medical school.

My private practice in psychology was in its seventeenth year, and there was no lack of patients. The only thing that seemed to change over the years was the problems. In recent years there were many more women coming for help with symptoms related to sexual abuse in childhood. This change was reflected in our professional workshops and supported by conversations with colleagues.

I thought about that as I drove my car that Monday morning in October from the West Mesa along Interstate 40 across the Rio Grande and into Albuquerque. I glanced upriver as I crossed the bridge. The wide expanse showed more mud than water. Great sandbars lined the middle area with side streams of water moving slowly around them. The spring runoff was long gone, and much of the water had been delivered into the irrigation ditches throughout the summer to serve the farmers of New Mexico, Texas, and even Mexico. The great cottonwood forests on either side of the river were what caught my eye. Hues of yellow with dashes of orange signaled the end of the growing season and the beginning of winter.

A few years earlier my interest in doing psychotherapy was slowly dying. Working with sexual abuse survivors had revitalized me. While ordinary psychotherapy required some fascinating detective work, with the sexually traumatized I had to accept the challenge to learn more about posttraumatic stress disorder, amnesia for traumatic memories, differential diagnosis, aspects of intensive long-term psychotherapy, and the biggest challenge of all, hypnosis. The study and learning of hypnosis to help survivors access and process memories of traumatic experiences had become my obsession.

As I walked into the waiting room of my office, Jan said good morning to me without turning around. She knew my footsteps as well as my mind. She had come to work for my associate, Marcia Landau, and me six years earlier after retiring from the university. She had been an office manager there, but had taken time off to pursue her passion for writing.

Secretaries are the guiding force of any organization, and Jan was more than a guiding force. She seemed to get satisfaction from caring for us in every way. If we didn't have time to get lunch, she would get lunch for us. If we needed some project completed by a deadline, she stayed late to help. She was attuned to our likes and dislikes and went out of her way to get us presents on special occasions. For my birthday one year, she had dolphin earrings and a pin made for me by a local artist.

I was routinely surprised to find a book Jan had placed on my desk that was just the work I needed to read at a given time. If it was fiction, often there were allusions to psychotherapy, spirituality, or life-changing relationships. Sometimes the books were descriptive of an area to which I would be traveling. I teased Jan about being a guardian angel.

This morning she followed me into my office and showed

me the list of scheduled patients. Most of the patients were regulars, but Jan pointed out two new patients she had scheduled. The first was a woman referred by a physician friend. My eye caught the second name, Barbara Maddox. I looked at Jan and she smiled.

"I knew you'd want to see her. You know who she is, don't you?"

"Of course. She's one of the most well known teachers in Albuquerque. A pioneer in education. She's won all kinds of awards. I'm pleased to get to meet her. It's probably some kind of consultation."

Dan's medical practice and my small medical audiocassette business, along with my therapy practice, had established us securely in the medical and business communities of Albuquerque. It was not infrequent that business and professional people would consult with me about management problems, office clashes, and other work-related issues.

I settled in for the day. With each patient I saw, I felt better and better. I was amused at the notion that by the end of the week I was drooping like an unwatered rubber plant, and that it was actually my work that began to nourish me with purpose each Monday. By four-thirty that afternoon I felt great.

Barbara was sitting in the waiting room holding the information sheet Jan had asked her to fill out. A tall, slender black woman, she wore a light pink suit with matching shoes. I was impressed with her clothing because in New Mexico the style is casual, even for teachers. Only lawyers and businesspeople typically dress in suits. But then I realized that this woman, because of her achievements, represented an entire profession. As symbol of a group, she would want to exert a positive influence for those with whom she consulted and spoke out for at sessions of the legislature.

I had another reaction, too: that any woman, especially a

black woman, who dressed that well in Albuquerque, New Mexico, was determined to make it in the world of the "haves." I sensed in her the same drive I had to participate in "the good life," regardless of how long and how much hard work it would take. I'll bet this woman's a fighter, I told myself.

Her longish black hair was pulled straight back, and her medium dark complexion with high cheekbones and large dark eyes gave her an elegant, big-city look. She was staring at me and nervously twisting the information sheet into a roll. I introduced myself and she stood up and put out her hand, saying, "I'm glad to meet you," breathless. Her eyes never left mine. They were direct and compelling . . . and fearful. I no longer thought she was there to discuss her work.

I was used to seeing that look. It invariably told me, "This person's been hurt." The story that would unfold would be a description of the hurt.

I closed the door behind us and motioned for her to sit in the large chair next to my desk.

"What brings you here?" I asked.

"I don't know where to start . . . sexual problems for one. I'm afraid my husband will leave me because I have so many problems. I know he's tired of them. We could have a good marriage, but I can't relate to him sexually. It has to do with my childhood. I think my grandfather sexually abused me because I hate him. I've always hated him. I go away when he touches me."

She sighed. "I have no memories though. I just remember him picking me up from school sometimes and taking me to buy clothes. I have a mental image of seeing his penis, so I think the clothes were a bribe so he could molest me."

I was dumbfounded at her ability to focus so quickly on serious issues. It was not unusual for people to announce that they weren't sure why they had come at all! Therapy was their doctor's idea. More typical was the awareness of unhappiness or depression, but very vague ideas about why the symptoms existed. The fact that she sensed sexual abuse had occurred and could even use the word *penis* was extremely unusual. When patients alluded to sexual activities, I often had to supply the correct anatomical name to the organ. I was impressed with this woman, but thought maybe she'd been in psychotherapy before. That could be the reason why her thinking was so focused. I filed that thought away for later. I had to follow up on her statement that she had no actual memories of abuse.

"What memories *do* you have about your childhood?"

"Poverty. My mother had me when she was fourteen. I never knew my father. My mother hated me because I was Grandma's favorite. They fought over me all the time. When I lived with my mother, I was her slave. I did all the housework and the cooking from the time I was six. Clothes came from the Goodwill once a year. She enjoyed not giving me birthday presents or Christmas presents."

"How could you have grown up to be who you are, so successful, without good mothering?"

"My grandmother. She was my lifeline. I knew she loved me. But she had to be careful how she showed it. She couldn't cross my mother too much, or I'd be kept away from her. Also, I had to raise my little brothers. My mother had two more babies by different men, and I had to take care of them. So, I learned how to be nurturing."

"To others, not to yourself?"

"Yes." Barbara bit her lower lip. "That's right. I have no self-esteem and I don't know the first thing about how to address my own problems."

I heard the words, but I heard more in her voice. It was low, resonant, clear, and unconfused. It was rare to hear a new patient speak without notes of exaggeration, defensiveness, or subtle pleading. I sensed a strength in this woman I had rarely felt about other patients during a first visit. I registered the history, but decided to drop the self-esteem issue for the present. I pressed for more information.

"Tell me more about your marriage."

"I met Cal when I was seventeen . . . on a city bus. He teased me and made me laugh. Then we started dating. I knew he was from a good family. We waited until our second year in college to marry. He's my first real friend, but I feel like he does all the giving. I don't know how to be close, and I have real problems with sex. I just seem to shut down."

Again, she went right to the problem. But she had made herself the problem. I needed to know whether her husband might be encouraging her to carry the burden for his problems. When this is the case, the husband often doesn't want his wife to have treatment.

"Does Cal know you're here today?"

"Oh, yes." Barbara laughed for the first time. "He said I had no choice."

"What does that mean?" So, maybe he's blackmailing her, I thought. Issuing threats about what he'll do if she doesn't come, but unconsciously planning to carry out the threats if she does.

"I've been in therapy before in different states, New York, Georgia. I dumped some stuff, but never seemed to resolve things. And I couldn't seem to feel comfortable enough with the therapists. But Cal knows I still have so many fears. They come out in horrible nightmares. He has to wake me up when I'm screaming. He said I had to come."

This sounded more to me like compassion than blackmail. So Barbara had been in therapy before. She had done some work, but hadn't gotten to the core problems.

"What makes you think this time therapy will be any different?"

"I feel strongly that I'm ready to work now. I'm committed. I'm so tired of feeling angry and scared all the time. Anger's my big problem. With Cal, I just 'go away' in my mind whenever I get angry. I withdraw and won't talk. With my daughter, though, it's much worse."

"How old is your daughter?"

"Seven. She's my youngest. I have a son, Paul, who is ten. I have no problems with him at all. Except I'm strict. Michelle, though, is a different story. I'm jumpy, irritable, and always angry with her. I'm afraid I'll physically abuse her."

This is a common report from those who were abused in childhood. The normal empathic feelings for one's child become contaminated by the impulse to attack the child during a conflict of wills, just as the parent had been attacked. A child of the same sex seems to be especially vulnerable. A parent can more easily project his or her self-hate onto a child of the same sex.

"Have you ever hurt her?"

"I've never beat her like my mother beat me. The worst thing I did was hold her head under the water once when she wouldn't cooperate when I was washing her hair. I just lost it. I'll never forgive myself for that."

I thought to myself, that's abuse? Had I done similar things to my daughters during fits of anger when they were young? Possibly.

"What about anger directed at yourself? Have you ever tried to hurt yourself?" Suicidal thoughts are nearly universal among survivors of childhood sexual abuse. Those who have suffered sadistic abuse or torture have almost always acted on the impulse to hurt themselves in the same ways they were hurt as children. They may cut themselves, make repeated suicide attempts, or do other self-destructive things, such as using drugs or alcohol or being sexually promiscuous.

"I think about suicide constantly. I almost drove off a cliff once when I was visiting in California. The impulse was so strong, I came very close. As a child, I remember climbing up a telephone pole to the top of a garage and jumping off. I was amazed that I didn't even break my legs. I didn't get hurt at all.''

''What do you think about doing to yourself these days?''

''I can't tell you yet.''

''Okay. Do you want to work with me, though?''

''Yes, very much.''

''Then, at least, you must promise me that you won't hurt yourself. Can you do that?''

''Yes.''

Her ability to make this agreement told me that Barbara was indeed motivated to resolve her problems. If she had hedged and suggested that she didn't know whether she could control the destructive impulses, I'd have considered referring her to a psychiatrist. Self-mutilators and suicide artists usually require repeated hospitalizations and close monitoring.

Her promise not to hurt herself was the beginning of her ability to trust in my care for her and to accept responsibility for her part in this special relationship we were about to embark on together.

''All right. I always view the first six weeks to two months as an evaluation period. You and I will both be coming to understand the extent of your problems and determining how we can work together. One of the most basic questions is whether you'll learn to trust me.''

''The word *trust* isn't even part of my vocabulary. I can't trust anyone,'' Barbara said evenly, looking right at me.

''That's common for survivors of childhood abuse. How about the word *safe*?''

Barbara laughed for the second time. ''That one's worse. I don't think I've ever felt safe in my life.''

Barbara's laughter was not of joy or even cynicism, but

seemed to ring briefly, like a bell, highlighting the truth of her statement.

"Those are goals then," I said. "Trust and safety. Two ingredients for a happy life. Let's keep this same time next week. Will this time work for your schedule?"

"I think so. I'll check my book and call if there's a problem."

"See you next week then."

When Barbara left, a familiar feeling of sadness passed like a wave through my whole body. Another child had been victimized instead of nurtured, I thought.

Mira came to mind. Her father was a prominent New York restaurateur who had sexually tortured her from the time he had returned from World War II and she was two years old. Her first two years were spent in the warmth of her grandmother's affection, but when her father returned, her parents moved to a secluded area outside the city. From then on, her life was an unpredictable living hell.

"Where was my mother?" Mira used to ask in the early years of her treatment. Her mother had been a passive accomplice, sometimes seeing and ignoring the abuse, often away shopping, or reading books in the kitchen while Mira was being tortured in the basement. At the end of her therapy, Mira would cry, sometimes for days, trying to come to terms with the fact that she simply "had no mother."

Thinking about child abuse and neglect made me angry. I felt it now. "Poverty!" Barbara had said. I wondered if she was aware that she'd described two kinds of poverty! Not only the absence of material goods, and even of food, but the most destructive kind of poverty for a child, the lack of love. That's the deprivation she was trying to deal with.

I came out of my reverie and went to the waiting room for my last patient of the day. After he left, I tried to organize my desk, but I was distracted. I kept thinking about the word *grief* and remembering a quote from a Marilyn French novel: "If the world became aware of its grief, it would drown in its own tears."[1] I wondered if Barbara could cry. Most childhood abuse survivors had been taught not to. If they cried, they would be brutalized even more.

On the elevator and then walking to my car I continued to think about the session with Barbara. I felt certain that sexual abuse was the predominant issue. Like all survivors, she would have to be helped to remember the trauma so that she could overcome the feelings of terror that were still attached to the repressed memories. No small assignment. It can take many years to help someone who has been abused from early childhood to unlock those traumatic memories. And if that isn't enough, after reliving the trauma, the patient then has to grieve over the fact that all of those horrendous physical and psychic intrusions occurred.

The thought caught me in the stomach. Did I want to keep working many more years? As Dan and I approached fifty, we teased each other about who would retire first. Of course he would, he'd say, since he put me through graduate school. He was ready to spend more time fly-fishing. No, I'd respond. I would retire first because I'd actually had two jobs all these years, one at my office, the other raising our daughters and running the household. Since we both knew that retirement was nowhere near and that we were really only trying to work through our feelings about becoming "old," the subject would be dropped.

It wasn't retirement I wanted anyway. It was some kind of relief. Relief from what, though? According to many of my peers, I had the perfect life . . . two healthy, happy, nearly grown children, a husband who was successful, outgoing, and fun to be with, plus a successful career of my own. And let's

---

1. Marilyn French, *Bleeding Heart* (New York: Summit Books, 1990).

face it, I told myself, about 80 percent of me *is* happy! It was that other 20 percent that worried me. It felt mysterious, elusive, and most of all, oppressive.

Maybe it was the commitment I faced. Taking on a case where the patient had suffered serious abuse was a little like adoption. After two or three years, you couldn't return the child and say, "I'm tired of all these constant demands." In the case of abuse survivors, many therapists suffer stress reactions from hearing repeated descriptions of sexual brutality.

Time requirements could be extreme during crisis periods. Family members of the abused might need counseling to understand symptoms that seemed bizarre to them. Hospitalization could be required. Consultations with adjunct therapists such as psychiatrists, psychodrama leaders, group therapy leaders, and art therapists could become time-consuming for the therapist.

Once a person was accepted into treatment, however, there was no abandoning him. The commitment was for the duration . . . as long as it took to heal. And sometimes, just as with my children, I wondered if I could hang in there until they were grown.

During Barbara's next session, she repeated her original worry that her husband, Cal, would leave her.

"Cal says I only have two emotional reactions: furious or withdrawn. There's no in-between. Cal's always complained, too, because I won't make an effort to make or keep friends. Every time we move, I just turn my back and leave. I never keep in touch with people. I don't know how to share myself.

"I'm a real good listener, but I get nervous and uncomfortable if someone wants to get close to me. Cal also wants me to be more sociable with his business associates. I just shudder at the thought of having company over. I don't know how to do that. My biggest fear is that Cal will get tired of all my problems and leave. It doesn't matter how often he says he won't leave me. I don't believe it."

"So basically, you're telling me that you have no friends, not even Cal, because you don't know how to let someone get close to you or you to them."

"That's right. I can't believe anyone could like me, so I'm only comfortable in my role as a professional. It's like I don't know how to be or do anything else."

" 'Anything else' would mean being yourself," I suggested.

Barbara gave an empty laugh. "I sure don't know how to do that, and I don't think I can because I have no self-esteem."

"You must know that you're likable. I hardly know you and yet I feel drawn to you."

"That's always puzzled me," Barbara said earnestly. "It's true. People seem to like me and want to be my friend, but I back away."

"Maybe our goal," I answered, "should be to find out when you stopped feeling lovable. It's when we feel unlovable that we are in mortal danger. As babies and small children we know we cannot care for ourselves. Therefore, if we feel unlovable, we realize we could be abandoned and then die. Our job is to help you feel lovable. That's when everything else can fall into place."

"It sounds impossible, but I want to change," Barbara said passionately. "I want to have normal feelings . . . for other people and for myself. I want to do whatever I have to, to get well. I want to get on with my life. I want to be a good wife and mother, and I have this desire to go back to school and get a Ph.D. or go to law school, so that I can be more influential in developing better teaching programs and also in-school counseling programs."

I thought about Sandra Murray, a social worker I had

tried to befriend in Los Angeles. We were both single and devoting most of our time to the black gang groups we were working with through an agency, Special Services for Groups. Meeting regularly with about thirteen girls plus their families, and doing the crisis intervention necessary to avoid gang fights and individual damage, was exhausting. I wanted Sandra to be my friend, someone I could talk to about the intensity of our work. Someone I knew would understand.

But Sandra was black. She was sweet and friendly, but I sensed that her work in the ghetto struck so deeply for her that whatever personal memories were evoked by our work couldn't be shared. After one visit to her apartment, I realized that I would never be allowed into her private world. I wondered if Barbara would be able to let me into hers.

Barbara interrupted my thoughts. "I think I have about two years before Cal's company transfers him. I want to be ready to move."

Two years! I thought to myself. That's an impossibly short time to resolve any abuse problems. But I couldn't share that thought with Barbara, so instead I asked, "What kind of work does Cal do?"

"He's a chemical engineer with one of the companies that contracts with the University of California at Berkeley to work with the labs at Los Alamos. That's why we live in Santa Fe."

"Santa Fe? I didn't realize you lived there. That means you have to carve a bigger chunk out of your day to commute back and forth here."

Barbara smiled. "Several people gave me your name as a therapist. I think I'm in the right place. The drive just confirms my commitment. It also gives me time to think."

I felt a fondness for Barbara from the first. I thought it had to do with the fact that we shared the same dedication to children: mine focusing on the area of psychology, Barbara's on education. Her commitment to developing children's programs had certainly surpassed my own, and her talent for community organization for special-needs children in the school system was remarkable.

I worried about the two-year time limit. I had never treated a sexual abuse survivor who was able to complete treatment in that time. At a recent conference on childhood sexual abuse, the presenter had stated that in his experience, eight to fifteen years was necessary to rebuild a shattered ego. However, Barbara seemed determined. Maybe she could do it. Or maybe her husband wouldn't be transferred, and the problem could be avoided altogether.

During our third session, Barbara talked more about her sexual concerns. "I want to work on my self-image and sexuality. I know I can enjoy sex because I have before. Cal is a very considerate lover. But somehow I don't feel it's okay, especially to initiate sex or to be active."

"Tell me what part of lovemaking is easiest for you. Let's go from the easiest to the hardest things."

"Being held is easiest. I love to be held. Next is being stroked. I like it when Cal strokes my back and legs. Kissing is okay. I like the kissing and I like to have my breasts fondled." Barbara stopped.

"So those are the activities that feel good. What about the ones that feel bad."

"I don't like manual stimulation. I hate penetration from behind . . . and anal sex would be the worst."

"So what is missing for you and Cal? What do you worry about?"

"I guess Cal would like to be able to touch me more. He's not interested in doing funky things like the anal sex. I guess it's just that I can't relax. I'm so tense all the time. And often my head or my chest hurts during sex. Like I'm being crushed. And if Cal wakes me up to have sex, I can't function at all. Then I can't go back to sleep, either."

"He wakes you to have sex?"

"Yes. Sometimes."

"That's a no-no. Even women who have no history of abuse can't tolerate their sleep being disturbed to satisfy someone else's wishes. Would either of you wake up your children in the middle of the night because you felt like playing with them?"

"No," Barbara said, laughing. "We'd never do that."

"Can you share this opinion of mine with Cal? That he simply cannot interrupt your sleep ever, unless it's an emergency or to wake you from a nightmare?"

"Yes. I can tell him that. As long as it's a message from you."

"Good. Now what about medical problems and other symptoms?"

"I mentioned the head and chest pains. I have those a lot. I've had vaginal and kidney infections all my life. I have high blood pressure and I'm on medication for that." Barbara looked thoughtful. "I'm obsessed with being fat even though I've always been skinny. And I can't stand to look in the mirror."

"We know that memories of abuse are stored in every area of the body, so it's typical that survivors have lots of physical fears and discomfort. They also tend to have eating disorders. Do you?"

"Not really. I was starved a lot as a child. Now, I like to cook for my family. I'm a really good cook, but I never have much of an appetite."

"Can you tell me yet about the fantasies you have about hurting yourself?"

"I'm ashamed to tell you. It sounds so crazy. You'll think I'm crazy," Barbara said in her clear voice. She looked nervously from one side to the other, then back at me. "I have the image of cutting myself open and pulling out my insides."

"Whew! It sounds more gruesome than crazy to me. We need to learn why you have these sadistic thoughts about killing yourself, instead of the more traditional images of doing yourself in quickly and quietly to avoid more suffering."

Barbara was staring at me, so I added, "Don't worry. I know you're not crazy. We'll get to the bottom of all this. Will you tell Cal about the new rule? No sexual intrusions after you're asleep?"

"Yes, I will."

"Okay. See you next week."

That night after dinner, Dan and I cleaned off the kitchen table. By October we had settled into our fall routine. Jasmine was away for her third year of college and Julie was in high school. The three of us would share the events of the day during dinner, but after dinner Julie disappeared to her room to study and Dan and I took an hour to sip coffee, read, and talk before getting to our own work.

"I heard a new method of committing suicide today," I told him.

"Oh, yeah?" he answered, more interested in his newspaper than in me.

"Yeah, it's pretty gruesome. You cut yourself open with a knife and pull out your insides. Sounds rather Japanese, don't you think?"

Dan put his paper aside. "What? Someone did that, or someone told you they thought about doing that?"

"Thought about it. A new childhood sexual abuse patient."

"A woman?"

"Yep."

"Sounds like a crazy."

"I don't think so. The crazy people don't lead functional lives. They can't keep a job. They're often isolated and unmarried. They have no friends. They're usually paranoid, or at the very least they have some thought disorder. This woman is one of the pillars of our community."

"How do they all find you? It seems like these sex abuse victims are the only people you see anymore. I don't think it's good for you. And I can't believe they're all for real. There just can't be that much abuse of kids going on. I think you're a soft touch," he said, and returned to the paper.

"Well, thanks for your vote of confidence. All I can say is, it's a good thing women are invading medicine. If they hadn't, none of the stories of abuse reported by children and their mothers would ever have been believed. We'd still be operating under the male illusion that child abuse didn't happen in America."

Dan shot me an annoyed look and went on with his reading. I swallowed my annoyance with the last of my coffee.

T W O

During Barbara's next session she spoke of her rages toward her daughter, Michelle.

"Cal is furious with me about my yelling. He says it has to stop. But I don't know if I can stop it. At work I have this real calm exterior and I would never yell at the children, but at home I'm a nervous wreck and always angry at Michelle. She dawdles in the morning getting ready for school. It doesn't matter how many reminders I give her, she just doesn't care about making me late. And eventually, I just want to hit her."

"So, do you end up dressing her?"

"Yes, or throwing her into the car with whatever clothing she hasn't got on yet."

"Why don't you just tell her she'll have to go to school in her pajamas if she isn't ready at the appointed time?"

"Because she'd go to school in her pajamas."

"So? She might get enough embarrassing feedback from her peers to motivate her to get into her clothes on time."

"I don't know if I could do that. I have this thing about being a good mother. You know, not being neglecting like my mother was. So I buy expensive clothes for the kids and make sure they always look just right."

"The good intentions are for you, though, aren't they? Would your kids complain if you didn't buy them designer clothes?"

"Paul wouldn't. 'Cept he's picky about his sneakers. Michelle wouldn't know the difference if I let her choose. I've just never taken them to K mart or any of those places."

"As long as Michelle knows that everything she does goes in your self-esteem basket and not hers, she's gonna balk and you'll be in a power struggle with her."

"Hmm. I see that now. Yes. My self-esteem, rather, my zero self-esteem. I feel like a failure, a nothing, if anything at all goes wrong. Did I tell you about Sheila?"

"No."

"Well, she was our foster daughter for a while. I couldn't make it work. She was a black teenager who was removed from her mother's home because the mother's boyfriend was having sex regularly with her. The mother chose the boyfriend over the daughter, called her a lying tramp, and moved to another state.

"That's a pretty typical reaction, as you know better than I, but the girl couldn't see the truth of her mother's rejection. She held on to a fantasy that her mother still loved her, and she saw me as the wicked witch who took her away from her mother. From my own background and from my studies, I understood how Sheila would want to pretend that her mother was really normal, but as the one trying to be a mother surrogate, I couldn't handle her rejection of me.

"Cal said I was just too sensitive and angry with her all the time, but that's just it, I *was* angry all the time. I couldn't stand it, so the social worker suggested she be moved."

"And you continue to beat up on yourself over it?"

"Oh, yes. I feel that I let Sheila down and that I let Cal down."

"Why Cal?"

"Because I couldn't make things work. When we married, I promised Cal we could have three children. He wanted three. But after Paul's birth, I couldn't face the prospect of having any more. I just couldn't go through it again. So after three years I asked if we couldn't adopt instead. He agreed that it would be all right."

"Was Paul's birth difficult for you?"

"Not really. He was born after a short labor for a first baby. But it was strange because I felt terrified and out of control in the hospital. I wasn't myself at all."

"So you adopted Michelle."

"Yes. And I can brag on her looks 'cause of that. She's really pretty." Barbara seemed to collect her serious thoughts again. "We picked her up from the adoption agency when she was just days old. The first thing I noticed about her were her eyes. I said to Cal, 'Look at those eyes, staring as if she can see right through you.' I've been intimidated by her, and she's always been very stubborn.

"So anyway, I didn't want a third, but I guess I tried to make a family with three kids to please Cal."

"Is he still insisting on three children?"

"No. I think he realizes we're probably better off with two. But I still feel like a failure."

"Do you suppose that every time you fail to control some part of your life now, it's a reminder that you couldn't control your life as a child and you learned to hate yourself because of that?"

"Yes. I was always trying to do the right thing, but it

always turned out wrong." Barbara seemed lost in thought. Finally she spoke. "When I was six, I was walking to the store with my little brother, Vaughn. We had to cross an empty lot. There were some teenage boys there. They raped me and Vaughn saw it all. After they left, we walked to the police station and I told them. They were white policemen and they laughed. When my mother got me home, she beat me for going to the police. I could never do anything right for my mother."

Barbara's statement, uttered so quietly, so matter-of-factly, evoked a reaction in me on two levels. My mind flashed to the injustice and I began processing ideas about it. At the same time, I reacted viscerally. I was used to reacting with emotion to events patients might describe. In fact, after all these years, my gut reactions helped me resolve discrepancies in patients' reports. My feelings merely fueled greater curiosity on my part.

This was different. I felt an intense pressure inside my body. I had to close my mouth so I wouldn't utter obscenities. The wish to express outrage battled with the need to nurture my patient. I was to deal with this conflict over and over again in Barbara's therapy.

If a white mother acted as Barbara's mother did toward her daughter, we would immediately think of her having a paranoid disorder. In a paranoid disorder, suspiciousness takes over. The mother imagines the daughter is doing horrible things and the mother is being blamed. She views the daughter as spreading lies to "outsiders," and this makes her feel that she's in great danger. The mother's solution is to punish the behavior, and so she beats her daughter.

I had spent enough time in the ghetto to know that while Barbara's mother's behavior may reflect paranoia, the mental illness model was not complete without adding in the cultural component. Blacks were isolated into their own social groups. Since they couldn't participate in mainstream America, they developed their own churches, their own medical care, their own bars, their own music, their own code of justice. All of this was based on distrust of whites. Barbara had been taught early that there would be a big price to pay if she ever confided in white authority.

Barbara's look of deep sadness in relation to her mother hung in the room like a dark cloud blocking her from any light. I had to attend to her self-esteem.

"You couldn't hate her, you know," I said softly. "To a little girl, mother is the whole world. You could only blame yourself. You could only hate yourself, thinking you had done wrong."

Barbara listened and I knew she had heard these support-ive statements. We only had a few minutes left, but I decided to make a connection to the topic she had begun with . . . her anger with her daughter.

"And Michelle is just a little girl like you were."

"Yes. That's right." Barbara looked tense and distracted. She glanced at her watch and said, "It's time for me to go. I'll see you next week," and she rushed from the room, leaving the last minutes to me.

I shouldn't have said that, I chastised myself. She's so smart and quick to process ideas, but she already feels so bad about herself. I just told her, basically, that she was projecting her self-hate onto her daughter. Great! I just added to her guilt.

I found myself listening to rock and roll music in my car after work that day. I was trying to drown the image of a little girl being gang-raped while her four-year-old brother looked on. But I couldn't get rid of the picture. I was used to individual suffering, the kind of abuse that takes place within the confines of one's family. This, however, felt more oppressive because Barbara was describing a much bigger problem. Barbara was describing abuse that was happening to thousands and thousands of children across the country.

I had worked with black teenaged girls in Los Angeles. I was familiar with the problem of racial prejudice, but I could never accept it. I was haunted by injustice. I remembered the arguments I had had years ago with my analyst.

"Why shouldn't I be depressed about the ghetto? We brought the blacks here as slaves and we'll never allow them to be equal citizens! It's not fair and I think discrimination is obscene!"

"Of course it's not fair," Dr. Stitzler would answer patiently. "You need to have a choice, however, between unconsciously identifying with the underdog and suffering, and being free to live your own life, choosing to help those who are suffering. The emphasis is on choosing."

He was right, of course, and over the years of my treatment I came to feel more and more capable of choice. But like everyone else, I had not sought analysis just for help in making choices. I'd sought help because I was miserable. Choices were but part of the problem.

No one knew about my suffering except my best friend, Carol. We had met in kindergarten, and since she lived within walking distance of my house and directly across the street from our elementary school, her place was my second home; especially after my family disintegrated when I was in the third grade, Carol's house was my refuge. My parents divorced. Who got divorced in 1948? I thought no one, except my parents.

It was as if my family had been afflicted, each member with a different contagious disease, rendering them incapable of living under the same roof. My father moved out and my mother went to work in an aircraft factory, leaving early in the mornings to catch the bus, and returning late in the evening exhausted. My sister had behavior problems and was sent to live with our grandparents, and I couldn't stand to be in the house alone.

So for many years I stayed at Carol's most of the time. Rickie, Carol's mother, drove us to movies and to all the important junior high and high school social events. She swore like a truck driver and taught us artless self-defense.

"If any guy tries to do something he shouldn't," she'd say, "you kick him in the balls hard as you can or gouge him in the eyes. Then run like hell!"

Carol and I went through school together including college at San Diego State University. We spent many evenings discussing our various complaints about our families, friends, teachers, and the world generally. My popularity, boyfriends, and straight A's never made a dent in my unhappiness.

"Gawd," Carol would say, "everyone thinks you're so perfect! If they just knew a tiny bit of how wretched you are, maybe people wouldn't envy you. I sure don't envy you. Maybe you ought to find a shrink."

So I talked to one of my social work professors one afternoon. Dr. Walker was a big, rangy man with wild curly hair and a distracted but gentle manner.

"What do you mean you think you need counseling?" he asked as he sorted through his mail.

"Well, I'm just never happy. I mean, I don't think I've ever been happy."

"How do you handle disappointment, anger?"

"What?"

"You know, angry feelings. What do you do when you get angry?"

"Nothing. I don't do anything."

"That's the problem, then. After you graduate and get settled, find yourself a good therapist."

After I got settled into graduate school at the University of Southern California, I found Dr. Stitzler. And sure enough, I'd get so tongue-tied with my anger and fear that he suggested I lie on the couch so I wouldn't have to look at him. It worked. As long as I didn't have to interact with the man, I could follow my thoughts and feelings.

And those thoughts and feelings invariably led to anger and deep sadness about feeling abandoned. I learned that I had felt abandoned as a girl when my father left. And I reasoned, as children do, that if my father could leave, so could my mother. I had lived in constant unconscious turmoil fearing that my mother would disappear, and when angry with her, wishing for her disappearance, since she hadn't been strong enough to keep my father around.

At times during my analysis I couldn't stand to think about my parents or speak to them on the phone. Occasionally, I'd drive to San Diego on the weekends and stay with my sister, avoiding my parents altogether. Very gradually, however, it became clear that although I had to be able to have my feelings of blame and rage toward my parents, venting feelings would not resolve my problems. I had to learn to feel strong enough to live my own life, forgive my parents for living theirs, and "be my own mother."

The therapy seemed like a powerful catalyst. I was always amazed that I seemed to be growing stronger every year after the therapy was over. Something mysterious had happened that I would be discussing with my patients in the years to come. The unique bond between my doctor and me had produced an awareness that I was smart and lovable. I had never believed that before, regardless of the messages I'd received.

For the first time, I was excited about my potential. I wasn't going to college simply to escape my working-class origins. I could not only recognize my choices, I could enjoy my life. I learned that psychotherapy is powerful medicine. But all that was long ago.

I tried to reassure myself that the feelings of sadness and anger I experienced following Barbara's sessions were normal. Her therapy, however, seemed to resurrect in me old issues of self-doubt. On the one hand, only a robot wouldn't feel anything after hearing revelations of pain and suffering in childhood. After all, one of the greatest writers on human development, Erik Erikson, believed that if one was emotionally healthy, feelings of "generativity" would develop as an adult. Generativity is the accomplishing of caring feelings for the next generation and for the community in which we live. I wondered if it was possible to have too much generativity. On the other hand, maybe my neurosis hadn't been resolved after all. Maybe I was still simply identifying with the underdog, feeling trapped in the same maze of hopelessness as the poor and the abused.

Dan would have agreed with that. Although he considered himself concerned and interested in social issues, he didn't believe in suffering over them. During my social-work days, he would say, "It's nice that you're helping these people, but you don't have to bleed for them. Leave the problems at work!" Now that I was counseling primarily sexual abuse survivors, he complained again that I was becoming depressed. Barbara was a particular problem for him.

Between my sophomore and junior years of college at San Diego State University, I worked as a medical social worker at the county hospital. The following summer I won a scholarship through the Western Interstate Council for Higher Education to work at a state hospital for the retarded. That was one sad summer.

I got to know children with such severe physical deformities they were tied to their beds and had no projected life expectancy, but their minds were active and normal and they delighted in company. And I got to know children in healthy bodies who had a normal projected life expectancy, but whose minds limited their ability to function in the world. They didn't know the first thing about caring for themselves.

We summer students were often overwhelmed by the hopelessness of the life situations we were observing. So we got together in the evenings and drank. I don't really like beer. I didn't drink it before that summer and I haven't drunk it since. But the summer of 1962 I drank a lot of beer and I cried in it. And I wasn't the only one.

After I earned my master of social work degree from the University of Southern California, I worked in many different settings: a state psychiatric hospital, the welfare department, a gang services agency, a halfway house for male prison parolees, a free clinic for flower children, and a children's psychiatric hospital. I supervised child-welfare workers who served the Mescalero Apache Indians in southern New Mexico and learned about the destruction of the Native American culture. My experience with people from all walks of life continued to expand when I worked on my Ph.D. in counseling psychology.

Growing up with a policeman father who had worked in all areas of law enforcement sensitized me to social problems from the time I was very small. I was taught that there were normal-looking people in the world who were doing abnormal things. There were gangsters, prostitutes, drug addicts, burglars, robbers, kidnappers, child molesters, and rapists. At all levels of society, people could be involved in perpetrating minor or major crimes. I was taught not to be scared, but I was to "keep my eyes open" and not be naive.

By the time I finished graduate school I was convinced that I knew all about human behavior. What my grandfather was so fond of saying, I thought, was absolutely true:

"There's nothing new under the sun," and nothing I didn't know about. I was to learn from Barbara just how naive I really was. I discovered that not only was I completely ignorant of the realm of evil, but I was ignorant of the realm of the spiritual as well.

In her next session, Barbara remained convinced that Cal was fed up with her behavior and ready to walk out, so I suggested he meet with us for several sessions. I've discovered that many of the women survivors of childhood sexual abuse have chosen partners who care very much for them and consistently demand that they work to resolve their symptoms of anxiety and depression. Cal was the first person Barbara tried to trust. As she told me what she knew of her family history, it was clear that Cal had become her way to leave her dismal past behind. I was eager to meet him.

Cal was a tall, black, well-built man with a direct, no-nonsense approach. I noted that he was tastefully dressed, in a perfectly fitted gray suit, white shirt, and a muted red-and-navy-striped tie. Barbara sat stiffly at the opposite end of the sofa and appeared uncomfortable being with him.

"You're not going to say anything, are you?" he asked Barbara.

"No," she answered, looking terror stricken. "Just go ahead and talk about how you see our problems."

He looked at me and sighed. "This is part of the problem. Barbara won't talk. She's afraid if she talks, it'll lead to a confrontation, and she avoids confrontation at all costs. You'd think I was a violent person or something. I get really mad sometimes, but I've never struck Barbara or the kids and I never would. I don't believe in spanking kids. It's Barbara who comes the closest to hitting them, and she knows I worry about that. She seems to be angry with the kids, especially

Michelle, all the time. Because of all her anger and fears, she acts cold a lot, like she's living in her own world and doesn't need us. I'm tired of that and I want it to change."

"You sound pretty firm about that," I said.

"I am firm about it. My family is the most important part of my life. I work hard and I have to be away from home more than I like, but family is everything to me. I know Barbara's family was a mess and she didn't have any role models, but I do want our family to be close. I want her to change."

"What if she can't? Barbara seems to think that if she doesn't change and quick, that you'll leave. Would you leave her?"

"No. Never. She would have to leave me. We're both stubborn people. But I know she can change. She's very strong and very intelligent. I don't know what her family did to her, but I know that's the basis of the problem."

I felt better after the first session with Cal. When Barbara had told me that he would interrupt her sleep for sex, I thought it possible we were dealing with a man with an unconscious need to keep his wife subservient and distressed. That was clearly not the case. Cal had simply reasoned that since sex is part of marriage and something people do at night, he should be able to have sex at night whenever he wanted it. Controlling the impulse would not be a problem for him, he assured me. I felt Cal would be an ally in our work. His commitment to Barbara seemed clear.

At Barbara's next individual session, she got down to business immediately, as usual, taking a piece of paper from her purse. "After Cal's visit here I came up with three areas that I need to work on: the first is that I do have to become more comfortable with confrontation and expressing my feelings instead of holding them in; the second is I have to figure out what it means to be me, instead of always trying to please others; the third is I have to work on being able to be a sexual person. I just realized in the past few weeks that I go away when we have sex. I'm just not there. I never noticed that before. Also, like I told you, if I initiate sex, I feel like a whore. It's a terrible feeling.''

Barbara slumped back in the chair and groaned. ''I have so many fears. It seems like I'm afraid of everything. Being out of food, not having money. I have such a panic of running out of food that I hoard it. I keep the pantry stuffed with more food than we could ever eat. At the same time I'm afraid to spend money. I never carry cash and I feel physically sick when I spend it.''

''What about your beautiful clothes?''

''I don't buy them, Cal does. He buys all my clothes. I can't stand to try on clothes and see myself in the mirror. And then I wouldn't be able to spend the money.''

Barbara laughed at the look on my face. ''It's true. He even buys my underwear.''

''Well, that's a switch. All I can say is, you're lucky he has such good taste.'' Then I glanced at her shoes.

''I may as well tell you,'' she said, ''I have two obsessions: one is shoes and the other is having my nails manicured.'' I had indeed noticed Barbara's beautiful hands, smooth skin, and tapering long fingers.

''People know that no matter what's happening, I make sure to get my manicure every week.'' She looked puzzled and added, ''I don't really understand why my nails are important, but I do understand about my shoes. We never had shoes when I was growing up. I mean our own shoes. I think I already told you that once a year my mother would take us to the Goodwill and let us pick out a pair, but I was always more self-conscious about my shoes than I was about my shabby clothing.

''You know how school kids are? I got teased mercilessly.'' She got a shy, little-girl look on her face. ''Shoes are the only thing I buy for myself. In the last few years, I like to buy shoes.''

My heart sank as I began to understand how pervasive the effects of Barbara's poverty were. "So Cal still has to spend the money, for the most part," I said. "You can't do it."

"That's right. I can spend money on the kids or on food, but not on myself, except for those two things.''

"Well, I'll say it again. You're lucky he has such good taste.''

As Barbara began to work on trusting Cal enough to speak up and express her feelings to him, I sensed that she was also working on trusting me. Trust is basic to any relationship, not just in psychotherapy. In the case of people whose privacy has been violated in the most extreme and sadistic ways by adults who were supposed to care for them, trusting seems like an impossible task. But little by little, I could sense Barbara's dedication to healing was gaining ground. She was allowing herself to feel close to me.

Each new revelation about her family was shocking, in that the human suffering that stems from poverty, discrimination, and child abuse is always shocking. It appeared that Barbara had been indiscriminately abused by many people in the family as well as in her neighborhood. What we were both totally unprepared for was the horror of a special kind of abuse, satanic ritual abuse.

Several months passed and Barbara continued to work on her childhood memories of feeling hated and abused by her mother. Her mother beat her regularly, inventing reasons to shake her, throw her to the floor and kick her, or grab a belt and whip her until she was bleeding. She remembered several occasions when she was sick and her mother refused to take her to the doctor. Her grandmother stepped in at those times, making sure that Barbara was given some type of medication (often herbal folk remedies made up by the grandmother herself), or that she was taken to a doctor.

Barbara forced herself to have sex regularly with Cal in spite of her fearful feelings and the fact that she would float away and be numb for the experience. She was also making herself talk more instead of withdrawing to her room and avoiding discussions. Although these were definite improvements, she continued to have horrific nightmares and felt bad about consistently interrupting Cal's sleep. Her feelings of inner rage also persisted.

"I can't stand this anymore. I can't stand the nightmares. I'm always covered with blood or someone else is covered with blood. Sometimes there're children or babies."

"How would you feel about using hypnosis to find out more about these nightmares?" I asked.

Barbara was entering the second stage of treatment—the harder work of getting to the bottom of her fears. In the first stage, she had worked on establishing a relationship with me, getting a grasp of what the problems were, and beginning to make some changes in her behavior. Cal had joined us for several sessions until she was more clear about his dedication to her and she felt a little more comfortable talking to him. Now, not only were her symptoms the same, they were intensifying. When I suggested the possibility of using hypnosis to help her access important memories, she was elated.

"I was hoping you'd suggest that. I knew you used hypnosis before I came here. I really want to work as fast as I can."

I had begun to attend hypnosis workshops about ten years previously. My first teacher, Erika Fromm, is one of the luminaries in the Society for Clinical and Experimental Hypnosis as well as in the American Society of Clinical Hypnosis. I came to feel that all the teachers in both professional hypnosis groups are luminaries. Each one dedicates extraordinary amounts of time to treating patients as well as writing and teaching about the healing benefits of hypnosis.

A few who influenced my learning in addition to Dr. Fromm are Dr. Harold Crasilneck at the University of Texas, Dr. Dabny Ewin at Tulane, Dr. Jack Watkins and Helen Watkins at the University of Montana, Dr. David Speigel at Stanford University, and Dr. David Cheek, past president of the American Society of Clinical Hypnosis.

My first interest in hypnosis was in learning to teach patients how to manage stress. Anxiety and chronic pain can be so disabling, I wanted to know ways of helping patients to cope with such discomfort. Then, as I began to see increasing numbers of women survivors of incest and childhood sexual abuse, I saw their frustration at not being able to remember details of the abuse. As I helped them access their memories through hypnosis, a remarkable and wonderful thing happened: self-doubt and anxiety dissolved and trust in the powers of their own minds appeared. Although this change happens in psychotherapy without the use of hypnosis, I could see the self-confidence evolving much more quickly by using hypnosis and getting right to those blocked memories.

Another advantage was that the memory work could be contained more readily in the office setting without so many feelings of being out of control and at the mercy of flashback images on the outside. Patients could be taught self-hypnosis to do their memory work on their own as well.

I always had to demystify hypnosis before going ahead. I told Barbara what Dr. Ewin and the others consistently stress: ''all hypnosis is self-hypnosis" and "there are only three states of consciousness: we are either awake, asleep, or in trance." The first message is stated to cut through the old ideas of authoritarian hypnosis, where people believe that they would be vulnerable to suggestions of behaviors that would hurt or humiliate them. With victims of childhood abuse, we have to acknowledge that they were subjected to suggestions that were coercive and destructive.[2]

I emphasized that I would help Barbara's mind to take the lead and would do nothing to harm her. I audiotape every hypnosis session, so the patient can take the tape home and listen again to her productions, and I did this with Barbara. Her tapes not only helped her to clarify her memories, but they became the basis for this book. All of the quotations in the story come directly from the tape transcriptions.

The second statement that we're either awake, asleep, or in trance helps to clarify the naturalness of being in trance. We daydream and go into trance regularly as we move through our days, and when we do anything on "automatic pilot," such as driving or cooking, we go into a trance state of focused concentration where we lose track of time and become totally absorbed in the activity. Hypnosis is a way of leaving the body alone to rest or to function automatically, while concentrating the mind on important work.

The process of helping a person into trance is called an induction. There are so many ways to do this that entire books have been written on them. Just asking someone to imagine a peaceful scene is all that's needed for a very good subject; or sometimes simply counting works. Prayer, meditation, imagery, repetition, or specific relaxation methods are all ways that people have learned through the ages to achieve what Harvard

---

2. I believe that anything parents or primary caretakers say to a child is a powerful suggestion to the child's unconscious mind and is therefore in a sense hypnotic.

physician Herbert Benson calls "the relaxation response."[3] Deep relaxation is renewing and healing for all bodily functions, in addition to freeing the mind to focus on important life issues.

I tended to use a combination of inductions, beginning with the Spiegel eye-roll technique. After asking patients to roll their eyes up as far as they can (eyes open), as though they're trying to get a look at the top of their head, I ask that they keep their eyes in that position, but slowly let the eyelids close: "Closing, closing, closed completely tight now." Then I ask that they "imagine a wave of relaxation pouring down over you from above, completely relaxing all the muscles in the head, neck, and shoulders, then let the wave of relaxation move down along your back, slowly flowing down like warm liquid releasing every tiny muscle and tendon, every nerve and fiber of your being. And let the wave move down into your legs, your upper legs and now your lower legs. Let that wave of relaxation wash all remaining tension right out the ends of your toes.

"Now concentrate on your breathing, knowing that every time you inhale, you take in a sense of peace and well-being; every time you exhale, you release any discomfort and go deeper into that peaceful, deep pool of calm that exists inside. That's right . . . going deeper and deeper."

Often, I add another "deepening" technique called the arm levitation. I ask that the person begin to feel the arm as light and weightless and being moved toward the forehead, as though a helium-filled balloon were gently pulling it up. Then when the hand touches the forehead, I suggest that the patient go into a very, very deep and comfortable trance.

I then establish finger signals, called ideomotor signaling,

---

3. See Herbert Benson, *The Relaxation Response*, 1st edition (New York: Morrow, 1975).

with the patient's unconscious mind. I simply ask the patient to lift one finger as they think yes, another when they think no, and yet another finger when they are thinking, "I don't know, or I'm not ready for my conscious mind to know that yet."

Barbara had looked at as much as she could consciously remember. Now it was time to let her unconscious help her do the work of recalling the trauma. The easiest memories had come first, though none of the memory work is easy. It's terrifying to remember even a small incident from childhood where personal privacy was not respected. If our personal boundaries are not respected, we know we can be killed. Terrifying, too, because when we remember, we feel, and the feelings of overwhelming fear and vulnerability crash in like a tidal wave. Work with Barbara would have to be done with great care.

THREE

Barbara looked more tense and nervous than I had ever seen her look before. But she also looked determined. "Are you ready for this?" I asked.

"Yes. I know I have to do this."

I instructed her to sit back and stretch out her legs on the ottoman, shifting the cushions of the chair until she felt comfortable. I asked her to place her hands flat on her lap so I could see them.

"Roll your eyes up now, as though you're trying to get a look at the very top of your head. That's right. Now leave your eyes right there, staring, staring. . . . Now leave your eyes right in that position, but let your eyelids close. Closing, closing, closed completely tight now. And let a wave of relaxation pour down over you from above. . . ."

I could tell right away that Barbara was a good hypnotic subject. She was able to leave her eyes positioned upward as the eyelids closed, so that I could see only the whites before they closed completely. I could see her body responding to the suggestions to relax. And her arm floated up easily to her forehead as she accepted that signal to let herself go into a deep trance.

"Now, I'm speaking to your inner mind, your unconscious mind. It's that aspect of your personality that has always been with you. It knows everything about you and is protective of you. When you think yes in answer to a question I might ask, what finger on your right hand wants to lift to signal me yes?" Barbara's little finger lifted. "Good. And when you think no, what other finger on that hand wants to lift?" Barbara's index finger lifted. "And when you think, 'I don't know' or 'I'm not ready for my conscious mind to know that yet,' what other finger wants to lift?" Barbara's middle finger lifted.

"Good. Now, again, I'm speaking to your inner mind and asking, is it all right for Barbara to explore experiences from her past that will help her to know why she's having nightmares?" Barbara's yes finger lifted. "All right then, I want you to slowly move back through the mists of time, slowly moving back to an event or experience that is important for you to know about. When you're there, simply say, 'I'm here.' "

"I'm here," a tiny voice spoke.

"How old are you?" I asked.

"I'm five."

"Where are you?"

"In the church."

"And what's happening there?"

"Granddaddy takes the special knife. He says he's going to fix the cat. There's something wrong with the cat and he's going to fix it."

The little-girl voice continues, "He's smiling now and ooooh"—she whispers—"he sticks the knife in the cat and there's blood all over and on me, too." She fidgets uncomfortably. There's a long silence.

I have the urge to fidget, too, but I stay still, trying to comprehend Barbara's grandfather's bloody activity.

"He lied," the little voice said finally.

"He lied?"

"Yes, he lied. He didn't fix the cat. The cat's dead."

"What do you do?"

"Nothing. I'm real quiet. Grandma taught me to be real quiet. I never scream and I never cry. If I did, Granddaddy would hurt me."

"What is he doing now?" I asked.

"He's cutting the heart out. He says I must eat of the heart and drink of the blood."

"Why must you do that?"

She makes a puzzled little-girl face. "He says it will give me power. I don't like it though. I feel sick, but I don't say nothing."

Barbara then tells me how her grandfather collects the blood from the cat and cuts up the remains. She is instructed to clean up carefully, putting the parts of the family cat in a bag and then into the furnace.

"Everyone says Muffin just ran off, but he didn't run off. Granddaddy killed him," little Barbara continued.

"Do you tell anyone?"

"Oh, no, I would never do that. If I did, Granddaddy said he'd do the same thing to me as he did to Muffin." But then, the little girl started squirming and shaking in her chair.

"What's wrong? You look really scared!"

"I'm in big trouble. I told my friend Bobby across the alley about the cat, and he asked my grandma about it, and now I'm gonna pay. That's what she says, I'm gonna pay."

She was so frightened, this little girl of five, I felt terrible about putting her through this. Too, our time was almost up, so I couldn't allow her to go on to the next trauma.

"Let those images fade away now, just fade away," I said. I barely had time to try to reassure her that she would be all right and that I would be there with her whenever she needed me. I restated suggestions for deep relaxation and calmness, especially during the night, to try to aid Barbara's sleep, and then I counted to ten and asked that she come back and again be in the room with me.

Whereas most people coming out of trance open their eyes slowly, blink, and look sleepy, Barbara's eyes immediately opened wide and questioning.

"Do you remember what you just described to me?" I asked.

"Yes, I remember everything. But I can't believe it. I must have made it up. I know my family was violent. At least a lot of them were. But Grandma and Granddaddy were the ministers of the Christian Faith Church. They were so rigid and strict. I just can't believe they were into that weird stuff!"

I shook my head in empathy. "I don't know what to think. I guess we'll have to wait and see how the rest of the story unfolds."

"Come on, this is too much!" Dan exploded. "Killing the cat is bad enough, but eating the heart and drinking blood? What do we have, a family of vampires? Maybe you'd better stop seeing her."

I rolled my eyes and said, "Sure," with sarcasm.

"Well, at least I don't have to hear about all of this crap," he said.

"Yes, you do. We're in this together."

"What are you talking about! You chose to be the psychologist, not me. Talk about it with Marcia or one of your other colleagues."

"I did, and she's never heard of anything like this. But you chose me 'for better or for worse.' And this is one of the 'worses.' I'll check it out with others, but I can't handle gory stuff by myself. Besides, you're the doctor. Blood shouldn't bother you."

Barbara's wish to deny that the cat-killing could have taken place was perfectly normal. Everyone's typical reaction to any shocking event is to say, "I don't believe it!" We need to understand the importance of the psychological defenses. I don't think they are respected for the lifesaving mechanisms that they are. As children, we would not be able to cope with fears about our personal safety without these defenses.

We quite naturally repress, deny, and rationalize frightening or horrible events. We need to believe that our parents, even if abusive or neglectful, alcoholic, or depressed, are just normal parents. We have to tell ourselves that everything in our world is as it should be and that we'll be okay.

Psychological defenses also enable us to repress and block out of memory altogether the most frightening events, so that we can continue to function. Without these wonderful defenses none of us would make it to adulthood. Our fears would overwhelm us and we would throw ourselves out the nearest window. (In fact, all of the victims of extreme abuse whom I have treated made suicidal gestures as children. They simply did not have the knowledge of how to go about actually killing themselves.)

When I heard Barbara describe the ritual killing of the cat, I knew why she had had to repress such memories. I also had a hunch that her nightmares were not just symbols of her fears, but were flashback memories of real experiences. I shared that idea with Barbara during her next session.

"I think that's right," she said. "It's hard for me to believe my family was into that kind of stuff because they were such religious fanatics. But I'm beginning to think that my dreams are about some things that really happened."

Barbara reported having been even more anxious following the hypnosis. She was having nightmares of suffocating and being dirty. Cal would wake her in the midst of her gasping and screaming for air and try to calm her.

"The feeling of having dirt all over me is unbearable. I've been taking about four showers a day," she told me.

She wanted to go ahead with hypnosis. After I helped her into her trance state, I suggested that her inner mind take her back to the experience that had caused her so much fear this week. Something must have happened to her in the past to make her feel that she literally had dirt on her.

Barbara stiffened in the chair, trying to pull her head down like a turtle does when frightened.

"What's happening right now?" I asked.

"They're taking me in the car. I don't wanna go. Something real bad's gonna happen now. I was bad and I hav'ta pay."

"You were bad? What did you do?"

"I told Bobby about the cat. Grandma says I hav'ta learn about keeping my mouth shut. I don't wanna go . . . something bad's gonna happen." She whimpers as she tries to shrink in the chair, stiffening her body.

"Where do they take you?"

"We drive a long time . . . Cherry Hill."

"What's that?"

"There's a graveyard there." She twists in her chair with fear. "I'm gonna die now 'cause I told."

"Tell me what happens to you now."

"I have to take off all my clothes. It's cold, too. They put me in this deep hole, this grave, and they bury me. All this dirt up to my neck." She's moaning and writhing in the chair, crying, "Please don't, please don't kill me. I'll never tell again. I promise, I'll never do it again. Ohhhh, no, now the Fat Lady throws her snakes in with me. Oh, no . . . I hate the snakes. Please don't! Please don't! Grandma! Grandma!" Her body goes limp and she is still.

"Where are you now?"

There's a long pause. . . . "I went away . . . to the Light. Jesus is here. He says he'll stay with me. He tells me I'll be all right. So I just stay here in the Light."

A graveyard, snakes, Jesus rescuing her . . . I was stupefied, but I couldn't indulge in my own reactions. I had to stay right with Barbara and help her move through this memory.

"Tell me what's happening at the grave."

"Nothing. They went away. I have to stay there all night."

"Who comes for you in the morning?"

"Grandma comes and gets me out of the grave. She helps me clean up and she takes me home."

It was striking to see the power of dissociation. I was to see it time and time again. As soon as the fear or pain was too much to bear, Barbara would "go away to the Light." My other abuse patients also used dissociation. One incest survivor went to "heaven, and I play there with God for as long as I need to." Another survivor of incest and child pornography went "to the clouds" and would make up nursery rhymes. It doesn't take a psychologist to recognize the adaptive value of being able to leave your body when the torture is unbearable.

In my hypnosis studies, I had learned about the continuum of dissociation. At one end is the normal biorhythm of daydreaming every 60 to 120 minutes, just as we cycle through similar dreaming states each night. When children are abused or tortured, they learn to "go away," just like daydreaming, only the reveries become longer and more intricate. At the extreme end of the scale are people who create alternate personalities to take the abuse, people who have multiple personality disorder.

The first woman I treated who "went away" floated up to the ceiling when her father was raping her. She would look down at the little girl on the bed being abused and from this "separate self" say, "She must have done something awfully bad. She probably deserves this." Barbara was the first patient I heard speak of not becoming a separate person but of going to "the Light." I was curious about this, but thought she must have learned about Jesus and "the Light" in Sunday school.

Barbara's telling me about being buried alive with snakes and left alone all night pushed me to look at my own powers of denial. These things were simply too strange and horrible to accept. I didn't want to believe that anyone could treat a small child in that way. My mind was like software unable to process information that had never been a part of the program. I called an analyst friend, who suggested that the memories were unconscious fabrications but of course, represented intense suffering.

I "knew" from the beginning, however, that everything Barbara told me was the truth. How did I know? I'm not certain, but I knew. One reason was that Barbara had no motive to make up bizarre stories. Her clear focus was to rid herself of the anxiety and fears that disrupted her family life.

I called another friend who ran groups for incest survivors. Did she know anything about patients who were reporting bloody rituals? Not much, she said, but she did know that the reports were increasing. Therapists who were seeing such survivors were calling it "ritual abuse." The practices were usually tied in with satanic worship.

"Some of the survivors of these cults have an ongoing

self-help group. But probably the best person to call would be Dan Kerlinsky, a psychiatrist at the Children's Psychiatric Hospital here in Albuquerque. He's been giving in-service training on this topic.''

I called Dan and met with him the following week.

I described some of what Barbara was telling me. Finally, I found myself sounding exactly like Barbara at the end of her last session: ''Well, what do you think? Am I crazy? Is she crazy? Does this stuff really go on? It's just too bizarre!''

My struggle to believe the memories was mild compared to Barbara's. Like other survivors of incest and sexual abuse, she wanted the memories to be imaginings that at some point she could sweep away and ignore. If she could just stop the memories, maybe she could be ''normal.'' Her family could be ''normal,'' too, except for being too strict and maybe containing a streak of cruelty. The problem is that if none of the events occurred, these patients know the alternative is that they are indeed crazy. Otherwise, where would such bizarre and terrible images come from?

Dr. Kerlinsky gave me an understanding smile. ''I wish this stuff weren't true,'' he said. ''But we have adolescents in the hospital here who have been abused in cults, and their treatment is a tremendous challenge. It sounds like your patient was in a traditional cult where the teachings pass from one generation to the next. These are often the hardest cases to treat because secrecy is paramount and most of the kids have been programmed to self-destruct rather than tell any of the cult secrets. The other types of cults basically are the dabblers, like the teens who are looking for magic and power and end up into drugs, sex, and violence, and the 'self-stylists,' the charismatic crazies like Charles Manson, who sometimes attract followers and who rationalize their criminal activities with their satanic beliefs. All of these groups murder.

''Then there are people like Anton La Vey, who wrote the

Satanic Bible, and Michael Aquino, founder of the Temple of Set. These people practice satanism openly and are therefore protected under the Constitution. Generally, you don't worry about the stuff that's out in the open. They're more into it for show business. In fact, La Vey worked in circuses and carnivals before he began his church.''

I moaned. "And all I ever wanted to do was psychotherapy. Now I'm into religion and homicide all mixed together.'' I shifted in my chair. "Oh, well, maybe growing up with a father who was a policeman has given me some preparation for this. But there's no preparation for hearing about atrocities involving children.''

"That's the truth,'' Dan said in a soft voice. "Do you know of any other therapists in the community who are dealing with these cases?''

"Not really. But I've just started asking.''

"If you come across others, we might consider starting a support group for the therapists,'' he said. "This type of work is just too emotionally draining unless you have extra help.''

Then Dan pulled open a file drawer and took out the fattest folder I'd ever seen. He held it up with both hands and said, "In the meantime, this would be a place to start.''

He allowed me to borrow his file for several days while I made copies of all the papers and bibliographies. His paper, written with Aurora Casta, M.D., "Psychiatric Aspects of Childhood and Adolescent Involvement in Satanic Cult Practices,'' was the first one I read. The following week, Barbara brought me the book *Michelle Remembers*,[4] and my education on the topic of satanic ritual abuse had begun.

"Have you read this?'' I asked Barbara.

"No.'' She smiled sheepishly. "I've always refused to

---

4. Michelle Smith and Lawrence Pazder, *Michelle Remembers* (New York: Pocket Books, 1981).

read or look at any material about violence or ritual abuse. Also, this book has my daughter's name. But Cal must think I'm ready. He brought this home. I'll let you digest it for both of us.''

I read the book quickly, eager to understand what kinds of rituals the satanic cults practice. I had to know what to expect.

Michelle Smith's mother had turned her over to a cult in British Columbia when she was five years old. The reasons why are not clear, but my hunch is that she was seduced by the powerful male leader, the sex, and the drugs. Michelle was used by the cult in many sadistic ways. She was kept in a cage or locked in the basement of an abandoned house. At one point, after having nothing to eat or drink for days, she tried to drink her own urine. The descriptions of satanic rituals and sex orgies performed by the adults seem bland compared to what had happened to her, a small child, cut off from all human care and used as an object for the most vile abuse.

After I had read the articles in Dan Kerlinsky's file, I ordered five cassettes from Sandi Gallant of the San Francisco Police Department, which arrived quickly. Detective Gallant began developing her knowledge of cults and ritualized abuse in 1978 when she worked on the People's Temple mass suicide. Since then she has become one of the leading law enforcement experts on cult homicide. I turned to history and anthropology books to expand my knowledge of satanism, witchcraft, black magic, and the occult. Yet with all I learned, nothing really prepared me for the experience of working with Barbara.

Barbara was having constant flashbacks now, terrifying images and physical symptoms. This was good in that it signaled us that she was ready to begin the memory retrieval in earnest. It was bad in that she couldn't sleep at all. The lack of sleep, plus her headaches, chest pains, and intense anxiety, were interfering with her ability to function. Cal could fill in for her with their two children, but no one could substitute at work.

As one of the state's foremost educators, not only did Barbara carry on with her routine teaching assignments, she had also been appointed by the governor to serve on a special education task force. Too, she worked as liaison with the probation department and the children's psychiatric department of the mental health center, organizing a first-offenders program for junior high and high school students. She was uniformly recognized as a woman dedicated to childhood education and the recognition and treatment of emotional problems.

But no one can work without sleep. Barbara's internist was willing to help by prescribing an antianxiety medication. Her blood pressure medication had to be increased. I told Barbara that we also needed to increase our sessions to two times a week so she wouldn't have to wait so long between meetings to let the memories come out.

"The hardest thing for me is having all these feelings," Barbara told me. "I'm sad and angry all the time, till I feel like I'll jump right out of my skin."

"Are these feelings new for you?" I asked.

"Yes. The anger has always been there, but never so close to the surface. I learned to cover it over, never express it. It feels real dangerous to have feelings. Like my heart will be broken into little pieces."

"Let's find out more about why your feelings frighten you so much. Are you ready?"

"Yes."

Once Barbara was helped into a deep trance, I asked her inner mind to take her to the significant event that she needed to look at and learn about at this time.

"Just go back and when you're there, say, 'I'm here.' "

Barbara said in a small voice, "I'm here."

"Where are you?"

"I'm hiding under the bed."

"Oh, whose bed are you hiding under?"

"Papa's bed."

"How old are you?"

"I'm real little. . . . I think, three or four."

"Why are you hiding under Papa's bed?"

" 'Cause there's a big fight goin' on. They're out back. Grandma says she wants to take me to Uncle Ted's house, 'cause they good people. She says I'm her heart, and just this one time to let her take me there. Papa is Granddaddy's father and he's the boss of the clan. He says, 'She's one of us and she stays here.' Grandma keeps asking and Papa's real mad. He says, 'Don't talk back to me.' Then he turns on his saw. I know that noise. I crawl over to the screen door and peek out. Papa and Granddaddy drag Grandma over to the saw. They push her leg into the saw. I close my eyes and scream inside me. I'm afraid they'll cut her leg off.

"It's quiet now and I open my eyes. There's lots of blood, but Grandma still has her leg. Papa says to her, 'Beth, don't you ever ever disobey me again, or I will kill you.' Then he tells Granddaddy to take her to the hospital and get it sewed up."

Barbara was still. "And where are you now?" I asked.

"I'm back under the bed. I just stay there for a long time. I don't want anybody to find me."

But then she stiffens and has that terrified look.

"What's happening now?"

"They're back and they're coming for me. They always find me no matter where I hide. I have to go in the car now. We drive for a long long time. Not to Uncle Ted's. I know we not goin' to Uncle Ted's. 'Cause Grandma doesn't love me anymore."

"You think Grandma doesn't love you anymore? She has

no choice but to do what Papa says. He won, didn't he? And you will be part of the clan."

"Yes, but it feels like she doesn't love me anymore."

"Tell me where they take you."

"We drive for a long time off the parkway and then we go down a road to this lady's house. She's real old, and bad, too."

"Somehow you know that she's bad?"

"Uh-huh. I can feel it. I'm sitting in the kitchen. I have to sit in this chair in the kitchen and I can't move. The old bad lady's name is Flossie."

"Do you know who Flossie is?"

"She's Dana's grandma. I think Dana's a cousin. They're somebody in our family. I don't wanna be here. And now Grandma's leaving. I don' want her to leave me, but Grandma gets that mad look and she says, 'Listen to me, girl. You stay right in that chair and do everything Flossie tells you, hear? Do just what she tells you.' So I sit and it gets real smelly."

"Smelly?"

"Yes. I have to smell the stuff she cooks on the stove. It's bad stuff. . . . It's brew. 'I am mixing your brew,' she says. 'It will conjure the master. The master will fill you with pure evil. The master will fill your soul.' My chest feels real heavy." Barbara is quiet and her breathing is labored. "The Light is coming. . . ."

"The Light comes to help you?"

"Uh-huh. It says I must see, I must sit and listen. It says It will keep the brew from going in my nose and inside me. And It will help me to be able to sit for so long. I have to sit there for many days, and the old lady says those words every day. That the master is claiming my soul and I must claim other souls. That is the burden I have to carry. And I must have no feelings so that I can do the bidding of the master." Barbara looks thoughtful. "That's why my chest hurts."

"Does your chest still hurt?"

"No, not now. I know the master is the devil. But I don't wanna be bad. And the Light will help me so the devil won't get my soul."[5]

When Barbara came out of her trance, she said, "Oh, gawd! That's why I'm afraid of my feelings. They mean I'm gonna lose someone like I did my grandma. She was the only one in the family who cared about me. I think my heart broke when she left me at the old woman's house."

"Your grandmother tried her best to keep you out of the clan, though, didn't she? And she paid a price for taking on your great-grandfather."

"It's amazing to me that I remembered that. I never knew it. I can't believe I never knew all that."

"Tell me," I asked, "what do you remember about your great-grandfather?"

"Only that I was scared of him. Everybody was. And he was white."

"He was *white?*"

"Yes. He was Irish."

"And here I was assuming the devil worship had African origins. If he started the clan in this country, it's probably Celtic in origin."

"Probably both Celtic and voodoo." Barbara looked thoughtful. "I remember hearing a story about Grandma's family being upset when she married into the McKelly family. Papa was known to be evil and violent. He apparently beat all the kids. All twenty-two of them."

"Come on, you've got to be joking," I said. "Twenty-two children?"

Barbara laughed. "It's true. I think there were three sets

---

5. In keeping with Scott Peck's efforts to develop a psychology of evil in his book, *People of the Lie*, I am not dignifying the concepts of the devil or satan by capitalization, thus making them proper nouns. I believe these are words that denote the entire class of "evil" and should be common nouns.

of twins. In fact, Granddaddy was part of the last set of twins. His mother died when she gave birth to him and his twin sister. Apparently, Papa's sister raised the kids and she was a real witch, in all regards. Beat the kids worse than Papa. God, what a family I grew up in!''

"How do you feel?" I asked.

"Much better than when I came in. I know why I'm afraid of my feelings and I don't have that pressure inside. That must have been the burden of feeling evil. Ugh. I just remembered what she said about the burden of claiming other souls. That would make for lots of pressure, too."

The release that came for Barbara following each session kept her able to function at work in a remarkably healthy way. She had a much harder time at home with nightmares, depression, and abrupt angry outbursts. Only when she trudged into my office would she slump in the chair and say, "I'm a basket case. I have lots of work to do today."

Our jobs were reversed, in a way. Barbara had to function outside of my office as well as she could and let down the barriers to the memories when we were together. I had to function most effectively in the office with her and could only let down the barriers to my innermost reactions at home. Only there could I be a basket case. Especially during hypnosis, I felt even more responsible for being supportive. If I was going to age-regress Barbara to ugly, terrorizing memories, I had to be right there tracking her every thought. I could not abandon her to reflect on my own reactions.

PART
TWO

SPRING
1989

F O U R

Spring had quietly appeared. The cottonwood forest along the river, dead like a pencil drawing for months now, began to come alive with green. I felt resentful. I kept getting stuck by the screen door with Barbara, hearing a saw that should have been used on wood. The only place I had been truly happy these past months had been on the ski slopes. But now ski season was over. It was time for the spring winds. The wind could be so intense that one year we had to use a wheelbarrow to carry the dirt off our driveway. We tried to joke that the dust and dirt were just the price we had to pay to live in the "Land of Enchantment." The "enchantment" was blowing around each spring, settling on the furniture and getting in your eyes. It also drove some people crazy.

"Every time I leave here I feel better and I tell myself everything will be all right. But it only lasts a few hours and then I sink back into the black pit," Barbara said. "All the horrible fears return. I still have that crushing feeling in my chest, and sometimes I can't sleep in spite of the medication. I get tense and rigid with fear and feel like I can't move."

"Would you like to see what thoughts come into your mind, or would you like to go ahead with hypnosis?" I asked.

"Nothing could come into my mind right now. I'm too tense. Remember, I researched therapists very carefully before I came here, and one of the reasons I chose you was because you use hypnosis. I need that help to recover my memories." There was a slight edge to her voice.

She caught me, I thought. I was hoping she wouldn't want to do hypnosis. I felt wary of learning any more about abuse and evil. She perceived correctly that I was backing away and got annoyed with me.

"Okay. Let's get started," I said, putting a tape in the recorder.

Barbara had taken easily to hypnosis. In addition to the fact that she was a good subject, she very much needed the peace and relaxation she could experience while in trance. She was learning to use self-hypnosis to cope with her often unbearable anxiety.

"Where are you?" I asked her once she was in trance.

"In the storeroom in the church." She was shrinking, stiffening her body, and shaking all at the same time.

"How old are you?"

"I'm four."

"What are you doing in the storeroom?"

"Grandma locked me in here."

"Why did she do that?"

"I dunno. I didn't do anything wrong. I didn't! She just

locked me in here. 'Grandma! Grandma!' I'm pounding on the door. But she won't come back. It's real dark in here and I'm afraid of the dark."

"Take a nice deep breath so you can calm yourself a little. That's right. Now, see if your eyes are getting used to the darkness. Can you see anything?"

"It stinks in here. It smells real bad." Barbara wrinkles up her nose and makes a face.

"What do you suppose that smell is?"

"I don't wanna think about it."

"Can you see yet?"

"A little. There's something in the corner." Barbara starts shaking even more in her fear.

"What is it there in the corner? Can you tell?"

"It's . . . it's . . . Sister Morgan."

"Sister Morgan?"

"Yes. . . . Oh! No! No!" Barbara screams.

"What's happened? What's happened to you?"

"I pulled at her dress and she fell over on top of me. She's dead and smelly and I can't move. I can't move at all to get her off me." Barbara is completely quiet, but moaning softly.

"What do you do now?" I ask.

"Nothin'. I just wait and wait till Grandma comes to get me. I can't breathe and I don't even want to. I just wanna be dead, too."

"When does Grandma come? How long are you there?"

"I dunno. Doesn't matter."

"Why not? What are you feeling?"

"Nothin'. I don't feel at all. I'm just there."

"What happens when Grandma comes?"

"She just pulls Sister Morgan off me and tells me to go upstairs and take a bath if I want."

We were both quiet when she came out of trance.

"I don't know what to think," Barbara finally said. "I have trouble believing this stuff. It sounds so crazy. On the other hand, why would I make it up?'' She was quiet for a few moments. ''You know how I told you I usually feel better after being here? I don't feel better today.'' She looked at her watch, dragged herself out of the chair, and said, ''See you.''

''You'll phone me if you need to, right?'' I called to her.

She turned to me and said, ''You know I will. I keep my word.'' And she left the office.

We had a verbal agreement that if she was thinking about suicide or hurting herself and couldn't stop the thoughts, she must call me. I worried about Barbara because of her fierce independence. She expected herself never to let down in her performance of duties, and she couldn't ask others for help. Her suicidal thoughts were horrifying. Most patients think of overdosing on pills or shooting themselves when they're distraught. I was afraid that Barbara might actually be capable of cutting herself open and pulling out her insides.

When she was with me, she would get anxious if we went over the allotted time by even one minute. Early in her work, she'd be on the edge of her chair ready to bound out the door five minutes before the end of the session. When I questioned her about her eagerness to leave, she smiled sheepishly. ''I just want to be very careful that I don't take advantage of your help. I'd worry that you might get mad at me.''

''The only way I might get mad is if you keep stopping your work early,'' I said.

On the other hand, I knew I could trust her to call me if she became dangerously suicidal. I knew she was telling the truth when she said, ''I keep my word.''

I continued to share the most shocking accounts of Barbara's past with Dan. I simply had to. With normal psychotherapy patients, confidentiality was easy. Albuquerque is sufficiently small that I would often run into patients while shopping or eating out. If they acknowledged me and stopped to chat, I would introduce them to my family, afterward explaining that the person was a colleague at the university or a student I supervised, or fabricating some other relationship.

Up to now, I rarely shared details of therapy with Dan, except when I had learned something I felt was important for me professionally. He, too, might share an epiphany with me about his work. For example, he intuited that certain patients with allergic symptoms might be suffering depression. The symptoms expressed the feelings without the patient's being aware of the substitution. We had decided to do a research project based on his hunch.

When disturbing or confusing psychotherapy sessions occurred, I had been trained to consult with a more experienced colleague. I tried to do that in Barbara's case, but no one, except Dr. Kerlinsky, had experience with what Barbara was describing. So on the days of my sessions with Barbara, after particularly upsetting revelations, I would share them with Dan.

"Are you sure she's not imagining all this?" Dan asked after I'd told him about the decaying body in the closet.

"I don't think so," I said. "She's the most stable person I've ever known, let alone treated. I know that sounds weird, but it's true. There are no signs of thought disorder or difficulty with reality issues as in schizophrenia. There's no secondary gain. She doubts the memories more than I do!"

Dan slumped back in his chair. "I just can't believe this stuff."

"I've pretty much decided that people are capable of anything," I told him. "Also, you know how you've always said, 'Truth is stranger than fiction'? We used to laugh at that. Now, I believe it's absolutely true."

We both lapsed into silence, and I knew we were thinking the same thoughts that any parent thinks when confronted with horror stories. The thoughts are always accompanied by a prayer: "Please, God, don't let anything even close to that ever happen to our children."

"I'm still not better," Barbara said in response to my inquiring look. "In fact, I'm not good at all. I'm afraid I'm really crazy. I think I'm just losing it and I'm making all this up. What I want to do is just focus on the incest with Granddaddy and get that taken care of. After all, that's one of the things I initially came for."

"Okay," I answered, "let's see what your inner mind has for you to look at today."

"Where are you?" I asked, once she was comfortably in trance and I had suggested she move back in time to a significant experience with her grandfather.

"I'm walking with Granddaddy. He picked me up from school and drove me to this house. We're walking up to the house."

"How old are you?"

"I'm twelve."

"What happens inside the house?"

Barbara stiffens and contorts her face with fear. "It's the Fat Lady's house. I hate her. She always puts her snakes on me."

"Tell me what happens here."

"She says, 'Well, if it isn't the little princess.' Then she and Granddaddy take off their clothes and they do their nasty stuff. I don't hav'ta do anything. I just watch. And she don't bring her stupid 'babies' out this time."

"What happens when they're finished?"

"Granddaddy puts his clothes on and says, 'Let's go, Princess,' and we go back to the car. He's driving and then he stops." Barbara stiffens again and says, "I have to suck his thing. I don't want to. . . ." She giggles.

"How come you're laughing?" I ask her.

" 'Cause I bit his stupid dick. And he doesn't hit me or

nothin'. I'm real mad and he knows it. I hate his guts and I'm moving back with my mother. I'm never goin' back there.''

Out of trance, Barbara began laughing again and said, "Now I do feel better. I never knew that that's why I moved back to Luciel's.''

"Luciel's?''

"Yeah, that's my mother's name. I never call her Mother. She was never like a mother, you know. She really hated me. Grandma was like my mother. But remember, there was this power struggle over me when I was little. This feels like the first time, this time when I was twelve, that I made the decision to move.''

For the next few sessions, Barbara was satisfied to discuss the incest with her grandfather. I was delighted to see her feeling good about herself and silently hoped the worst was over. I slowly realized she was avoiding using hypnosis or looking at any new memories. Knowing she had stood up to her grandfather had given her a boost, but it was only temporary.

"This isn't working,'' Barbara said as she slumped into the chair. "I thought maybe I could just have simple incest, and I could work through it and feel halfway normal.'' Barbara caught herself on the "simple incest'' statement.

"Isn't that stupid? I know nothing about incest is simple. But somehow, it seems more acceptable than this. I can't stand to think about this satanic stuff. I can't handle it. At work, when I've heard people in probation, the court system, or even other teachers talk about satanic or ritual abuse, I'd just walk away. I never wanted to even think about it. It makes me too anxious and I'm having a hard enough time functioning.

"I keep waking up at night feeling slimy, like I'm covered

with some kind of slimy stuff and I can't get it off. Oh, and I took the kids to the zoo and they wanted to see the snakes. I couldn't even go into the Reptile Building. Snakes terrify me."

"Now, that's not a surprise, is it?" I asked her.

"No. But it still seems silly to me. Not real."

"What would you like to do?"

"I think I need to use hypnosis and find out what's going on."

Once Barbara was in a deep trance I gave her the instruction to move back through time to a significant event. "I'm hiding. In a tobacco field. Grandma told me to go here and hide. It's in the country."

She sounded little. I matched my voice to hers, speaking as I would to a very small child. "How old are you?"

"I'm three."

"Why does Grandma want you to hide?"

" 'Cause lots of people are comin'. All the McKellys. And she don' want me to be there."

"How come?"

"My mind says 'cause there's evil all around. But there're snakes in the tobacco field. Brown with greenish spots. An' they're poisonous. So, I run when I see 'em. I run back to the house. An' they're all there. Everybody."

"Who do you see?"

"Silas, Grandma, Granddaddy, Aunt Lilly, Papa, Auntie, Ben, Robert, and that nasty Donald. I can't stand him. I don' know the rest of them. They're Granddaddy's relatives. We all have to go to the McKelly property. We go in the cars, and we go past the barn and down a dirt road to this house." Barbara starts scrunching up in her chair as though she's trying to shrink herself away.

"I cannot see the house." Barbara's voice goes deeper as she clearly speaks someone else's words. " 'Death will surely fall upon you if you ever see this house.' "

"Who says those words to you?"

"Papa says those words."

Barbara is trying to shrink herself again. She's obviously terrified.

"They tied something over my eyes and I'm freezing. And I don' wanna go into that house alone."

"You have to go in alone?"

"Feels like it, 'cause they don' care 'bout me."

"No one's there for you."

"No. And I'm freezing. I don' have no clothes on."

"And what's happening now?"

"They're touching me . . . smearing somethin' on me." In addition to her plaintive voice, Barbara moves her hands as though she's trying to brush something off her. She's very obviously scared and uncomfortable.

"What does it smell like?"

"I don' know. Tar. They put it on my eyes . . . on the stuff over my eyes. And on my chest. It's sticky and kinda hot. Not burn hot."

"And what else?"

"They sayin' their bad words." Barbara's voice drops again as she mimics a grown-up: " 'We commend this soul to you, as we lower her down into the depths. Take her and take all that is left of her. She will do your bidding. If she does not do your bidding, you shall claim her soul at the right time. Not even the enemy, who thinks he is so great, can save her, because your power is great, almighty father. And we commend her into the jaws of your mouth, so you will have her soul forever.' "

"What do they do now?"

"I'm spinning and spinning. They spin me all around. An' now they're wrapping stuff all over me . . . like cloth."

Barbara's voice is so small, I can barely hear her.

"They put a rope around me. I can tell 'cause it's tight

—
67

around my arms. I don' wanna go down the hole. There's a monster down there. I don' wanna go. I don' wanna go. I can't see, so I can only think what's down there. An' I don' wanna go to the monster.''

''You'll be all right,'' I try to reassure her. ''Tell me what happens next.''

''They lower me down . . . down . . . into a pit. I don' know . . .''

''Is it a cellar?''

''I guess so, but I can't see nothin'. I'm listening. The Three-in-one[6] says, 'I will help you. I will keep you safe.' It's the Light in my mind. It feels warmer now. I'm down there. My feet . . . the only thing that sticks out, so I can walk around. It's not a floor. Feels like rocks.'' She starts shaking one foot and then the other.

''What are you doing?''

''Creepy things. Slimy things here and cold. They're on my feet.''

''What could they be?''

''I can't pick 'em up to tell. Maybe worms.'' Barbara gives a sigh of resignation.

''How long do you have to stay down there?'' I ask her.

Again, Barbara's voice lowers into that of an adult: '' 'The master shall keep her for five days and five nights. Because the master can do his work in a shorter time than the enemy. The enemy took seven days. The master shall devour her in five days, and she shall belong to him.' That's what they said.''

I had the same aching sad feeling for her that I'd had when I read about Michelle Smith's being left in a basement alone for days. ''That's a very long time. What do you do there?'' I asked.

''I know how to count, so I move real slow all round the

6. The *Three-in-one* was a term Barbara's family had used for Jesus Christ or God, probably resulting from the Christian reference to the Godhead as Father, Son, and Holy Ghost.

place. I count the walls with my nose. I can tell when one wall ends and then another one starts.''

"What a smart little girl you are.''

"Yes. I can count and there're four walls there. The floor's just dirt an' rocks. An' all those . . . those things. I hate 'em an' they're all over.''

"Five days and nights. That's such a long time,'' I say. "What happens when you have to go to the bathroom?''

"That's how I know it's a long time. 'Cause I can hold it a long time. But I do hav'ta go potty, so I go over in the corner like dogs do, and I sweep those things away with my feet. They're bigger than worms.''

"Bigger than worms? Could they be little snakes?''

"I don' want them to be snakes. I'm afraid of snakes. If I think they're snakes, I'll get too scared. They put snakes on me before.''

"Do you go to sleep?''

"No! If you go to sleep, the things'd be all over you. I'm afraid they'd eat me. I get real tired and I yawn, but I'm too scared to go to sleep. So, I step on things with my feet and try to figure out what they are. Mostly rocks and those things . . . they're snakes and I don't want them to be.'' Barbara is quiet. "That's mean,'' she says after a while.

"Yes, it is mean to make a little girl be there with snakes. Don't you get hungry or thirsty?''

"I hate water. I don't drink water. I hate it 'cause they make you drink lots and lots of it. I get hungry, but then it goes away. . . .

"They're coming to get me now. Granddaddy says, 'Barbara, I'm lowering a chair down there, and I want you to sit on it.' So I sit on the chair and I put my feet around so I won't fall. They take the stuff off my eyes. I can see now, but it hurts my eyes.'' Barbara starts shivering with fear again.

"What's wrong?''

"The Fat Lady has short red teeth. She says, 'Come to me, my little darling. Oh, you precious little thing. Yes, you have survived all the things the master has asked of you. You are definitely the one. You shall be crowned the princess. You shall lead the clan.' The Light says, 'Don't listen to her.'"

With surprise Barbara says, "They put white stuff on my legs! Why'd they do that?" Then after a thoughtful pause: "It wasn't tar on me. It's grease, and they're tryin' to get it off." Barbara starts shaking again. "I wanna go home."

"What are they doing now?" I ask her.

"I can't tell you." She whispers, "The Fat Lady is very wicked. I don' wanna tell you what she does."

"It'll be all right. I'm here with you. Take a nice deep breath." Barbara does as I suggest and I can see that she's gathering her courage to speak.

"She licks me. And she puts her tongue between my legs. I shiver and shake inside and she laughs. She says, 'See, I can bring the jaws of the master out of a mere baby!' I feel real bad. I wanna go. It's all black. The Light is gone and it's all black."

"You feel real bad. Is it because you had a pleasant feeling?"

"Yes. That means I'm bad like them. It means I'm one of them. It means I'm evil, too." The little girl, Barbara, sitting before me looks completely distraught.

"You're not bad or evil. They just want you to think that. You're only a little girl. Did you know it's normal to have pleasant feelings if someone touches you down there in a soft or gentle way?"

"No. I think it's bad."

"It's only bad that they do it and you have no choice. You're too little. Grown-ups aren't supposed to do things like that to children. You aren't bad, they are."

Barbara listens to me, intent. "I'm upstairs now and there's a bed. I'm real cold and tired, but I don' get to go to sleep. Granddaddy comes in and he has no clothes on. He says, 'I hear you're ready to experience the master. You do what you did for Nonnie' . . . that's the Fat Lady's name. 'You do that with me.' I wanna go home. Jus' take me home. But he doesn't. He lays down beside me 'cept he's not actin' mean. I'm very cold. He stinks, too.''

"What does he smell like?''

"Like wet hay. He's touchin' me on the chest and tellin' me I'm a beautiful little girl, but I don' believe him 'cause he always called me a 'nappy-haired little nigger.' He's tryin' to make the evil come again between my legs. It's all black again.''

"You know it's wrong, don't you?''

"Yes, but he does it anyway . . . an' he shakes all over . . . then he falls asleep and I go under the bed so nobody else'll come and do it. Grandma's at the door and she has clothes for me. She says to come on and be real quiet. She takes me down the stairs and carries me. I'm a little scared 'cause we might get caught.''

"Where does Grandma take you?''

"Not home. She takes me to Anna's. That's her mother. She's real dirty. House is dirty, too. She smokes a pipe. There's a bed by the door and a chair with a straw seat. It's one room and she's got it real hot. There's no bathroom and no closet either. Grandma says, 'I'll make a cot on the floor for you and you go to sleep.' But I don' go to sleep. I listen. Grandma says she's scared. She says she's afraid they're gonna get me. Anna says, 'I tol' you not to marry that black-ass man. I tol' you the McKellys were nothin' but of the devil. I tol' you, nothin' but evil!'

"Grandma says, 'Yes, but I'm in charge now and I gotta protect her.' Anna says, 'You gonna be the death of me 'cause I can't save your souls from those devils.' And Grandma says, 'I am the smartest, the biggest, and the lightest . . . the one

with the prettiest hair. I can do it. I am the queen of them all.'
Anna gets real mad. 'Get your yellow ass out of my house! And
leave that one here. And don't come back and don't touch that
baby.' So Grandma left and I'm jus' cryin' and cryin' for her
to come back. I don' wanna stay here. Anna's dirty.

"Next morning Anna takes me to Joe's house. That's
Grandma's brother. They have children. She says, 'Don' you
let the McKellys take her. They're not gonna destroy this
child.' But they say I have the sign of the curse and I'm
wicked. They tell Anna it's too late. They say they can't keep
me. I'm glad. I get to go back to Grandma.''

When I brought Barbara out of her trance, tears were rolling
down my cheeks. She looked at me incredulously. "Why are
you crying?''

"I'm overcome with feelings for that little girl you were
who endured so much all alone. The more important question
is, why aren't you crying?''

Barbara looked thoughtful. "I could never cry. It wasn't
allowed. I could only cry on the inside or I'd be punished. I'm
amazed that you would cry for me. I feel like such a nothing
. . . like nothing, as small as an ant. That's what I feel like, an
ant. I feel so ashamed and embarrassed, as though no one
could possibly like me.''

"I believe you're a very special person. And I hope you'll
learn to believe that, too,'' I said.

I couldn't believe I had dissolved into tears with Barbara.
That's not something I had ever done before, and identifying
completely with a patient's problems is discouraged during
training. Most of my training and supervision as a psychother-
apist was Freudian and neo-Freudian, or what is often referred
to as ego-analytic. In that framework, the therapeutic relation-

ship is carefully guarded, and the therapist works to maintain a neutral stance. Within that neutral relationship, the patient can then look at early traumatic experiences from different angles, like carefully inspecting all sides of a puzzling object with no contamination from outside suggestion.

I had been through a five-year traditional psychoanalysis. I wondered what my analyst would say about my lapse in "abstaining" from inserting my feelings into Barbara's therapy. Naturally, it would be counterproductive for the patient to have to worry about the effect of her material on the therapist! Would Barbara be afraid to bring up important memories now for fear that I'd fall apart?

Then I pictured my analyst. "If that's all you did, indulge in your own feelings," he would say, "yes, you would be harming your patient. But in fact, you used your feelings to make an important interpretation—that she was never allowed to have her feelings in response to any of the abusive behavior and that she blamed herself. As a result, her self-image has suffered tremendously."

That felt better. I also thought of one of my favorite social-work supervisors who used to tell me to "use" myself in therapy. "As long as you're tracking the patient properly, don't be afraid to be right there with her." Maybe that's what I'd unconsciously done with Barbara. I was right there with her. I felt cheered by the possibility that my response had been therapeutic. I could not feel anything but tension and outrage, however, about what I was hearing. I found it difficult to comprehend the notion that adults would band together and inflict evil on a small child. In fact, I found it altogether difficult to comprehend how anyone could embrace evil.

My religious background was varied. As a girl, I tried to concentrate on being good. I wanted to have a sense that God was smiling down on me blessing all of my endeavors.

My mother and grandmother were Christian Scientists,

the church founded by Mary Baker Eddy, and as a young child I attended services each Sunday eager to see what kind of long gown the woman who led the services would be wearing. Once, when I asked my Sunday-school teacher why I was having nightmares, she replied that it was because I had bad thoughts. I wasn't prepared to take that much responsibility for my thoughts at that time, so I found reasons to get out of going to church after that.

Later, after my parents divorced, I began going to the Episcopal Church with my neighborhood girlfriend. The attraction there was Father Robinson, who was truly good-looking. I think half the congregation consisted of teenaged girls, transfixed by that handsome face, thoughts everywhere but on his sermons. Then I attended the Lutheran Church for several years because there were attractive boys at the youth-group meetings. I began to teach Sunday school but gave it up because I couldn't stand to tell small children about the devil. What all this adds up to is that I never wanted to think about evil. And I certainly never believed in the devil.

Free will was a concept I believed in, and I assumed anyone in his or her right mind would choose good over evil. I believed that only people who were mentally ill could hurt their children or commit murder. In college and graduate school, I learned that genetic predisposition and early childhood experiences are responsible for people's behavior. Poverty, social conditions, lack of appropriate parenting . . . these were the factors that might cause someone to become mentally ill and hurt others.

What Barbara was telling me about the perpetrators in the satanic cult was shaking the roots of everything I had understood about human behavior. I was beginning to see that some people embrace the dark side of the psyche. My diagnostic manual of mental conditions failed me when it came to categorizing such people. I continued to read broadly about individual and also group perpetration of evil acts.

Molly Harrower, a noted American Rorschach expert, obtained the Rorschach and other psychological tests of the Nazis on trial at Nuremberg. She matched them with Rorschach tests of American men of the same age and level of education. The disturbing results were that when the two groups of tests were anonymously evaluated by other experts, they could not tell any difference in the character of the men. Top-ranking Nazis functioned easily on the two diverse levels of being good family men and of efficiently carrying out mass murder. Douglas Kelley, the psychiatrist appointed to the Nuremberg trials, had already stated the unthinkable in 1946: "From our findings we must conclude not only that such personalities are not unique or insane but also that they could be duplicated in any country of the world today."

I was fascinated to receive an article from a friend at the University of California who was doing computer searches for me on satanism. The article was from an Italian journal and described a satanic rite practiced throughout the 1930s by the SS, Hitler's elite corps. They dressed in sleek black uniforms with special insignia, lightninglike *S*'s, death's-head badges, and silver daggers. German banners and symbols were part of the decor, and the rite, called *Die Elektrischen Vorspiele* (The Law of the Trapezoid), used a pentagonal enclosure, mirrored, with a hanging trapezoid above. Stroboscopic lights and electric organs playing the music of Morganrot or Wagner were used to imitate the lights and sounds of hell and to invoke the devil. In place of a nude woman as an altar, a human skull was used. We aren't told about the rite itself, but it apparently ended with the proclamation: "We desire power! We shall have power! We desire wealth! We shall have wealth! Hail, Loki! Hail, Satan!" Loki, I found in the *Satanic Bible,* is the Teutonic name for the devil.

Being evil was beginning to seem quite distinct from having a mental disorder. I had heard a saying once: "The mind is like a parachute. It works best when it's open." I felt as if my mind were being opened by a gust of wind, periodically so shocking that it threatened to take the very breath out of me.

From my reading, I was attempting to develop a historical context in which to understand satanic practices. I learned that from about 7000 B.C. to 2000 B.C., goddess religions and paganism were predominant.[7] Matrilineal descent was practiced as part of the matriarchy of that time. Around 1800 B.C., Indo-Europeans began moving south into Anatolia, Mesopotamia, and Canaan, those areas that we now call the Middle East. Archaeologists refer to this as the Aryan Invasions.[8] What began to evolve over the next two thousand years was a violent repression of the matrilineal religious cultures and substitution of the patriarchal religions of Judaism, Christianity, and Islam.

While it was possible to eradicate matrilineal descent and establish the dominance and power of men, it was never possible to stop completely the practice of the ancient customs of worship. Goddess figures and pagan rituals were believed to gain favors from the unseen supernatural powers regarding the seasons, crops, fertility, illness, and death. High priests and priestesses ran many sects and traditions all over the world. Magic, witchcraft, and paganism survive in almost all cultures and are prominent in preliterate cultures even today.

Devil worship seems to have evolved in response to the control, dominance, and power of the Christian church. In their eagerness to spread the belief in Christ as the representa-

---

7. For more on goddess worship, see Merlin Stone's *When God Was a Woman* (New York: Dorset Press, 1976) and Marija Gimbutas's *The Goddesses and Gods of Old Europe* (Berkeley and Los Angeles: University of California Press, 1982).
8. Merlin Stone conjectures that because German archaeologists were making these discoveries, Hitler may have read about them and changed his last name from Schickelgrüber to a name most resembling that of the first group of Aryans to invade the Middle East, the Hittites.

tive of the one true God, early church fathers denounced any form of paganism or witchcraft as devil worship and thus ascribed real power to the devil. Those who worship satan and use black magic believe that satan, the Adversary of the Old Testament, is more powerful than God.

Witchcraft was an offshoot of paganism, referred to as "the craft." (Barbara's grandmother referred to it as "witching.") The emphasis is on using magic to influence the gods to help achieve a desired goal. According to Bronislaw Malinowski (1884–1942), the founder of social anthropology, there are three main elements to magic: the spell, the rite, and the condition of the performer. The spell uses incantations, or chanting, using special words in a certain way. Medicines, poisons, or potions are also used. The rite means practicing the magic in a formal and defined ritual situation. The condition of the performer involves purification rites and taboos in order to invest the ceremony with sanctity or holiness. Barbara was describing all of these aspects of magic used in satanic worship.

Satanists completely reverse Judeo-Christian values and practices. The Black Mass, for example, is an obscene version of the Roman Catholic requiem (mass for the dead). The satanic version uses a nude woman as the altar and uses black magic to invoke the devil. The entire mass is said in reverse. Every aspect of the ritual, including murder, is designed to mock the prevailing values of preserving life, denying lust, and respecting the dead.

Babies and small children are especially valued because they give satanists the opportunity to achieve their highest goal: the corruption of innocence and goodness. The adults dedicate the child into the service of "the master" through symbolic "birthing" rituals. They also force the child to participate in learning about evil and to find others who can be used by the cult to increase the number of souls they corrupt and thereby, give to the devil. Babies are especially valued for human sacrifice since satanists view them as having "pure hearts," that is, untainted by a belief in God.

Barbara's family referred to the devil always as "master" or "father." She never heard them use the words *devil* or *satan.* Her family, by day, were strict fundamentalist Christians. At night, during their satanic rituals, they rarely spoke the name Jesus Christ but referred to Him as "the enemy."

F I V E

he historical reading was both engrossing and infuriating. I had never been interested in history before and now I knew why. History, for me, had meant the imperative to memorize the dates of men's violence. War after war after war. The history of men killing. I had always memorized just enough to get through the required high school and college history courses. Then I ignored history and focused on literature, psychology, sociology, the sciences of personal interaction.

Dan loved history and liked nothing more than talking about it with his middle brother, Will, the family's walking encyclopedia. They could spend hours debating governmental decisions, military strategy, and the different possible outcomes in terms of international power. I pounced on them once in the middle of one of these intellectual exchanges.

"This is exactly what's wrong with the world. Men only care about control: how to control and who will have the power to control. Who will send which army where. And of course in that context, women and children are quite secondary."

I waited for one of them to attack me or at least answer my accusation. All I got was perplexed looks. Dan then turned back to his brother and continued right where they had left off. I was furious. That night I insisted on reading to him several of the passages about the Aryans sweeping down from the north and the Hebrews coming in from the west to destroy the land of Canaan, "the promised land."

"It's no different from what the Europeans did to this country! They massacred the Indians and then enslaved the Africans. In the Middle East, men decimated the peaceful matriarchal cultures and gave us the three male-dominated religions of Christianity, Judaism, and Islam."

Dan just looked at me.

"And the look you're giving me right now is simply patronizing," I said. "Like I was speaking some unintelligible foreign language."

Dan scrunched up his chin and shrugged. "It's interesting, but I don't remember reading about any of that in school. If it's really true, why aren't we taught about it?"

With teeth clenched, I answered, "Because men run every institution in the country. The women may teach, but the men run the schools and write the history books."

"I think that part about Hitler taking his name from the Hittites is interesting," Dan said. "I'll bet that's right. But I don't believe that the Jews killed all the inhabitants of the Fertile Crescent to take over that land."

"Not only to take over the land, but to develop a new culture. Why do you think all the early kings had hundreds of wives? In order to destroy the goddess religion and matrilineal descent. But you don't have to take my word for it. You can read these books, or better yet, read the Old Testament. Yahweh's commands to destroy every living thing are right there."

I wanted Dan to share my outrage about the discoveries I was making. I didn't know what we could do about the steadily swelling river of violence flowing through our present society, but I wanted his help. It was clear, though, that while he could side with me over an individual case of violent abuse such as Barbara's, he couldn't separate himself from everything he had learned growing up about men: that their rightful place in any society was to be the most powerful. If male power is the dominant value in society, then women and children will continue to be used and abused. I felt completely disheartened.

Barbara was sitting on the edge of her chair, alternately wringing her hands and twisting her wedding rings. "I've been having a strange reaction to the color white. My daughter needed a new dress for a special event, and as we were shopping, she saw a white one she liked. I freaked. I couldn't look at it or talk about it. She realized something was wrong and went on to look at others. That evening, I started thinking about my wedding and how terrified I felt walking down the aisle with Granddaddy.[9] I got out my wedding pictures and brought one for you to see." She reached down into a bag and brought out an eight-by-ten photo.

"It's a beautiful dress," I said, "but you do look sad and scared, as though you're remembering another time that was unpleasant. Should we try to discover what happened before in a white dress?"

---

9. Although I was stunned at the realization that Barbara's grandfather had not only allowed her to marry but had participated in the ceremony, later in therapy we learned of the price she had paid for this freedom.

"I have to."

"Where are you?" I asked when Barbara was deep in trance.

"I'm sitting alone in the back of the church."

"What are you wearing?"

"Nothing. I don't have any clothes on. I'm just sitting in the back waiting for them to come."

"How old are you?"

"I'm six."

"Who is first to come in?"

"Grandma. She says, 'Come here, Barbara. I have something for you.' So I go and she has new clothes for me. She says I have to go upstairs and take a bath first 'cause I'm real dirty."

"How come you're real dirty?"

" 'Cause I was laying in the dirt."

"Where were you laying in the dirt?"

"In the graveyard."

"Oh, and now it's morning."

"No. It's afternoon."[10]

"What happens now?"

"I hav'ta go upstairs and take a bath . . . a hot bath with oils."

"With oils?"

"Yes. Special oils and special scents. Then Grandma comes up and puts the clothes on the table and tells me to put on the clothes when I get out of the tub. These are my princess clothes, she says."

---

10. Therapists who use hypnosis have been accused of "suggesting" that their patients have certain memories. I have been impressed by the fact that patients are very clear about refusing to accept "suggestions," just as Barbara did here. Not only did she consistently correct my statements, in many sessions she argued with me about her view that she was bad and the clan was good because they were grown-ups and therefore, whatever they told her must be right.

"Your princess clothes."

"Uh-huh. And so I put them on. They're all white. White panties, a white undershirt, a white slip, and white socks and white shoes. The white dress. I hate the dress."

"How come you hate the dress?"

"It's ugly. Ugly things happen in that dress."

"Ugly things?"

"Yes, but I don't want to talk about it now."

"Okay. Tell me what happens next."

"I ask Grandma if I can go 'cross the alley to Bobby's, and she says there's enough time, but I better not get dirty in that nasty house. So, I go there and we sit at the table. They don't have any food. And I tell Bobby that I'm a princess and he says, 'Nuh-uh,' and I say, 'Uh-huh.' He says, 'Who told you?' and I say, 'Grandma.' So he comes to the side door of the church with me and asks Grandma if I'm a princess. She says, 'No,' and looks at me, and I know I'm in trouble again."

"You're in trouble."

"But she didn't tell me it was a secret. I wouldn't have told him. I would have told him to promise. She didn't tell me it was a secret!" Barbara began to wail.

"You didn't know. And now you're in trouble?"

"Big trouble. I have to go to the upper room. I have to take off all the clothes because I wasn't fit to be the princess. That's what Grandma says."

"So you have to take off all your clothes. Now what happens?"

"I hide in the closet because I don't like the men finding me, the Keepers."

"Keepers?"

"That's what they call 'em. The Keepers of the Rite. But Granddaddy finds me. He's yanking on my arm. He says, 'Get your ass on the bed now!' He says I'm gonna pay 'cause I broke the Rite. But I didn't know it was secret." Barbara pauses and looks completely despairing. "I shoulda known. Everything they do is secret."

Barbara is shaking and stiffening in the chair now. "I didn't know," she whimpers. "You didn't tell me. . . . I didn't know it was secret." She's very still. "There's things on the bed."

"What things are on the bed?" I ask.

"Snakes . . . they're on me." Her whole body is shaking.

"They put those snakes on you. You're so scared."

"And the snakes . . . and there's somebody there . . . hiding . . ."

"Who's there, hiding?"

"It's the Fat Lady . . . and she has more snakes, in a cage."

"How many snakes are on the bed with you?"

"Four. Four black ones. And now she ties my legs . . . she ties my legs to the bed and she takes out one of her black-and-white snakes. She says her 'babies' is gonna eat the evil inside of me so I'll be a good princess. The snakes are on my legs now . . . crawling up my legs." Barbara is stiff and shivering uncontrollably.

"It'll be all right," I say softly, trying to reassure her. "What happens next?"

"She's laughing and pushing the snake up inside me."

Barbara stopped shaking and her body went limp. She dissociated and went away from the torture. I had to help her to come back and face the horror of what had happened to her. Survivors of abuse, battle, and torture have to be able to know consciously most of what happened to them in order to work through their feelings of rage and grief. Only then can they integrate the experience into their personalities and go on with their lives without displacing those feelings onto themselves or their current family members.

"You've gone away to the Light. That's good that you know how to do that. Take a deep breath so you can be even more comfortable. . . . That's right. And you and I know that you can always go to the Light when you need to. Now I want you to come back and tell me what happens. You can do it. Tell me what happens now.''

"She's mad. The Fat Lady's real mad. She says I killed her pet. She says I killed her pet 'cause there's poison in me." Barbara winces and her head jerks.

"What happened?"

"She hit me hard in the head. And Grandma comes in and says, 'Now you can't put any marks on her. She has to be perfect.' "

"So at least she can't hit you anymore."

"I don't care. Nothing hurts anymore. I'm gonna die."

"You're gonna die? How?"

"Make the men kill me. I'll make 'em so mad they'll kill me. That's what I'll do on that special day."

"What special day is that?"

"The Rite of the Princess. I have to marry the devil, but it's really Granddaddy. He says he's the devil, but he's not. He's a shit." Barbara begins using a grown-up voice: " 'Once you become the princess, then you have all the power over the clan. Then you can choose who the king will be. And you will decide who will die. And you are the queen forever through all eternity.' "

"Move forward in time to when that ceremony begins to take place."

Barbara shifts in the chair, cocks her head. "I'm there, but I'm still mad. I had to put on these white clothes again. But I tore the ribbon off. Grandma doesn't hit me. She just sews it back on and acts like nothin' happened. Now I'm waiting in the dining room. I'm waiting for the Keeper to bring me the key. And now I have to unlock the door and it's all white in there. Lots of candles and everybody has on white, including Granddaddy.

"Ugh! There's snakes all over the floor. Grandma's across

the room at the altar and she says, 'Don't be afraid, Princess. They're there to carry you over into the righteous phase. You will walk with them and they will bring you over to us, and you will be a part of us forever to eternity.' So I walk through the snakes to where Granddaddy's standing . . . with his shitty grin. He takes my hand and we walk between the special candles to the table where the parts are."

Barbara starts squirming in her chair. "I can't do this, I can't." Her voice lowers as she imitates an adult. " 'As you come to this table to partake, we each share part of the heart. Each will have one foot, one hand, one eye . . . for these are the symbols of eternal life.' "

Barbara now speaks in her own little girl voice: "Now I have to eat one eye, one toe, and a piece of the heart." She began to gag so severely that I was concerned she would actually throw up in my office.

"What's in your mouth?" I ask her.

"It's an eye. It's Charles's eye! It's terrible!" Her whole body is shaking as though she were convulsing. I quickly told her to go to the Light, go away from that scene and become comfortable. I did that as much for my benefit as for hers. I was nauseated and having trouble accepting my visual images of what was happening.

Barbara relaxed again in the chair, and I asked her to continue to observe this Rite of the Princess and tell me what was happening.

"Now I have to drink some blood, but only fresh blood." Her voice drops. "This is a symbol of the bond between us, the blood of the most purest heart, one that was conceived by the master.' Granddaddy says that, and now they bring the baby. It's Aunt Connie's baby. She's not here. She's always drunk. Grandma lied and told her she'd give the baby to somebody to raise."

Barbara went on to tell how her grandfather placed the

ritual knife in her hand, put his hand over hers, and together they killed the infant. I was completely startled by this revelation, but all I could do was listen as little Barbara described the clan's collecting the baby's blood, and passing it around for everyone to drink. Following this, they began chanting and disrobing. Barbara was forced to kneel in the circle of people and remain silent while each man ejaculated on her, then lift her face up as each woman squatted over her and rubbed their vaginas on her face, symbolizing each celebrant's participating in giving birth to her. Barbara was now the princess of darkness, the clan's representative of evil on earth.

When Barbara came out of trance, we were both exhausted and speechless. Barbara stared at me for a long time. Finally, she said, "I don't know how I can live with this."

I had a similar helpless reaction. I felt drained and sick. How on earth could I help her to get over anything this dreadful? But I had to offer her hope. "It's been hard for you to live with these secrets. I think the Light will help you as you continue to bring them out. And I'll be here to help you. When did you learn about the Light?"

"What do you mean?"

"Did you learn about it in Sunday school? And what does it mean to you?" I remembered reading that Michelle Smith had seen a light when she was undergoing satanic torture. She also described Jesus coming to her as well as Mary, whom she called *"ma Mère."*

"I learned about Jesus in Sunday school," Barbara answered wearily, "but there was never any mention of the Light. I feel like I've always known the Light. But I don't know what it means and I can't think now."

"I think you may need extra help with these memories of murder. I've never referred anyone to a minister or a priest before, but I think you could benefit from consulting a spiritual adviser. Would you consider doing that?"

Barbara pursed her lips and said, "I'll think about it." She checked her watch and got up to leave.

"Is Cal at home this weekend? I want someone to be available to you."

"No, he'll be out of town. I'll be all right."

"Whom else do you trust? I know you've said you have no friends, but there must be someone. Whom could you call if you need to?"

Barbara gave a little laugh. "Sharon. Sharon's one of the administrators I work with who knows me like a book. She won't let me push her away. Very strong and caring. She raised three children, one with Down's syndrome. She's always checking in to see how I'm doing, even though I've not told her much about me. I think she intuitively knows what's going on."

"You must promise me to call her if you need some companionship. And if you get too scared, call me. Here, write down her number for me and leave it with Jan, and let her know that she'll hear from me if I get concerned about you." Cal and I had agreed in Barbara's presence to contact each other if either of us became alarmed about Barbara. Now I felt I needed other allies to help Barbara feel safe and to discourage her from hurting herself.

I certainly did need allies. I felt I couldn't help Barbara by myself. My own emotional life had become chaotic. *Cyclothymic* was the old term I thought of. It meant cycling though moods in an uncontrollable manner. While on the outside I functioned normally, inside I felt jittery and upset, and often those feelings plummeted to lows that I could only define as an ongoing "anxious depression." I explained it to Dan one evening on our deck in the following way: "It's like coming across the scene of a bloody accident and for days afterward you can't get the gruesome images out of your mind. Plus, your body has its own reactions. For me, anxiety hits me in the gut. I feel like I'm twitching all the time.''

"I know about your tendency to have irritable bowel," he said, "but it sounds like the primary diagnosis is posttraumatic stress syndrome.''

"Always the physician," I teased him. "But you're right. I'm sharing Barbara's diagnosis. Except her symptoms exceed mine by geometric proportions because she lived this stuff. What amazes me is that I continue to function perfectly well on the surface. I can finish a session with Barbara and immediately move into a session with another patient without a ruffle.''

"We all do that," Dan said softly. "Remember last year when that little boy died suddenly in the hospital? I saw the rest of my patients that day, but then I was a wreck when I got home. Took me a long time to get over it. We doctors don't do death. We're only taught how to prevent it, so when death occurs, we feel like failures. We cover up our insecurities pretty well, don't we?''

"What's the alternative?" I asked.

The following week, I was shocked when I greeted Barbara in the waiting room. Her hair was nearly shaved off. She smiled a little uncertainly. "Do you like it?''

"It makes you look like a model from *Vogue* magazine. Is that what you intended?''

Barbara shrugged and snuggled into the big chair in my office. "I was just tired of fooling with my hair. I almost didn't come today. In fact, I wasn't going to come back at all. I got through the weekend okay, but that last session was too awful. I didn't say anything when you mentioned finding a priest 'cause I just wanted to stop all of this. It makes me feel so crazy. But then last night something really weird happened.'' Barbara paused, seeming to gather her courage. ''Jesus came to me.'' She looked at me with that inquiring look I had come to know so well. The look posed the question, ''Do you think I'm crazy?''

I nodded for her to go on.

''Jesus told me I have to tell you everything about the Rite. He said I have to tell you all that happened to me so I can grow up and not feel like an ant.''

I sucked in my breath and answered evenly, ''In that case, we'd better get to work.''

Barbara knew that there was more about the ''Rite'' that she had to remember now, and she was very frightened. She told me she thought we needed some kind of a verbal signal to keep her going at times when she was regressed in hypnosis and was fearful of telling clan secrets.

''I know there are times when my mind feels like it just can't tell you things. Maybe if, when I get stuck, you could give me a key. Say, 'It's all right. It's me, Gail. You can tell me.' That'll remind me that it's you and you're safe and connected to the Light.''

I agreed to say those words to reassure Barbara of her safety whenever I thought she was having a hard time moving ahead with her memory work. And then I put her in trance.

''The parts, the parts! They're here!'' Barbara said in an agonized voice.

''What is that? What are the parts?'' I asked her.

''The parts . . . Charles, Michael, James, Adam, David, Paul. And their . . . the bodies. I'm crying inside. I liked them. Especially Charles. I liked him.''

''Where are you?''

''In the graveyard. It's cold and scary. I have no clothes

on. I'm six now. Six is a special birthday. Did you know? Grandma told me."

"Is Grandma there with you?"

"No. I'm all alone. I must stay here until dawn." Barbara's voice lowered as she began quoting the words of a grown-up: " 'We celebrate the rule of our master over his kingdom. Earth belongs to him here and in the eternity. Come unto me, little children, for I will show you the power of darkness. I will show you strength. You will never be afraid or lonely again. Come unto me, little children. Prepare to enter the gates of hell. There shall be special parts . . . the eyes, the ears, the hands, the feet, the penis, the heart. The penis is the symbol of penetration. She will always be protected. The heart is her ability to conquer souls throughout the world.'

"I can't remember what the other parts mean. Then Granddaddy says, 'She shall be adorned with the parts for twelve hours. I will come to her and make her worthy of the words. Then she alone shall rule and be powerful. These are the most sacred of days. The ignorant spin their wheels looking for the coming of Christ, the fake one. Save us, Master, from the fools who know not your strength and goodness. You've given us power to rule the earth they do not deserve. We commend her soul to you, Great One." Barbara was quiet.

"So now you stay there in the grave until dawn?"

"I'm on top of a grave of someone who's supposed to have power. There's a big cross. The bodies are around me. Two on each side and one at my head and one at my feet. And the parts are on top of me. And I have to stay here 'cause they called out the special spirits from the grave, and if I get up, they'll get mad and kill me. Grandma says if I'm quiet and don't move, the spirits will come into me and I'll be special and strong like them. But I don't want to be like them and I'm ascared, so I ask Jesus to help me, and He keeps me warm and says He won't let the evil spirits come into me."

"You've learned that Jesus will take care of you, haven't you?"

"Uh-huh. Jesus comes with the Light and keeps me warm. Not real warm but warm enough."

"Who comes back at dawn?"

"They all do."

"How many people are there do you think?"

"Lots. They all come back and they make an aisle. They take the parts off me and I have to walk down the aisle. First Granddaddy says, 'The princess has come. She has arrived and she is ready for the preparation of the feast.' They're all clapping and saying, 'Welcome, Princess, welcome, Princess.' I hate that! They're disgusting."

"You know they stand for evil, don't you?"

"They do. They do really bad things."

"They kill children," I add softly.

"And grown-ups, too. I saw them do that. They killed a man once 'cause he lied."

"What did he lie about?"

"I don't know. Grandma and Granddaddy said he lied and so he had to be punished. But he wasn't worthy to eat his heart, so they just killed him with a big knife from the kitchen and put him in the alley like a bum that somebody had killed. If he was a pure heart, they would have eaten his heart after they killed him in a ceremony. And they'd cut off his hair and save his fingers. But they didn't."

Out of trance, Barbara looked as despondent as I'd ever seen her. "Now I know why I do the work that I'm doing . . . trying to help children. I can't stand the thought of those little boys."

"Do you know who they were and how they were killed?"

"I guess I've been saving that part. I've been having nightmares about killing little boys and being covered with blood." After a long pause Barbara said, "That's probably the real reason I cut off all my hair. I hate that feeling of being covered with blood." After a long pause: "I think I'd like Cal to be here for the next session. I need for him to know more about the horror I'm trying to live with and that he's having to live with. And I want him to know I'm not crazy."

"What about following through on finding a spiritual consultant?" I asked.

"I'll do that now. I'll find an Episcopal priest. I stay far away from fundamentalists, and Catholicism is a little too far in the other direction for me. Episcopalianism somehow seems safe. I'll do it."

We had an hour and a half reserved for the next session, and Cal was there with Barbara, as she'd requested. I pulled up a chair on Barbara's right for Cal to sit in, as I always sat on her left near my desk and close to the audio equipment. Cal began by expressing his concern about whether Barbara might need to be in the hospital.

"She's probably told you she's smoking again and drinking a few glasses of wine each evening. I'm really worried that the next step is that she'll hurt herself."

I looked at Barbara. She said steadily, "All I can do is promise that I'll ask one of you for help if I feel desperate."

"And I can promise both of you that if and when I feel Barbara needs to be hospitalized for her own safety, I will make that happen," I said. "I hope we can avoid doing that, though."

"Me, too," Barbara added. "I'll be furious if I have to go to the hospital! My family has ruined my life enough."

The three of us got as comfortable as we could to prepare for a long session, each of us recognizing it wasn't the length of time we were trying to prepare ourselves for.

"Where are you?" I asked Barbara. Her eyelids were

fluttering as they do during REM sleep and dreaming. I could tell she was watching a picture.

"I'm in the hospital."

"How old are you?"

"I'm six."

"What's happening there?"

"It's nighttime and the nurse is pushing me in a wheelchair. I don't like this nurse. She takes me to an elevator and we go down to the basement."

"How do you happen to be in the hospital?"

"They say I have boils on me. The nurse says she's taking me for treatment, but I'm getting scared. Oh, and there's one of the Keepers. He opens a door for us and there's this big room all filled with people."

"Who are these people?"

"Some of 'em I know, but lots of 'em I don't know. And I can't find Grandma. I can't see her. I'll be really scared if she's not here! The Fat Lady comes over to me and says, 'Welcome, little princess. The little darling is finally here.' But she doesn't say it in a nice voice. An' I still can't find Grandma.

"The Fat Lady grabs me and tells me to get up out of the chair and get over on that table. I do, and oohhh, the monster is over by the window. The doctor tells me to take off my robe and get on the table and lie real still. He says I have boils down there, but I know I don't."

Barbara is shaking all over with a look of terror . . . and then she's limp.

"Know that the Light is with you, Barbara, and I'm here, too. It's Gail, and you can tell me what they're doing to you."

Her body stiffened again and she began to speak in a tiny voice.

"The doctor put some kind of clamps down there and it hurts so much. And then the Fat Lady sucks on me. She says she's sucking all the bad stuff out of me to purify me and prepare me for him . . . for the monster who's dancin' around over by the window.

"I say I hav'ta go potty and the doctor gets mad. He says he'll put a ca . . . catheter in me so I don't hav'ta get up. They don't want me to stop the ceremony. Everything hurts down there. And then they stick something in my butt and there's stuff going inside of me because it hurts my stomach. And then the Fat Lady's biting me and biting me all over and now on my neck."

Barbara's body is twitching as though she is being physically attacked in all the ways she's describing. "The doctor says to the Fat Lady, 'You are one sick bitch,' but she just laughs and starts dancin' around saying the evil words. They're not real words. They're different. And I always try not to hear them. They can make me look at things, but they can't make me hear, so I like to not hear the evil words. They sing them sometimes, too."

"What happens next?"

"I don't wanna see. I don't wanna know what happens next. The people move away from the table and I can see boys laying in circles on the floor."

"How many boys?"

"There's one . . . oh, that's Charles. He was in the room with me upstairs. But then they took him away and said he'd died. He's not dead. He's not moving very much, but I don't think he's dead. I bet they gave him a shot or made him drink somethin'. And there's Michael and Adam and James, and David and Paul. They all belong to someone here. Their mothers are here. Oh! There's Grandma. She's there in the corner. I thought she wasn't here, but she is."

"Six boys in circles. Are they six years old, too?"

"I think so. And the Fat Lady's putting her snakes on each one. The special candles are on the floor, too. Now I have to wait in the other corner, and Grandma comes to the table.

They call it the altar, but it's a funny table. Grandma starts saying her words, 'In da no we do, in da no we do,' and sometimes I hear the word *evil*. Then she says, 'Say-ay-ay we now. Say we now. Bring unto us these gifts. The gifts of man to the master. We bid your pleasures, Your Blessed One. For you are the one and only master of the land. Spare us your vengeance. We offer unto you these sacrifices. Spare us, O Great One. Spare us, O Great One. We do your bidding. Accept these as our bounties and save us from the wrath. Give us all power as we drink the blood and eat the flesh for the master.'

"Charles starts screaming, so Sister Miller gives him a shot. She's a nurse. But then they bring him to the table and the doctor tells me to sit on him and I do it wrong. They get mad at me 'cause I'm supposed to sit on his penis. So I do and the doctor gives me the special knife. I pretend I don't know what to do, so he has to put the knife in Charles. I'm crying inside. Then they give me this other knife. It's very small and narrow. I've never seen one like it before. Grandma tells me I must cut out each eye very carefully. I drop the knife and act like I can't do it. Grandma says I must do it just as she tells me and do it right. 'Lift the eyelid with your left hand and now cut carefully around the white part. Be careful to take out the entire eye. And now do the other eye. The eyes will give your heart the power to see.' "

Always something more shocking than I could ever imagine! I thought quickly. A six-year-old girl who was familiar with knives, of course, was not familiar with a scalpel.

"And then they take Charles away and bring Michael," Barbara continued. "I have to sit on his chest when they cut him open 'cause they make me cut off his penis and his testicles, 'the organs of penetration,' Grandma says. She says her words while each boy is killed and some parts are cut off."

"What parts are taken?" I ask.

"Two eyes from one, two ears from another, two feet from another, two hands from one, a heart, and a penis."

"What are all the people doing while this is happening?"

"They're all dancin' around and singing. Nobody has clothes on, so sometimes they do nasty things to each other. I don't feel good. It's dark in my mind. The Light went away from me. I don't feel good."

I didn't feel good either and I could tell from looking at Cal that he felt worse. He had his elbows on his knees, knees spread apart. He looked so close to the floor that he might fall there if just a feather pushed him. I wanted to end this ghastly session, but I'd learned to check in with Barbara's unconscious mind to see if she was ready. I asked her if she had done enough work for today, hoping beyond hope that her answer would be yes. Her voice said yes, but through our prearranged finger signals, which were a more direct link to her unconscious mind, the answer was no. I took a deep breath and suggested she move back to the event that she needed to learn about.

"I'm back there with the boys. Grandma says, 'She is ready now for the master.' There's blood all over me! And now the monster's coming. . . . Oh, no, not the monster! I'm too scared. Oh!" Barbara's eyes almost opened right up. "It's not the devil! It's Granddaddy!"

When I brought Barbara out of trance, she smiled and said, "There's no devil. It was always Granddaddy with a mask." That was the information that Barbara had had to retrieve before she could finish that session.

I had been confused about Barbara's belief in a literal physical devil. She had many nightmares in which she would see the devil and was convinced that he was a physical presence. During other hypnosis sessions, she had mentioned that she knew the presence wasn't really the devil, but was her grandfather. However, she was slightly older during those age-regression sessions, and she was very angry and thus feeling stronger. This was her first clear realization that her grandfather dressed up to look like the devil. It was a tremendous relief for Barbara. But there was no way to relieve the horror of the experience of the killings.

Barbara looked increasingly tense and nervous as we discussed what had happened. I asked if she knew in what hospital the ritual had taken place. She told me, "It was the only hospital for blacks. I was born there."

Cal added, "It's been closed down. I think it's an apartment complex now."

"I have a lot to learn about these perpetrators," I said. "I simply can't understand how mothers could willingly turn their children over to be sacrificed. I just don't get it."

"I can't understand any of it," Barbara said in a wooden voice.

"I'm sorry," I said to both of them. "I just got caught up in the defense of intellectualization. If we talk about the hospital and the perpetrators, then I don't have to share your pain. What are we going to do about your pain?" I asked Barbara.

She shook her head. Cal was staring at her intently. "I'm going to be worried about her," he said. "Especially when I'm out of town."

"When do you next leave?" I asked him.

"In three days."

"I'll be fine at work," Barbara said.

"We know that," I told her. "You function wonderfully well within the structure of your job. Most of us do. It's outside of that structure that you'll be the most vulnerable to suffering." I suggested that we add a third appointment time to our weekly therapy schedule. Both Cal and Barbara looked relieved.

"Oh, and I just remembered," Barbara said, "I have an appointment to meet with the priest tomorrow."

"Good. And let's promise to call each other if we get worried."

I postponed telling Dan about that session. I often felt that in my anger about male aggression, I was dumping information on him that he couldn't possibly know how to respond to. But there was another reason I didn't tell him. A much more important reason. Death intervened.

It was a Friday night, May 19, 1989. Dan and our daughter Jasmine had flown to Mexico to climb a mountain. Her college classes had finished, and as the strongest athletes in the family, the two of them usually planned one strenuous climb each year. Julie and I had gone out to dinner, stopped at the Gap, her favorite clothing store, and had gotten home about ten. She was sleeping and I was in bed reading a novel.

The phone rang at eleven-fifteen. "Dr. Feldman, we've been trying to get hold of you all evening." It was my answering service. "You have an emergency call from the Hemmings residence."

I hung up and began to dial our best friends' house. After living in Albuquerque for twenty years, we had lots of wonderful friends. Robert and Ellen Hemmings were special because their youngest daughter was Julie's best friend ever since they attended Montessori preschool together. It felt rare that four adults shared as many interests as we did, and over the years our two families had traveled together for skiing, fishing, and hiking.

Dan and I had been coping with our sadness about their impending move to Vancouver. They were Canadian citizens, both having grown up in the wilds of Canada and later, Montana. Right after their marriage, they had built a rough cabin in the forest, with their own hands. Now, they planned to build a permanent home in Vancouver. Although Robert had trained as a lawyer, he had stopped practicing law and developed his own oil business. He was carefully nursing financial contacts in Hong Kong and the Far East that would enable him to relocate. We were to be their first visitors the following summer and sail with them along the Inside Passage.

My heart beat loudly as I waited for someone to answer the phone. A strange voice was at the other end. "Gail, this is Stephen, Ellen's brother. I don't know how to tell you this, but Robert killed himself today."

My throat tightened and "No!" came out at the same time. "No! No! No!" My stomach knotted. "That couldn't be! What happened?"

"He hanged himself."

"Oh, God. How's Ellen? What about the girls?"

"Well, they cried for so many hours this evening, I think they're sleeping. They're exhausted."

"Should I come over?"

"No. I flew in from Vancouver this afternoon and Ellen's other brother came in this evening. What we'd really like is for you to come over in the morning and talk to the kids about this. We don't know how to explain it to them."

I hung up and began running up and down the stairs, sobbing and screaming. Then I remembered what Ellen's brother had said. They wanted me to talk to the girls. I couldn't possibly do that. I couldn't think at all. I ran to the phone and dialed a retired pediatrician and psychoanalyst living in Santa Fe. I had participated in one of his semester-long seminars at the medical school on psychoanalytic interpretations of literature. I was very fond of him and respected his wisdom. I got an answering machine. I was crying and sobbing my message, spilling out words about Robert's suicide and how I didn't know what to tell his children. I hung up and threw myself on the bed to let my crying continue.

Then I thought to call Marcia Landau, my office partner. She and I had met nineteen years earlier when she was pregnant with her youngest child. She was about to go on maternity leave from the Child Guidance Center and I was asked to fill in for her while she was away. By the time she returned, the Center had found enough money in the budget to hire me part-time.

Marcia picked up the receiver and uttered a sleepy "Hello." I told her about Robert's suicide.

"I'm coming right over," she said.

"You can't do that. It's the middle of the night and it wouldn't be good for you." Marcia suffered with chronic asthma that had landed her in hospitals, not only in this country, but several times when she was traveling in Europe.

"You can't be alone with this," she said definitively. "I'm coming over, so put the outside light on for me. I'll stay the night."

"I should have known what was happening," I said as we talked at the kitchen table. "I think this one big deal must have fallen through for him. He was completely preoccupied with it the last two trips we were on. He'd leave us on the ski slopes to go make phone calls. And Dan told me that when they took the girls' class on a field trip to Mesa Verde a couple of weeks ago, Robert went to bed at eight. We didn't know what to make of it. But he was obviously depressed! I'm a psychologist! I, of all people, should have seen it!"

"You're a friend, not a psychologist to them. You couldn't have helped him with anything. Ellen's the one you're going to have to try to help with *her* guilt. She's going to be a wreck."

I felt completely deflated. Like a flat person. "Robert was my best male friend. He was like a brother I never had. We'd share our novels-in-progress that we knew would never be published. But, we always told each other, 'this one's really coming along. This one may have possibilities.' And he helped me with legal questions. He was so enthusiastic and supportive of my work. He understood me . . . even more than Dan." I put my head in my hands and cried some more as Marcia rubbed my shoulder. Then I looked up. "I don't know what to say to the girls."

"Yes, you do. You've explained suicide to children many times. Remember? It's a mind sickness. Depression is an ill-

ness where a person's thinking becomes more and more narrow until they can no longer see alternatives or solve problems.
Where normally the person can figure out how to get around
a problem, the depressed person sees no way except suicide.''

Yes, that would come back to me, I thought. I could do
that. Then I returned to my own sense of guilt at not having
realized how much pressure Robert was experiencing. Marcia
patiently explained again that although mine was a natural
reaction, I couldn't have helped Robert out of his depression.
He wasn't the type to go for help. He could help others, but he
would never have accepted help for himself.

"You're right," I cried. "But I never even realized that!
That's the problem! Robert had an alcoholic father, who
robbed him of his childhood. He had to be the man of the
house and run the farm and take care of his younger brother
and sister. Shit! He only learned how to be a caretaker. He
didn't learn how to take help for himself." I cried and swore
some more. It was three A.M. by now.

In the morning, I went in and sat on Julie's bed. Her eyes
opened immediately and she could tell by looking at me that
something was very wrong.

"You look gray," she said. "What's happened?"

"I'm sorry, honey, but Robert died yesterday." Julie cried
and asked many questions, preparing me, I thought, for how
I would try to explain suicide to his daughters.

Over the next two days, many friends helped Ellen and
her brothers continue the packing that had already been
started. Along with many of their friends, we packed and
sealed boxes, cleaned areas of the house, and cried on each
other's shoulders. Instead of moving to Vancouver, Ellen and
her family would drive the U-Haul trucks to Laramie, Wyo-
ming, and leave everything at her brother's. Then they would
drive on to Montana where they would bury Robert. There
was a special place there, Ellen said, where Robert had said he

wanted to be buried. It was on a hill overlooking a beautiful, peaceful valley.

Sunday night we were still working at the Hemmingses' when Dan and Jasmine came home. They were dirty and tired-looking, still in their climbing clothes, but glad to finally be a part of the mourners.

"I'm so sorry we weren't here," Dan said as he gave Ellen a long hug.

"How are we gonna get along without Robert?" Jasmine asked through her tears. Jasmine loved Robert as we all did. She and I held each other, and I felt a surge of thankfulness that my family was all here, close and loving. I have to remember to be more appreciative of what I have, I thought. And a vision of Barbara came into my head. There are levels of love, I thought, and levels of betrayal.

A group of us organized a memorial service for Robert, to take place the weekend of his burial in Montana. We held it at the Friends' Meeting House, a place we thought Robert would approve of.

It continued to amaze me that I functioned so well at work. I never faltered in carrying out normal duties, except for several hours that Monday morning when we were helping Ellen and her family, her family without Robert now, prepare to leave town. We continued to grieve, however. Julie missed her dearest friend, Polly, and Dan appeared shell-shocked. He heaped blame on himself for not recognizing Robert's depression and helping him.

Dan had another reason to feel guilty. The Monday morning after Robert's suicide, he got a call from a physician friend in Los Angeles who told him that Gilda Radner had died over the weekend. Dan had grown up with Gilda in Detroit. Her older brother, Michael, was Dan's closest boyhood friend.

They wanted Dan to come to Los Angeles for the memorial service being organized there.

"How can I go?" he agonized. "I never even went to see her in the hospital!" While we kept in touch at Christmastime, and Dan had gotten regular updates from one of her doctors, he chastised himself severely for not visiting Gilda before she died. "What is wrong with me anyway?" he asked.

Of course he flew out for the service, but returned feeling guilty that he enjoyed the memorial appearances by Gilda's famous friends, instead of spending time with Gilda herself before death arrived. I felt like Dan, that we weren't "doing death" very well.

Work with Barbara continued unabated. I was impressed at how consistently she did her memory-retrieval work. Regardless of the horrifying experience for her of being immersed in fear and trauma, she pressed on relentlessly. I had rarely seen such a combination of motivation and stamina. When she was suffering from intense nervousness and lack of sleep, my inclination was to slow down, hers was to keep going. She was absolutely driven to master her fear and gain the upper hand over her past. Like vomit, the memories were ugly, but the more that came out, the less toxin was in the body and the better Barbara felt.

My affection for Barbara was so strong, I puzzled over it. Although I became attached to many of my patients, I felt especially close to Barbara and looked forward to each of her sessions. Why? I think now that it had something to do with recognizing how badly she needed me and my responding to that need. The affection was similar to the greater love one might have for a handicapped child in recognition of his greater need, and the deep respect for the courage required by him to overcome his limitations.

Occasionally, I thought about Barbara's visitation from Jesus. Could that have really happened? At a conference I had attended, the leader did a guided imagery where he had us imagine white light pouring through a funnel into the top of the head. It was a peaceful feeling and also the type of meditation that was supposed to heal areas of the internal body that might be attacked by virus, bacteria, or cancer. I began to practice that meditation, allowing the light to pour through my insides. I also began to imagine the light surrounding me on the outside, making a protective bubble. I never had any sense of spirit visitation, but the white-light imagery helped me to be more calm.

I also began to ask the Light to take care of Robert. If there was an afterlife, I thought he would be mad as hell at himself. Let him know how much we still love him, I thought. We will always love him. Then I asked for guidance in my work with Barbara. I thought of her Light and said, "If you are like guardian angels, help me do just the right thing in order to help Barbara."

PART
THREE

SUMMER
1 9 8 9

S I X

The summer heat had settled on Albuquerque, but I was unaware of the weather. Jasmine had two jobs, one at a health spa and the other hostessing at a downtown restaurant. Julie was away most of June and July at a camp she loved in the Pecos Wilderness outside Santa Fe. I was working on an article on satanic ritual abuse in the evenings.

My thoughts went to the satanic rites Barbara had been describing. In the anguish of hearing her memories, the sequence of events became confused. I began to organize the rituals in my mind. The first formal ritual, when she was made princess of darkness, appeared to have taken place when she was three years old and the family gave her to the devil for five days by putting her into the cellar. The next formal rite was what Barbara had called Induction to the Rite, which was the torture in the Upper Room when she was six. Then came the sacrifices of the boys, which the group called Keeping the Rite.

Following that was the marriage ritual to the devil, also at age six, which they called the Rite of the Princess. There were many other sessions of torture and confinement during those years, all of which satanists refer to as "purification" rituals. They were attempts to "break the spirit" by inducing fear, confusion, and the belief that the child is totally controlled by evil and belongs to the devil.

Articles on satanic ritual abuse were beginning to appear in the professional literature. Barbara was by no means a lone survivor. The victims and survivors of sadistic abuse in general, and satanic abuse in particular, were turning up frequently all over the country. The treating therapists were networking, writing articles, and developing institutions in order to treat and study the symptoms of dissociation and multiple personality disorder. The most noted clinics were those affiliated with Chicago's Rush-Presbyterian Hospital and the National Institute of Mental Health in Bethesda, Maryland. And now there was a new journal, *Dissociation.*

With fascination, I read an article titled "Satanism: Similarities Between Patient Accounts and Pre-Inquisition Historical Sources," written by Sally Hill and Dr. Jean Goodwin. I knew Dr. Goodwin from years earlier when she was doing her training in psychiatry. Since that time, she had published several texts on treating sexual abuse and incest and numerous professional articles.

Not so many years ago, they wrote, children were not believed when they told about sexual abuse and incest experiences. Because of physicians such as Dr. Goodwin, childhood abuse was being recognized and the children were receiving the care and treatment they so badly needed. Dr. Goodwin had now discovered another area of human suffering where patient credibility was a hindrance to their help and recovery. Many of the survivors of sadistic abuse were thought to be crazy and were misdiagnosed as schizophrenic.

In her research, Dr. Goodwin found that as early as the fourth century, the following elements of a satanic mass were well described: (1) ritual table or altar, (2) ritual orgiastic sex, (3) reversals of the Catholic mass, (4) ritual use of excretions, (5) infant or child sacrifice, and ritual use of (6) animals, (7) fire or candles, and (8) chanting. When she extended the historical search from A.D. 400 to 1200, three additional elements were found: ritual use of drugs, the circle, and ritual dismemberment of corpses. Barbara had been remembering scenes and experiences where her family used every one of these rituals.

I was to learn that there were others in my field who dismissed reports of satanic ritual abuse as fabrications typically made by hysterical women who were trying to get special attention. I smiled bitterly to myself when I thought of the added pain and humiliation these survivors of such extreme abuse would feel if they knew that they were not only disbelieved, but were seen as having pathological motivations for their excruciating memories.

It made me think of another fairly recent controversy in my field, the attack on Sigmund Freud for changing his beliefs about child abuse. Freud treated a number of women who had symptoms of dissociation, physical disorders, and what we now call posttraumatic stress disorder. The women invariably revealed a history of incest or sexual molestation as children. Freud believed that these seductions were the cause of the women's symptoms and he used hypnosis to treat them.

But over the years as he wrote and lectured about his views, his male colleagues were disbelieving of such reports. They were scandalized at the notion that fathers could mistreat their daughters, that men, just like them, might sexually abuse a child. The opposition to Freud was intense. He eventually relinquished the "seduction theory" and settled on the idea that such symptoms could develop from unconscious sexual longings and fantasies. When he stopped using hypnosis and gave up the seduction theory, Western women and children were sentenced to seventy more years of abuse without the possibility of being believed, and of symptoms for which they would not be helped with hypnosis.[11]

My reaction to the disbelievers softened, however, when I reread *Michelle Remembers*. Many months had passed since Barbara had brought me the book. During that time, I had read numerous books and articles on every aspect of child abuse. As I prepared my paper, I realized I needed to go over the book again. It was one of the only survivor reports I knew about.

What a shock to discover I had completely blocked from my mind the horror of the murders that Michelle had participated in. I had forgotten every scene of killing. I remembered only the confinement and nonphysical abuses, as well as the descriptions of satan and those who appeared to be possessed by the devil. I was learning how normal it is to deny, repress, or intellectualize possibilities of experience that are just too strange or frightening to accept into awareness.

This reminded me of Jean-Paul Sartre's comment that the difference between Americans and Europeans was that Americans don't really believe in the existence of evil. I believe he was right. I realized now that allowing for individual acts of evil is much easier than crediting group acts. After all, an individual isn't so frightening. We can call him such names as *madman, psychotic, homicidal maniac*. Too, these names

---

11. For more about Freud's retreat from the seduction theory, see Jeffrey Masson, *The Assault on Truth: Freud's Suppression of the Seduction Theory* (New York: Farrar, Straus & Giroux, Inc., 1984).

imply a mental derangement, not a moral, spiritual, or societal aberration that might affect us or the people we know.

I thought about what happened to Dr. Bruno Bettelheim, the renowned psychologist, when he came to this country after being released from a concentration camp in Nazi Germany. He tried to tell about what was happening in the concentration camps, and few would believe him. In fact, he was accused of indulging in "paranoid distortions." Americans could not take the Nazis seriously. They could not believe that a group of people would organize themselves to perform such atrocities as torture and mass murder.

During the same period, Americans were alternately shocked by and disbelieving of reports of a nationwide group of extortionists and murderers who came to be known as the Mafia. Some responsible newsmen and law enforcement officers denied its existence entirely. Yet, the historical fact is that "criminal brotherhoods" came into being in the 1400s in Spain and other parts of Europe, and that the Mafia was one of these groups that had established itself in America around the turn of this century.

In order to understand sadistic acts by groups, I found it helpful to study the effects of peer pressure and obedience to authority. Here in America, social psychologist Stanley Milgram showed that people of all ages who were unlikely to be cruel in everyday life were willing to administer what they were told were dangerously high levels of electrical shocks to others simply because someone in authority told them to. This branch of psychology has proven that "normal" people in groups will commit behaviors toward others that they would not do on their own.

Milgram's work was done in the experimental laboratory. The My Lai massacre in Vietnam on March 16, 1968, was done in real life. American soldiers of C Company, Task Force Barker (First Battalion, Twentieth Infantry of the Eleventh

Light Infantry Brigade), frustrated because they could not engage the enemy after they had sustained a number of casualties, killed between five hundred and six hundred unarmed villagers including children. They rounded them up into groups of twenty to forty and slaughtered them using rifles, machine guns, and grenades, shooting some as they tried to run away.

It had been easy to read about the Nazis committing brutalities. Accepting the truth that Americans, given the right situation, would also follow commands that go against everything our country and its citizens stand for left me feeling weak.[12] It was dawning on me that we humans all share the same task: taking the ultimate responsibility for our own power by not giving it to authority or abusing it when we have authority.

My mind was devouring all this new information, but my heart and soul couldn't accept it. I felt sick with sadness when I would put myself in Barbara's place as a child forced to submit to and participate in atrocities. I felt sick with rage and self-hate when I tried to put myself in the place of the perpetrators bringing mutilation and death to other human beings.

So I was relieved to get a call from a social worker, Dr. Wendy Fideo, who had much experience treating patients with multiple personality disorder. She, too, was working with survivors of satanic and ritual abuses.

"I'm having a meeting at my office next Tuesday night for a group of us who are trying to treat these folks," Wendy said. "I got your name from Dr. Dan Kerlinsky."

Finally! A support group. It was none too soon. My own levels of anxiety continued to increase, and I wasn't able to hide it from Dan. My nightly meditation and relaxation exer-

---

12. For a more thorough discussion of the My Lai incident, see Scott Peck's book, *People of the Lie* (New York: Simon & Schuster, 1983), beginning page 212.

cises sometimes helped. At other times, I simply couldn't fall asleep no matter what I did. Dan found me one night downing a sleeping pill.

"Looks like you're hooked on these," he said, inspecting the bottle. "This was full last time I looked. You better think about cutting down. You don't want to be taking these for more than a couple of months." He stared at me. "And I won't continue to supply you with them for more than that."

"Don't worry. It's a small dose," I answered, not telling him that I often needed two of the pills to calm me down enough to sleep.

S E V E N

Normally I enjoyed summertime. My friends back in California had sometimes asked how we could stand the desert heat. "You're confusing New Mexico with Arizona," I told them. "New Mexico is about a mile high, so the heat isn't so bad, plus we don't have the humidity of the East."

Summer was a time for swimming, tennis, hiking, bicycling. But this year I couldn't seem to look forward to anything. I worked out to *Jane Fonda's Challenge Workout* video at least three times a week, ran, and played tennis, but I seemed to be doing the exercise because I needed to.

"I've been having a lot of trouble breathing," Barbara announced at the beginning of one of her sessions. "I feel like I'm suffocating all the time."

"Have you ever had asthma or allergies?" I asked. "It's summertime. Could there be any physical reason for the trouble?"

"No. I've never had anything like that. I think it goes back to something the clan did to me."

"Well, let's take a look," I said as I reached for a tape and placed it into the recorder.

Barbara got comfortable in her chair, stretched her legs out on the ottoman, and placed her hands palms down on her thighs. She moved easily through the relaxation suggestions of trance induction, and her arm moved slowly up toward her forehead when I suggested the arm levitation. "When part of your hand touches your forehead, you can allow yourself to go into a very deep trance," I suggested. "And as your hand floats back down to your lap, you can go deeper and deeper and deeper." I then established finger signals with Barbara and asked her unconscious or inner mind if it would be all right for Barbara to explore what it was that was making her feel as if she were suffocating. Her yes finger lifted.

"Move back through the mists of time until you reach an important experience or event. Let me know when you're there."

"I'm eight and I'm sittin' on the side steps in the alley, and it smells like dead rats," Barbara says. "It's not dead rats, though. It's dead people. I tell my little brother, Vaughn, and he wants to go tell Bobby. They both come back and I tell Bobby there's dead people stinkin' up his alley. They're lookin' in the window to the cellar. Grandma comes out and says, 'What you all doin' down there? Nothin' down there but rats. Better get away from there before you get rabies.' Then she looks at me and I know I'm in trouble.

"When Mother comes to take us home, Grandma says, 'I'll bring her home later.' She makes me sit in the back of the church till she's finished in the kitchen, then we drive to Reverend Conrad's. Grandma don't talk to me either, so I know she's mad. Reverend Conrad's got a funeral home an' his mother's an old lady and she says I'm nosy. 'You know what we do to nosy kids? We fix their nose so they can't snoop.' She takes us downstairs to the basement where they take dead people who're supposed to be dead. There're these long silver tables and things hangin' from the ceiling like the bottles in the hospital. And there's a big furnace where they burn people whose bodies are decomposed. That's the word he says, 'decomposed,' and they can't go in a coffin. There're no coffins in this room. It's cold in here. The coffins are upstairs so people can pick.

"First, Grandma says I hav'ta stay here, then she says, 'Let's go.' We drive in the car again and she says we're goin' to the country. I'm scared. Bad things happen there." Barbara shrinks up and says in a whisper, "I don' wanna go, I don' wanna go, I don' wanna go.

"She takes me to that old lady's house again, but there's another old lady there, too. She says, 'Well, look here. Look what sweet thing Bethie brought us today!'

"Grandma says, 'This is where you get when I can't control you. Remember this.' I don' want her to go! I'm screaming!" Barbara's body goes limp.

"Are you with the Light?" I ask.

"No. I'm pretending I'm dead. I'm not scared anymore. They drag me up the stairs and into the house. I sit on the little chair I sat on before and they cook the brew. It smells like dead rats. They say their stupid words: 'We will cook the brew for her and she will become one of us. The brew will bring out the impurities in her. As she breathes in the air of the brew, she will know and do the biddings of the master. The more she smells, the more she'll give up the enemy's ways. The more she smells, the more she'll be one of us. As you hear us say the words and smell the brew, you will be the master's.'

"They go in circles around and around me, and the brew

has a funny cloudy smoke and it stinks. I just sit on the chair. 'You cannot go to sleep,' the old lady says. 'If you go to sleep, the master will come for you and you'll never see anybody you care about again.' So I just sit and sit. They say, 'We do the Dance of the Feast. You must walk with the beast, to be a pure heart, a pure self, so you won't be contaminated by the enemy. You won't accept the enemy. We will not have one in our camp who is leaning toward the enemy. We will expel him.'

"Now they put some brew in a glass and I have to drink it. It's nasty." Barbara's body goes limp and she has a look of complete peace.

"Where are you now?" I ask.

"The Light came and Jesus said, 'Come with me. I'll help you.' He says I have to do this by myself. He says I'll be able to do this. I shouldn't worry. He'll help me."

Barbara then moved the scene to the farmhouse where she had been lowered to the devil when she was three years old. The entire clan was there. She began struggling to breathe, gasping, panting, and twisting. "They're touching me. Lots of them. Putting stuff on me. All over me. I have no clothes on. It's the brew they're putting on me. Get offa me!" Barbara cries. "Please!

"They open my legs." Barbara's voice drops to that of an adult. " 'We have to fill every opening, so we will suffocate the enemy. There will be no escape. The enemy is within her. We feel it. We feel the heat from the enemy within. We will fill every cavity, every opening.' . . . They put things in me . . . cotton in my nose that smells real funny and in my ears. They tape my eyes shut and my mouth. They put something up my butt and something up in my vagina. I don't know what it is.

"They're lifting me up. I'm very cold. I can't see and I can't hear the words they say . . . lots of words. Fire! There's fire underneath my back. I feel it. It's hot, but they don't put me in it. The words . . . 'As we commend this soul, as we bury and suffocate the Light in her, we will return her to the warmth of the almighty master. The master is rising through her. The master is rising through her. The master has conquered the enemy.'

"Not mine! My Light isn't stuffed in my body! They don't know. They think everything's in the body! They just don't know!" After a long pause, Barbara says, "I'm cold. When they finish, they put me on a table. I'm really cold." Her voice lowers, " 'The first thing she shall hear is the words of the master. Come, all ye beautiful little children. Come unto me. Come unto me, little children. Come unto me. I will give you the joys of the darkness. I will take away all your pain. You shall never feel the sadness that so many feel. Come unto me. I will bring you the joys of the gift of darkness. I shall bring you the joys of the gift of darkness. Come unto me, little children. Come unto me.' Grandma said that.

"Then, we shall give her the sense of smell. She will be able to smell death. She will enjoy the scent of fresh blood. She will have a keen sense of smell.' Then they unplug my nose. 'As you breathe, you will breathe in the master. This is the scent. We all carry the scent. You will be able to tell us from all others. You will know who is a true follower of the master, a true member of the master's clan.'

"Now they take the stuff out of my butt. They don' say nothin'. Out of my vagina. . . . 'We have sealed the sign of penetration. She shall never be penetrated by anyone. If anyone should think of defiling our most secret princess, the one who has just been given to the master, he shall die. She shall never be penetrated by them.'

"Now they take the tape off my mouth. 'She shall only speak the words of the master. Only the truth of the master. From these lips she will bear witness to the master.' Now my eyes. It's hard to see at first. Grandma says, 'As you look with your eyes, look straight to the soul. See if it's a worthy soul. If it's unworthy, you shall strike it dead. You shall strike it dead! Especially those who try to interfere with the master. You must do this!' That's what they said."

Barbara moaned as she came out of hypnosis. "I feel like screaming!" she said.

"I think you should!" I answered. "After all the ways they violated your body and tried to take your soul. Maybe you could come up with some creative outlets for your rage."

"Maybe I'll prune trees tomorrow," Barbara said in a grumpy voice. "Suffocating Jesus." She shook her head. "Can you believe what concrete thinkers they are?"

"Yes. They don't get high marks in abstract reasoning, do they? There's research showing that a very large number of the population, the majority, I think, never develop the ability to think abstractly and to reason logically."

"Well, my family fits into that category. It's strange that even when I was real little, I knew that what they were doing was wrong and stupid, too. And I knew that I didn't want to be part of their evil. I hated all of them except Grandma. I know without her they would have killed me. Especially my mother and Nonnie, the Fat Lady. They both really hated me."

"They were jealous of the little princess of darkness, eh?"

Barbara laughed and shook her head. "And I'd give anything if it had been them or someone else, but not me." She took a deep breath. "My breathing is fine now. They didn't suffocate anything."

When Barbara returned, she gave me a little grin and said, "Cal told me I have to find another outlet for my rage. I almost pruned every tree and shrub to the ground."

We laughed conspiratorially together. "Seriously," I said, "how are you doing?"

"Okay. I'm sleeping better and I've cut down on the cigarettes a little. It's weird. I won't smoke at work, and at home I have this one corner where I sit and smoke. It's the only place I smoke at home."

"We'll continue to monitor that. What about the drinking?"

"I'm still drinking several glasses of wine at night. I'm afraid if I don't, I'll come apart. I can't really explain it. I want to quit both the smoking and drinking, but I don't think I can do it right now."

"You're right. Now is probably not the time to try to give up addictions that help you manage your anxiety. You'll conquer them later on."

I gave myself the same advice. If I was addicted to sleeping medication, I would just have to taper off it at some later time when I wasn't so stressed.

After July 17, it seemed as if that time might never come. Dan woke me that morning to tell me that Kait Arquette, the eighteen-year-old daughter of my friend Lois Duncan, had been shot the previous night. Kait, an outgoing, attractive blonde, had been shot in the head as she drove down Lomas Boulevard at about eleven P.M. She was the daughter of Lois and Don Arquette, though Lois was referred to in our house as Lois Duncan because that is the name under which she has authored over forty books, many of them for young people. She was Julie's favorite writer.

All of Albuquerque was stunned and frightened. A "drive-by shooting" it was called. As I write this two years later, the case has not been solved. Although at one point arrests were made, the suspects were later released. Lois and her family continued their own investigation, which seemed to implicate crime rings in southern California. Kait had been breaking up with her Vietnamese boyfriend. She had been to California with him over spring break her senior year and had learned about auto-accident scams and drug dealing. She may have known too much to be allowed to live.

I knew none of that in July. All I knew was that a beautiful young woman, the daughter of my friend, had been gunned down. Parents' normal fears for their daughters involve rape if they are on foot, accidents if they are driving. Now we could add to our worries being shot in the head while behind the wheel of a car. I felt revolted. And I felt an intense ache for Lois.

On my way to work the next morning, I looked up at the sky and said, "So what is the message here? Am I supposed to be learning about violence and death? Okay. Okay. But there better be more!"

In hypnosis that day, when I asked Barbara's unconscious mind to take her to an important event, she said, "I'm waiting. I'm just waiting at home for Grandma to come over. Mother went across the street and called her from the neighbors'. She told her that I was runnin' up and down the street telling people things. I never did. She lied, but I can't say nothin', so I'm waiting. I chew on my lip tryin' to eat myself up, but it doesn't happen. Then I curl up inside. . . ."

"Trying to make yourself disappear?"

"Yes, so I could die before Grandma comes. But I don't."

"How old are you?"

"I'm seven. Grandma's here now and my mother's laughing when she takes me away. She knows I'm gonna be hurt." Under her breath Barbara says, "Bitch."

"What happens now?"

"In the car, Grandma says I hav'ta go to the Upper Room. She says, 'If you're not gonna live with us, you have to learn to obey the rules when you're not with us.' We're at the stairs to the Upper Room now, and everybody's there singin' the Upper Room song."

"Who's there?"

"Grandma, Granddaddy, Sister Miller, Miss Nonnie the

Fat Lady, Sister Catherine and her husband, Gordan, Miss Ava, that's Fran's mother.''

''What is the Upper Room song?''

''It's ugly. 'Come into my room, come into my Upper Room. In the Upper Room there's no song, there's no peace, there is no happiness. Come into my room. Come into my Upper Room.' ''

Barbara looks terror stricken. ''There're snakes in the chair! And I hav'ta sit there with 'em. And I wasn't even bad. I didn't do anything wrong! I wasn't bad. . . .'' Barbara whimpers.

''What happens now?''

''I hav'ta sit there till it gets dark. Then Grandma stands at the table and says, 'Hear ye, hear ye, hear ye. It is the seventh hour of the seventh day in the seventh circle. Hear ye, hear ye, hear ye. O Great Master, it is time to perform the task of the clan.' Then the door swings open and we must walk into the church. They walk up the aisle and then they turn around and look at me, and then they lock the doors. And it's all men there. It's just men.''

''How many men?''

After a pause, Barbara answers, ''Twenty-one. I counted them and Granddaddy makes twenty-one. That's three times seven. Seven is an important number only this year, Grandma says. And I'm seven.''

''What do they do now?''

''They must start exactly at seven, so they take off their robes and they have no clothes on, nothing. And they sing the 'come to me, little children' song. And Grandma stands up at the pulpit above everybody and she says, 'Come to me, little children, come to me. He will give you the fruit and you shall bear the master's name.' But there aren't other little children in there. There's only me.'' Barbara continues in a puzzled little-girl voice, ''Usually there's other kids. It's only me this time. Oh, there is somebody else. But they're not seven. It's Allen and Nacy. Allen's nine, two years older than me. And Nacy's only six. They go in the circle, and they don't have clothes on either. They don't give 'em a table though. They sit on the floor.

"Now the Fat Lady comes and pulls me by the ear. But I don't wanna go to the circle, so I won't. So, she pulls me, she's dragging me up the steps to the Upper Room."

Barbara's body goes limp and she has that peaceful expression.

"It's all right. It's Gail and I'm here with you as well as the Light. Come back now and tell me what happens to you."

"I ran to the corner to try to hide. But there's a Keeper there. He says I've been turned over to them because I must learn to hold my tongue and be silent. He grabs my tongue. I don' wanna tell what happens now. . . ." Barbara is twisting and looking devastatingly sad. "There's no Light either. It's just gray.

"He pulls my tongue . . . then he puts his penis on my tongue." Barbara moans and talks so quietly I can hardly hear her. "Now he takes one of the snakes and he puts the snake on my tongue. And I have to take my clothes off 'cause I'm going to get a beating, he says. He tells me to bend over and I do, and he hits my butt real hard. Now, he's sticking his penis in my butt and it hurts really bad . . . so bad." Barbara's body is tense and shaking.

"It hurts so bad you don't know what to do," I say gently.

"Yes. And he says bad things, too! He says, 'You're a tight little whore.' He squeezes my butt and keeps saying that. I don' wanna hear that! I don' wanna be called that! I'm not a whore!"

"Of course you're not. You're just a little girl. He wants to hurt you and he wants to hurt your feelings."

"And he put things inside me."

"What do you mean?"

"He said he put things inside me that will be there forever. And no one can get it out and I can't poop it out either. And he said the evil will 'grow and flourish.' So I guess I hav'ta be like them."

I made a quick mental note that this information corresponded to what I had read about most survivors of satanic abuse. They were told that something was placed inside them that they could never get out. Whatever the substance is, the child believes that it binds them to the cult. They can never escape from evil. Some children are told that an explosive device has been placed inside and that if they ever tell what has been done to them, the device will blow up and kill them.

Barbara's voice was getting smaller and more hopeless with every word. I decided I should bring Barbara away from the victimization of that event and focus on positive suggestions. I counted back from ten to zero as I instructed her to stay in her comfortable trance state, but to come back to her present age. When she acknowledged that she remembered what the Keeper had done to her, I emphasized that nothing he did could change her from the good person she is and always was. Nothing he did could make her evil or change all the things about her that make her special. She agreed that she had a tendency to believe that the bad things, the "ugliness," was still inside. She promised me she would continue to work in therapy on building her self-esteem.

E I G H T

felt as low as I could get after that session. The rage imploded upon itself and dissolved into a bleak sadness. That adults would systematically work to destroy a child was more than I could bear. I felt completely helpless, powerlessly listening to one description of criminal violation after another.

What is this urge that men have to dominate and destroy? I wondered. What is it about the makeup of men that they deem it appropriate to band together to torture and terrorize others, the sheer power attracting occasional women like an unrelenting magnet? For women, depression tends to obscure anger, I believed, and for men, anger tends to obscure depression. It was clear to me why more women in society would tend to be depressed. They had no power. They aren't allowed to get safely in touch with their healthy anger, which is a life-energy force.

I could understand why men might be drawn to anger . . . it's a more powerful emotion. It feels strong. But why would they need to abuse their power? And if anger covers depression, what is it that men are depressed about? These thoughts were to pass through my mind constantly as I tried to understand male violence.

Jan, my secretary, was the first to notice that I was losing weight. One day she actually made me get on the scale in my office: 118 pounds. Normally a thin person, I didn't tell her that my weight hadn't been that low since high school. "You better not lose any more," Jan cautioned. And I knew she'd watch me.

I had learned from Barbara that specific words could cause more psychic devastation than some of the sadistic actions she was subjected to. She couldn't shake the effect on her of being called a "whore." I couldn't understand how being called names could have such a powerful effect until I read Dr. Leonard Shengold's book, *Soul Murder: The Effects of Childhood Abuse and Deprivation,*[13] where he describes the effects of sadistic abuse on the child's sense of identity. While the child's body may heal, the child feels his or her soul, the innermost self, has been irrevocably twisted and distorted into badness, if not destroyed altogether.

At the beginning of one of the next sessions, Barbara said she was having flashbacks of crying. We had talked about the fact that she had trained herself not to cry and that it was difficult for her to allow herself to cry even now in order to grieve about her childhood. However, Barbara felt that several times as a girl she had done little else besides cry.

---

13. Shengold, *Soul Murder* (New Haven: Yale University Press, 1989).

Once in hypnosis, Barbara saw herself the summer between her seventh and eighth birthday crying constantly, at home and at school. "Ever since he called me a whore," she whimpered, "all I can do is cry. And I'm at school now and the teacher is yelling at me."

"Why would your teacher yell at you?"

"Because she's one of them. It's Mrs. Mattes. She doesn't go to our church, but she's one of them. I call them 'devils.' "

"And you have seen her at some of the ceremonies?"

"Yes. She was at the hospital, and she was at the graveyard sayin', 'Welcome, Princess.' And now she's yellin' at me sayin' I'm a smart, intelligent girl and I must stop this crying. . . . But I can't stop. And it's close to my birthday and bad things always happen on my real birthday and after that, too. I hate birthdays."[14]

I asked Barbara to move ahead in time and tell me what happened on her eighth birthday.

"I'm in a church but it's not my church. There's lots of people, but I don't want to see any faces and Jesus says I don't hav'ta see any faces. There's lots of smoke from the brew. The room is all steamy and crowded and purple looking. It smells real bad, like dead rats. But it could be dead people, too."

"Do they cook parts of bodies sometimes?"

"Yes, but they don't eat it."

"Do they do anything with it besides smell it?"

"They make things . . . like the special candles. And they use the special candles when it's a special time . . . like now."

"What is this special time?"

"This is the special time for all the princesses to get together so they may choose one princess to lead the whole area."

"How do they choose?"

14. The most important satanic holiday is the individual's birthday. Barbara's birthday is in early October, the same month as the satanic high holy days, which begin on October 28.

"They say you have to carry the sign. But I don't know what the sign is."

"What happens now?"

"There are eight girls from eight regions and we're all eight years old. They don't let us sit together 'cause they're afraid we'd talk. So we have to sit in different places against the wall. It's like a big contest and then your clan becomes the strongest if you have the princess. My back hurts 'cause we have to sit with our face to the wall, kind of bent over. And it's cold in here. It's a basement."

"Have you been here before?"

"Yes, but it's not a church like I've been in before. It's a temple."

"A temple?"

"Yes, where Jews go."

"And are there Jewish people there, too?"

"No. No Jews. The janitor is black, so they don't know they're doing this to their temple. They don't have to paint anything on the floor 'cause it's already there. They don't have to do anything except put the candles out."

"What is it that's already there?"

"On the floor, there's a big Star of David. But that's not what it means."

"What does it mean to the clan?"

"It's the sign of strength." In a lower voice: " 'We are the strongest of all our master's followers. We rule the earth. We are the strongest of all. The other ones are idiots, trying to follow the master, but they don't know how. This is the sign of the most powerful clan of the most powerful set of our master's followers.'

"Now they get the special candles that they made from the people, and then they make a kind of circle. The candles have aisles around the circle and there are eight spokes on the circle. We each have to walk down our spoke. And then we go into the circle and there's a fat fat, ugly black man in the middle of the circle. And we have to sit down.

"He doesn't have a penis!" Barbara exclaims.

"He doesn't have a penis? How do you know it's a man?"

"It's a man. It's not a woman. It really is a man."

"What do you suppose happened to his penis?"

"I don't know. Maybe they cut it off. They do that, you know."

"When do they do that?"

"They always do it when they kill people in my church."

"What happens now?"

"He dances around with no clothes on and sings his song: 'I am the most powerful and powerful one. I am the one who sings. I am the one who does not carry the sign of penetration. I am the one who is powerful.' He is disgusting."

"And what happens now?"

"Each princess has to be served by eight men from her clan. That means they stick their penis in your mouth and you have to swallow the stuff and not let any dribble out of your mouth. But Grandma told me before that I should let it dribble out of my mouth so I won't get to be the princess of the region. So that's what I do."

Our time had run out for the day, and I didn't really miss hearing more details about the princess pageant. I had a suspicion that Barbara's grandmother knew more than we did about what eventuality awaited the grand princess of darkness. She may have saved Barbara's life again, but she only saved her for further torturous satanic rituals.

Barbara and I were developing wonderful facial expressions to communicate our sense of disgust, amazement, and exhaustion at the end of a session such as this one. She scrunched up her mouth, rolled her eyes, and pretended she was pulling out her hair. I stuck out my tongue and pretended gagging.

131

I was beginning to understand why sexual abuse survivors usually have eating disorders. When my weight first began to drop, I was pleased. I remembered the saying "A woman can't be too thin or too rich." I paid little attention to my food intake, even after Jan's warning. But now, my lack of appetite and my skipping meals began to alarm me. I realized the abuse stories, plus my upset about Robert's death and Gilda's and then Kait's, had left me feeling that I wouldn't care if I never ate again. I simply could not enjoy food.

Satanic abuse survivors have been alternately starved and forced to swallow human parts and sexual excretions. Consequently, they may have little knowledge about good nutrition, nor the "stomach" for feeding themselves appropriately. Barbara had told me repeatedly that as a girl, she was "skinny as a rail," and I surely believed her. Some sexual abuse survivors become overweight as adults. They put on the weight to symbolize a protective barrier against further physical intrusion. "I don't want men to find me attractive," one woman said. "I don't even want them to look at me."

I was struck by the sick irony of the "special candles"; candles that are made from human beings used in a satanic ceremony in a Jewish temple. Barbara had been referring to "special candles" for nearly a year. I had never thought about where the candles came from.

I was also beginning to understand why sexual abuse survivors are typically dysfunctional sexually. I was becoming more and more disinterested in sex. We discussed this reaction at one of our therapists support groups. I had come to look forward to these small meetings of women, women who, like myself, were trying to handle their reactions to stories of overwhelming abuse.

"I'm having a hard time remembering that my husband is actually a nice man," one woman said.

"Yeah, but he is a man," said another sarcastically. "I met a gorgeous Nigerian woman psychologist at the APA [American Psychological Association] meetings last year. She was saying that she thought we American women were really stupid. When I asked her why, she said we let our men get too close to our small children. I defended our wish to include men more in childrearing, but she just harrumphed and said, 'As long as men have penises, they're going to want to stick them in anything that moves.' I hate to admit it, but I think she may be right."

"I think I'll write a paper called 'The Bad Penis,'" I joked. "I attended meetings on group violence in Washington, D.C., last year. All the presenters were males, and all described group violence perpetrated by males. When I asked them to comment on the contribution of patriarchy to all of this violence, they had little to say. One of them actually fell back on the old 'bad breast' routine.[15] 'Well, you know, all of the men were raised by women,' he whined. I'm really up to my ears with that one."

We all agreed that we could rant about men as much as we wanted to in our group, but that we really needed to be more neutral with our husbands. The arrival of a caring and gentle male psychiatrist at later meetings helped us to stop viewing all males as the criminal perpetrators we were hearing about in our offices.

I still had a hard time at home. I went through the motions of sex, but I couldn't imagine when feelings of passion would return. And I was hard on Dan. Every time a new act of violence against women hit the newspapers (which was about every other day), I'd be all over him.

"You're a father of daughters!" I would shout. "What are you going to do about this male abuse of power? The least you

---

15. The "bad breast" is a psychoanalytic metaphor that blames mothers for "poisoning" their children and thus causing mental illness or criminal behavior.

could do is join the men's movement! They're trying to get men in touch with their feelings. You know, sensitivity and intelligence, instead of dicks for brains!''

Poor Dan. Arguing with a madwoman could get him nowhere. Sometimes he'd try and I would just increase the decibel level. Once, he stared at me and said, ''I am not a sexual pervert or a criminal. I work as hard as I can, and I love my kids. Maybe these guys were raised by screaming banshees like you and that's what made them turn weird! Now lay off!''

He was right. I realized I was dumping my grief on him. Sometimes I felt so deeply despairing after listening to a story of abuse, and I heard many each day besides Barbara's, that I felt complete hopelessness about the human species.

''You know how I've talked about my mother hating me?'' Barbara asked at the beginning of a session. ''I'm not sure you understand how much she hated me. I think she sold me to men when she needed money. I need to know about that.

''It's the Fourth of July,'' Barbara began once she was into her trance, ''and Vaughn and Chubbs and me are in the closet. They broke the leg off my dolly and put their things in her.''

''Their 'things.' Do you mean their penises?''

''Yes. They put them in the dolly and then they were gonna put them in me . . . we're doin' the nasties.''

''Sex play. Yes. Children do that sometimes, you know.''

''Mother's really mad. She found us and told me to go get ready for an ass whipping 'cause I know better than that shit. And she says, 'I don't care what your grandma says, I'm going to beat the shit out of you.' And she's hitting me and hitting me. . . .''

''With her hand?''

''No, with a belt. All over. 'Specially on my shoulders

and my back. It really really hurts. . . . Now, her friend Jimmy's over. It's nighttime. They're on the sofa together and I'm tired. I just want to go to bed. He's kissing her and she says, 'I have some fresh meat for you.' That's what she says. 'The Fourth is coming up and I could use some money.'[16] The man laughs and she tells me to 'get upstairs and clean the room up there where you guys made a mess!' But I'm afraid. It's dark up there. But I go and the man comes up. I ask Jesus to help me.

"The man says, 'I'm gonna ride your pussy all night. And there's no need to be callin' for that bitch. She hates your guts. That's why you're up here.' He's touching me and I don't like that. I just want to die. He hurts me a lot. It hurts so much, I cry for my mother, but he says, 'Forget it. Nobody loves your little ass anyways.'

"It hurts too much. I just want to die. And I can't get away all night 'cause he has his leg over me when he's not doin' stuff to me. An' it hurts more than Grandma's."

"What do you mean? What does Grandma do that hurts you?"

"She stretches it so the men won't hurt me. That's what she says."

"She stretches your vagina?"

"Uh-huh."

"How does she stretch it?"

"With her fingers."

"When did she start doing that?"

"A long time ago. When I was real little."

"And what about your anus? Your bottom?"

"She doesn't do that. Only the men at the church do that.

---

16. Barbara had begun the hypnosis saying it was the Fourth of July, but it was actually a few days before. She had apparently encoded this memory associating it to the Fourth and therefore thought all the events were occurring on the Fourth.

This hurts so much. And my head hurts, too. 'Cause it always happens to me. The men always do things to me.''

"Mother lets them, doesn't she?''

"Yes. And sometimes she gets money for it. She tells them I've never been touched, so it'll cost them extra. That's what she says.''

Once out of trance Barbara said, "Well, I guess this is why I haven't even been able to touch Cal, let alone have sex, for the past couple weeks. I've been a mess again at home, and I'm sure there's more of these memories.''

I was filled with disgust following this session. The image of a grown man not only forcing intercourse with a little girl, but doing it repeatedly while saying no one cares about her, was beyond sad. And what about Barbara's mother? How could she prostitute her small daughter? I found myself in Dan's position. Confronted with female violence, I had to try to fit it into my self-perception. I realized how hard that is as I tried to comprehend Barbara's mother's purposely subjecting her offspring to sexual abuse. Was I capable of having that much hatred and causing that much sadistic violence? Under the right circumstances, I didn't know, and I didn't want to consider it.

One hypnosis session that summer of 1989 was almost too much for me to bear. Barbara's unconscious mind recognized that this memory could be too devastating for her to relive, so during the induction stage of helping her into trance, her "mind," which is how she referred to her unconscious, told me that it would have to tell the story. It could tell me so the little girl wouldn't have to suffer so much.[17]

---

17. Prior to this, I would have viewed the "mind" as a combination of her unconscious, her adult ego-state, the executive function of the personality, and that aspect we refer to as "the observing ego." I now believe that her

"She's there hanging."

"Where is that?"

"In a basement. Her mother sold her to two drunks in a car. She thought they would just use her in the car, but they drove away. They took her to their house where there's a basement. She can't talk. They've stuffed a rag in her mouth."

"I'm glad you're with her. How many men are there?"

"There are seven. They put a rag in her mouth so she can't scream."

"Does she have clothes on?"

"No clothes. . . . First they beat her."

"What do they beat her with?"

"It's not a belt. It's not a razor strap, but it's some kind of a leather strap. Then they stick needles in the back parts of her arms. Not where the veins are. 'We're gonna make a junkie out of you,' is what they said. 'So you'll always come back to us.' There was nothing in the needles. Barbara knows that because she knows what it feels like when fluid is going into the flesh from a needle."

"And now what happens?"

"They take the rag out of her mouth and say, 'If you scream, if we see one tear drop, you'll be in one of those cages over there and we feed 'em rats for food. There is a little boy in one cage and a little girl in another. The little girl is clearly starving, and her eyes look hollow and empty. The little boy just looks wild. So I didn't let Barbara cry. She didn't cry one drop. It was very hard, though. We had to do all the work. No one came to help. And it was very hard. She would have fallen apart and died if I let her see the children."

"What do they do to Barbara?"

"Different things. One stuck his penis in her vagina and one stuck his penis in her butt. One stuck his penis in her

---

"mind" is all of those parts of her self or soul, as well as her connection to the Light, Barbara's manifestation of God.

137

mouth, and one beat her. That makes four at one time. And so we played a game.''

''A game?''

''We played hide-and-seek in our head. So she wouldn't wake up and see them. I had to help her live.''

''Yes, of course.''

''And when the four of them finished, they didn't come inside her; they creamed all over her and smeared it into all the little prickly sores that they made from the needles. And then it was three men at one time. After that, they sat and took out their drugs. They did have drugs. They didn't use them on themselves, but they got the little girl out of her cage and chained her up and used them on her. And, and . . . the screaming!''

At that moment, it seemed that Barbara, the nine-year-old little girl, had emerged. She sat holding her ears and rocking back and forth in her chair, a look of agony on her face.

''Does it go on for a very long time? The screaming?'' I asked her softly.

''A very long time. And they hurt the little girl more. I think they hurt her more because she struggles. She gets hurt more!''

''And when they are through with her, what do they do?''

''They kick her over to the cage and call her really bad names . . . 'slut,' 'whore,' 'bitch,' 'cunt,' and they throw her in the cage and she's crying. But I don't cry.[18] And then they take out the little boy, saying what they're gonna do to him. But he turns around and he has a rat in his mouth, and they decided they didn't want to get rabies so they left him alone. And then they looked at me and I decided to look straight at

---

18. Here, Barbara switches to the first person. She did this after recognizing the presence of the other child victims. From here, she is able to relive the experience from the strength of her total integrated self, at the end returning to "mind" in order to tell me how to help her.

them. I would look straight to their souls. I decided that if I died tonight, they would never sleep another night as long as they lived. I gave them the evil look. I know that look.

"I just stared, and one guy said, 'This bitch is crazy. She is crazy! Do you see that look she's giving us?' And the other guy says, 'I know her mother. She's part of that family with crazy-assed niggers . . . the family that kills people. Didn't you hear 'bout what they did to Joe and them people? They work roots on you and they eat hearts and stuff.' Then another guy says, 'Let's go get a heart and see if she'll eat it,' and laughs. I just looked at him and I wouldn't say anything. I just looked and I sat there all weekend and stared. They chained me up again, but they didn't do anything this time. They just sat there and watched me and waited for me to cry, but I didn't.

"They must have fallen asleep because my back was to them, and when they woke up in the morning, I was still awake, waiting. And I did not pass out. I was waiting. One was named George, and he said, 'Where'd you learn that from?' but I said nothing. I just looked at him. So he unchained me and said, 'Go over there and put your clothes on, bitch!' But I just looked at him, so he went and got my clothes and threw them at me. I put them on and we went up the stairs, just me and him. When we went through the kitchen, there was a lady sitting there and she said, 'I told you 'bout bringing your fucking toys in this house!' And I looked at her and she said, 'That one's not a toy, is she?' and he said, 'No.' He put me in the car and drove me back to the alley and said, 'If you ever think of comin' back to that house, I'll have somethin' waitin' for you. You may work your magic, but it has nothin' to do with me. I ain't scared of your ass!' But he was. He was really scared."

"You did such a good job of taking care of yourself."

"I had to."

"What do you call this part of your personality that knows how to care for you?"

"It's my 'mind' and it's me. The strongest part of me and the smartest part of me. It is the part that holds all of me."

"How can I help Barbara with this experience?"

"She didn't want the kids to be hurt. That is the hardest part for her . . . when kids get hurt and she can't do anything about it. That is why she tries to run away from herself and cries inside."

"Does she like the ocean?"

"Yes. She loves the ocean, the beach, and the sand. Water is very special to her."

"Good. I want you to help her, when she feels so very sad inside about the children, to think instead about the ocean. Help her to begin to release the sadness, release the bad feelings, and identify with the timelessness of the ocean, of the grains of sand on the beach that number so many that we could never ever count them. She can begin to feel that timelessness . . . feel the warmth and feel the goodness in the water. Maybe begin to float on that water, and when she needs to cry, let her tears mingle with the water. She is part of the water, she's part of the earth, she's part of the universe . . . and even though we cannot understand why there is evil, why children are hurt, why she is hurt, we can understand that feeling of being a living creature and of being a part of everything else that is living, including the water . . . including the water that gives us life, including the air that is all around us and gives us breath . . . including the Light and that time when the Light gives us to God, to Jesus, to the good spirits that live beyond, that we can't see, but we know of their helpful presence. And we identify them, too, with this sense of infinity and timelessness . . . no beginning, no end. We can't understand it, but we know it.

"Let Barbara experience this feeling of timelessness, of floating, of peacefulness. Let her see the ocean, the water, the sunlight sparkling on it, the golden flashes and sparkles of sunlight that warm the water and warm her, too, so that she can become one with nature and one with God, not questioning, just being. . . ."

It was strange to hear myself say these words. I hadn't considered myself a religious person since I was a teenager. And as an adult, I had converted to Judaism when I married. I had great respect for the high ethical standards taught in Judaism as well as the strong commitment to family life. As a young adult I had gone through my atheist stage, and when I finally came around to believing in a Greater Power, I never tried to fathom my thinking about it. I had little use for organized religious groups. My historical reading told me that throughout the ages, men have tended to use religious dogma to justify gross misuse of power. In spite of my pessimism, here I was sounding like a New Age Christian.

This growing sense of spiritualism was only expressed in my sessions with Barbara. Although I was using a great deal of hypnosis with my other patients, I stuck to traditional relaxation imagery and ego-strengthening suggestions following their memory work. I tried to dismiss any thoughts about Barbara's visitation from Jesus, but sometimes, as at the end of this session, I felt as though the important words were being put in my mouth . . . the words that would be most useful for her to hear. And I remained intensely curious about her description of her "mind" as "the part that holds all of me."

N I N E

needed a vacation. We were due to go to Hawaii for ten days, but I was more nervous than excited. I was worried about Barbara. With a vacation of that length, I inform my patients about it at least six weeks ahead of time. Barbara and I were anticipating the separation. She assured me she'd be all right, but I arranged for her to see one of my associates at least one time during my absence. Helene Fellen was a social worker from Los Angeles who had joined our group several years earlier. She had an additional master's degree in developmental psychology.

"It will be good for you to see Helene. You'll be practicing trust," I told Barbara. "You've come to trust me, but you need to know there are lots of other people in the world who could help you, too."

Barbara gave me a look of tolerant disbelief. "I'll do it just because you're asking me to, not because I want to. It's real hard for me to talk about myself at all, and to someone I don't know, it'll be even harder."

I spoke with Sharon, the one person Barbara had said she could turn to if she needed someone. The telephone conversation was brief, almost cryptic. I realized immediately that Barbara's judgment of character was accurate. Sharon was attuned to Barbara's suffering without a need to rescue her or to know details. She simply said, "I've told Barbara she can call me any time of the day or night."

Maui was colorless that summer, the usual wild tropical colors turned gray. Napili Bay, our warm "bathtub," with its surging undertows and the surf above, was huge, uninviting, and dangerous. Rather than my usual five novels, I'd brought only books pertaining to cults, child sexual abuse, multiple personality disorder, and perversions. The topics seemed to go with the inclement weather.

The last day on the island was bright and the surf had calmed. We spent much of the day snorkeling. I left my family and friends way out by a rocky point at the north end of the bay and said I was going to swim to the middle of the bay and then go in. I'd meet them on the beach.

It felt good being by myself in the water. Alone, I could feel more a part of the ocean. I followed a "herd" of ever-present goatfish along a bank of coral, then focused on a small school of yellow tangs darting about. I swam on, about to go toward shore, when I caught sight of a single huge parrot fish. It swam ahead of me, as though beckoning. I followed easily with an inexplicable feeling of peacefulness and joy that made me want to laugh. This parrot fish was not the usual mixture of greens, blues, and yellow. It was nearly all iridescent lavender. It would stop every now and then as if to wait for me. The message seemed to be, "Isn't it nice to go your own way?

Don't be afraid to be alone. You can discover the world by yourself."

My lavender parrot fish made the entire vacation worthwhile. I had a feeling of inner calm I knew would continue to be accessible. All I needed to do was remember that it was there, a deep pool of inner calm with a lavender parrot fish swimming inside. On the plane home, that thought made me smile.

Barbara seemed happy to see me. She reported that she had done "okay" in the session with Helene and felt good that I had arranged it for her.

"It felt kind of like a good mother getting someone really nice to baby-sit while she's away," Barbara said.

The theme of not having had a mother kept returning to Barbara. She'd say plaintively, "I know that all the abuse was awful, but it was about them! Not having any love from a mother feels like it's about me!"

Uncharacteristically, I'd argue with her, saying things she already knew, such as the fact that every child victim of hate, abuse, and neglect blames herself for her parents' behavior. It comes with the inability to reason cognitively, as well as the powerlessness of not being able to hold adults accountable for their behavior. Barbara would give me her big brown-eyed look of patience and say slowly, "I know that." Then I'd get down off my high horse of denial and let her do the work she needed to do that day. (If only it were possible to talk someone out of their troubles!)

Hypnosis always reminded me of how easy and seductive it is to intellectualize issues of therapy. When hypnosis is done well, the patient runs the therapy. The person's unconscious mind focuses in on what is of primary importance at that moment. It's also reassuring to know that the unconscious protects the patient from moving into frightening areas before she's ready. I found consistently that if something comes up in hypnosis that a person isn't ready to handle, they either say so or come out of trance.[19]

On this day, Barbara's mind took her to an important event involving her mother. I was surprised when I asked how old she was and she answered, "Twenty-two. I'm at the house to pick up my mother and she's not dressed. She's not coming."

"She's not coming where?"

"She's not coming to my wedding."

"How does that feel?"

"I'm hurt, but I have to leave and get to Sam's and Julie's. The photographer's there and I can't be late. But when I get there, I start to cry and Julie says, 'She's never been there for you, so don't waste any tears on her.' And when Granddaddy and I get in the car to go to the church, I told him. He said, 'Don't worry 'bout her. Don't ruin the day for her. She'll pay.' And I remember that he's always been mean to her and I don't know what he'll do to her."

"And what do you think of when he says, 'She'll pay'?"

"That they'd hurt her. There's nobody to watch out for her. I'm afraid they'll hurt her because of what I've done."

"What do you mean because of what you've done?"

"Because I left the clan, and when I did, I told her some of what I knew. And she told Auntie. And now, she'll have to pay. They'll take her to the Upper Room. I don't think she

---

19. One nineteen-year-old girl came for help to access memories of incest by the father. Her family had told her not to come and to forget her "crazy ideas." We agreed before the first hypnosis session that she wasn't ready to barge in and see what had happened to her, but toward the end of the session, one of the incest images flashed in her mind. Her eyes flew right open and she came out of her trance. I then helped her to relax deeply again and gave positive suggestions regarding her ability to handle any memories of abuse when she was completely ready.

could take it. She's only good at being mean to others. That's all she knows how to do.''

"Let that image fade away now, and when I count to five, move to the next significant event. One, two, three, four, and five. What comes to mind?''

"I'm in the tenth grade and I'm sick. Really sick. Mother's fussing at me to get out of bed, but I can't. B.J., her husband, comes in and feels my forehead. He tells her I'm burning up and she better take me to the doctor. She is really mad and says it's my fault she has to miss a day at work. We don't go to the hospital. She takes me to this old man on a side street. He asked me when was the last time I ate, and I said I didn't know. Then he asked me when was the last time I went to the bathroom, and I said I didn't know. He went and got my mother and said she should take me to the hospital. He said I had a high fever and my body was shutting down.

"She told him she would, but when we got out to the car, she said, 'You dumb-ass little bitch! I can't believe you don't have sense enough to go to the goddamn bathroom! Cost me all this damn money. It's a good thing he's a friend of mine 'cause I didn't have to pay him, and I'm damn sure not going to pay no hospital bill for you! Get your ass in the car and I'll take you home.' I said I had to throw up and she said, 'You better not throw up in my car. You better throw up on the sidewalk.' So I did, then she cussed me out all the way home. Then she told me to take off my clothes and get in the tub, and she gave me an enema. I was still sick for a long time, but I only stayed home for three days, 'cause I couldn't take her. I don't know when I started eating again.''

"Did your mother try to feed you?''

"No. I did all the cooking. In the three days I was in bed, she didn't make anything for me or send anything upstairs for me.''

"What do you suppose is important for you to know about that time?''

"I didn't want to live. I was trying to pass over."

"You were trying to die?"

"Yes, but I didn't. My brother, Vaughn, would bring me water, but he got a beating for that. She beat him hard and he ran away. Then I went right to the Light, and I said I wasn't going to live anymore and fight anymore. The Light didn't say anything. It was quiet, so I just stayed there."

"Did you start to get better?"

"Yes. When I slept in the Light, I was getting better."

"It wasn't time for you to pass over, was it?"

"No. But I felt so sad, so very sad. She doesn't treat me like mothers treat their daughters. I've seen other mothers."

"She doesn't know how to love you."

"She hates me. She tells other people that she loves me, but she doesn't."

"It is sad that she couldn't love you and appreciate you. Sad for both of you. But the Light warmed you and you began to get well."

"Yes. But I was real different in school. I didn't care anymore. I didn't care if I had friends. I didn't care if I did well or not."

"You'd been too hurt."

"Yes. It's the kind of hurt that makes your chest and back hurt."

"It hurts your heart."

"Yes. And this is when I found out. I didn't really know before that she hated me, but I know now."

When she came out of trance, Barbara asked, "How are you handling all this stuff?" I'm sure I looked as low as a human being can look. I'd become incredibly attached to Barbara. It was unlike any relationship I'd ever had, with patients, friends, or family. It felt as though in these other relationships I took the love for granted. In this one, I was being required to feel it, inspect it, talk about it, and ultimately learn more about its meaning.

147

"At times I feel overwhelmingly sad about the things that happened to you," I answered. "Other times, I feel anger and outrage toward the perpetrators. But I'm okay with all this. I know I'm supposed to be learning from you."

"That's what Father Collins said," Barbara exclaimed. "He said he was learning from me. He's really helping me, too. I'm glad you made me find a priest to talk to. I'm not sure anyone else besides you two would believe me. Do you believe all of these memories?"

"I do. Strangely enough, I have the hardest time with your mother. I understand mob psychology and peer pressure and the greed for power, so I can accept the notion that a bunch of people worship satan because they think it'll give them more power. And I associate power with white people. Since the Nazis were white, Europeans were white, and all the satanic abuse survivors I know about all over this country are white, I have no trouble believing the satanic ceremonies. Plus, they fit with all my historical readings. And blacks, no doubt, learned a lot about sadistic violence from their white masters.

"What I have the most trouble understanding is your mother's hatred. I can't comprehend where that much hate comes from, and of course as a mother, I can't identify at all with enlisting others to harm and possibly kill my child. I've had flashes of hatred for my children, but I could never act on them. I just have to say again that your mother's hate is about your mother, not about you! It's got to be about the evil in her, her entanglement in her own narcissism. That's what it is! It's the individual evil I have the most trouble understanding!"

"Hmmm, yes. I think you're right. As you know, I feel tremendous anger toward Michelle sometimes, and I'm afraid I'll act on it, but I really don't want to, and on some level I don't think I ever would. My mother, though . . . Do you know there were bullet holes in the walls of our house? She'd get pissed and shoot at people. No, I could never hurt Michelle. I really enjoy her sometimes.''

"Do you? I've not heard you say that before.''

Barbara smiled. "I've been taking her shopping with me and she likes it, and she likes having lunch with me. It's helping me get over my shopping phobia. I keep a limit on what we can spend, so neither of us will get carried away.''

"Feels good?''

"Feels really nice being with her at those times.''

PART FOUR

FALL
1989

T E N

September was approaching. Part of the reason Barbara was shopping with Michelle was to buy school clothes. Barbara was feeling more jittery and we discussed several reasons why she might be having trouble at this time of year.

"September is when school starts, so our real sense of the new year from the time we are small is based on the academic year," I said. "Fall is a reminder of all the feelings we ever had about being sent off to school. And then it becomes a reminder of all the feelings we ever had about being successful or about being a failure."

"That's right," Barbara said. "And when I had good teachers, I wanted them to take me home with them. When I had bad teachers, they were an extension of my family's abuse. I thought I would never get away from hurt and evil."

"What other thoughts do you have about fall?"

"It means my birthday is coming up and also the satanic holidays. That's probably why my blood pressure is going up again."

"Let's go ahead with hypnosis and find out what the inner pressure is all about," I said.

"Where are you?" I asked Barbara once she was into her trance state.

"I'm at Grandma's, in the church. I'm in the closet on the way to the little bathroom. Tommy told me about where they hide things. Tommy's older and I have to help him clean up before church. He told me where they hide the heads of people. So I'm on my knees trying to move the big drain thing away so I can look down there. It's not really a drain, but it's supposed to look like one."

"How old are you?"

"I'm nine."

"What are you thinking as you work to remove that drain filter?"

"I wanna see the heads. It smells a little, but not too bad. I think that's 'cause the rats eat all the flesh off the bones."

"There are other bones down there, too?"

"Some. Like the fingers. They always save the fingers. But other parts they take to Reverend Conrad."

"Why do they take them to Reverend Conrad?"

" 'Cause he has that funeral home where they burn up dead people."

"What happens next?"

Barbara scrunches down in her seat and begins to shake. In a little voice she says, "Grandma found me. She's really mad. She says I hav'ta pay for snooping. She's moving the 'frigerator away from the wall and there's a door. She says I have to go down there and think about what I did. So she drags me to the door and makes me look in, then she pushes me down the stairs and slams the door.

"I could see all the snakes everywhere. Even hanging down from the ceiling. I think the snakes will eat me up. That's how I'll pay for snooping. I'll die and go be in hell."

"What does happen now?"

"I try to look for a place with no snakes and I see a light in the corner, so I go to it and the snakes slide away."

"Where does the light come from?"

"It's Jesus! The Light is Jesus, and he says, 'Don't be afraid.' "

"And no snakes come there?"

"No."

"Are these the kind of snakes that bite people?"

"I don't know. . . . I don't hear any rattles. They're mostly black snakes."

"How long are you down there?"

"I can't tell 'cause there's no windows. I don't know if it's all day and night or if it's longer than that. . . . Grandma doesn't love me either."

"Grandma doesn't love you? Did you always think before that she loved you?"

"Not all the time. No. But she was nice to me. Now I know she doesn't love me. They don't know how to love."

"The clan and people who worship evil don't know how to love?"

"Nobody I know does. My mother, Granddaddy, Grandma, nobody does. Only Jesus."

"You know that He loves you, don't you?"

"Sometimes I do, but sometimes I forget. I only see Him when it's really bad. Like now, with the snakes. I'm scared of snakes. But if He thinks I can do it by myself, He doesn't come. That's what He said. So there're things I've learned to do by myself."

"Yes. What happens when Grandma comes back?"

"She lets me out, but she says if I ever tell what I saw, that all the snakes will raise up out of hell and finally get me."

"What does that feel like when she says that?"

"Not as bad as the other thing she said. She tol' me that she never did love me. 'The only reason that you are here,' " Barbara said, using her grandmother's voice, " 'is because of Papa and because you were born with the gift. But I could never want a child born from the heart!' That's what she said. So no one's ever loved me."

"But you know that Jesus loves you," I said softly.

"But that's not people!" Barbara says, crying. "And it hurts my heart."

"And you know in your heart who you are and what you stand for. I think that you have a gift that the clan is jealous of. I think that you have the gift of being with the Light. You know how to love and it makes them angry."

"I jus' wanna cry. I hurt. . . ."

"Do you know, Jesus gives us all tears so we can cry when we're hurt?"

"No."

"It's true. We all have tears so we can cry when we hurt. It's how we love ourselves and love others when they get hurt."

"They won't let me cry."

"Because they don't know how to love. But you can cry now, and you must know that the Light is in your soul and they can never take that away from you. They can never take love away from you."

"I know that," Barbara said, trying to control her tears. "And Jesus tol' me once that when I get bigger, they'll be people who will love me."

"Believe that," I said. "Believe it."

I know in retrospect that my own defenses saved me from overwhelming sadness. In particular, intellectualization. I became enormously curious about snakes after that session. Where did Barbara's family get all the snakes that constantly turned up in cages and inhabited their cellars? What did the snakes mean to satanists? How did snakes get to be associated with evil and with sex?

First, I consulted a book on reptiles. I learned that the snakes Barbara seemed to be describing were, most likely, the black rat snake. These are not poisonous. Since they lay eight to fifteen eggs at a time and even when tiny can feed themselves on slugs and earthworms, I suspected it wouldn't take long to accumulate a mob of the creatures. Also, since eggs are fertilized internally, the sperm may live on in the reproductive tract of the female for months and even years after copulation has taken place. Female snakes can keep producing offspring even if the males disappear. What independence! I thought.

Thinking of snakes and sex led to one quick association: the snake as phallic symbol. One didn't have to study psychology to know that most people view the snake as a penis, and the penis as a "one-eyed snake."

Historically, I learned that the snake was maligned at the same time as women. Prior to the advent of patriarchy, snakes were revered as symbols of life energy, life-giving power, and even of immortality. Archaeologists found that the snake and its abstraction, the spiral, were dominant motifs of the art of ancient Europe, reaching its peak of expression around 5000 B.C.

Ancient cultures explained the mystery of life with symbols of water, the snake, and the bird. "The universal snake winds around the universal egg like a continuous flow of water," writes UCLA archaeologist Marija Gimbutas.[20] Later, around A.D. 900, in the Americas, the Toltecs' god, Quetzal-

---

20. Marija Gimbutas, *The Goddesses and Gods of Old Europe* (Berkeley: University of California Press, 1982), 95.

coatl, was a feathered serpent, one part resplendent bird, one part rattlesnake. As one, they had the power to drive the winds, bring the rains, and actuate fertility.

During the approximately five thousand years of goddess worship (7000 to 2000 B.C.), the snake represented wisdom. Headbands of some of the ruling high priestesses were adorned with the rising cobra, and the snake emerged from the forehead of the wearer as the Eye of Wisdom. The Levites, the only group of Hebrews who were accepted into the priesthood of Yahweh, are credited with writing the tale of creation we read in Genesis. Moses was one of the Levite priests. The goal was to discredit the goddess religions and their practice of matrilineal descent.

Because women could chose who would father their children and could freely practice their sexuality, women of these cultures were referred to as "temple whores" and "prostitutes." With the destruction of the goddess religions, the only good woman was a woman who belonged to a man. She no longer had status. Her wisdom was suspect as it came from that emissary of satan, the snake.

When Dan and I decided to buy a set of the *Encyclopaedia Britannica*, I was pleasantly surprised when they arrived with coupons for free library searches on listed topics. I sent off for articles on cults and religious sects. One of the articles returned was titled "Serpent-Handling Sects." I was fascinated to learn that among the fundamentalist Christian sects in the South are groups that believe that Mark 16:17–18 is a test of faith: "Faith will bring with it these miracles: believers will drive out demons in my name and speak in strange tongues; if they handle snakes or drink any deadly poison, they will come to no harm; and the sick on whom they lay their hands will recover."

There are an estimated one thousand members of serpent-handling sects in West Virginia alone. Migrations into urban areas of the Midwest led to serpent-handling churches in Northern cities as well. Services last from two to five hours culminating in speaking in tongues, handling poisonous snakes, handling fire, and occasionally drinking strychnine.

Yes, members die. One sociologist ties the behavior to ignorance and poverty. The members of this religious sect call themselves the "chosen people," and they choose salvation and even death over the destitution of being "in the flesh." So, I thought, some fundamentalist Christians use snakes in their religious practices. Timber rattlers, copperheads, cobras. If a member dies, it's God's will. In Barbara's family, if a member died it was satan's will, except death wasn't usually caused by the snakes.

The question kept repeating in my mind: Why would people embrace any extreme sect? A book by Arthur Deikman provided some answers.[21] Dr. Deikman suggests that due to the structure of childhood, we all long for a wise, strong parent figure to care for us. In describing this "dependency dream," he asserts that four basic behaviors are played out in cults: dependence on a powerful leader; forced compliance with group values; consistent devaluing of outsiders (every group I've read about views itself as the "chosen people," including Barbara's clan); and forbidding dissent.

Dr. Deikman helps the reader see how easy it is to go along with accepted ideas and to acquiesce to group pressure because of the longing to "return home" and be cared for. I remembered a left-wing bumper sticker from twenty years ago that I thought then was rather silly. The sticker said, "Question Authority." I wondered briefly if I might be able to find one of those bumper stickers now.

The thought persisted that I could no longer be shocked.

---

21. Arthur Deikman, *The Wrong Way Home: Uncovering the Patterns of Cult Behavior in American Society* (Boston: Beacon Press, 1990).

Each startling new revelation from Barbara under hypnosis had to be the most upsetting and abhorrent. But I was always proven wrong.

As Barbara's birthday approached, she felt more and more tense.

"I know it has to do with the satanic stuff 'cause I always feel awful around my birthday. I think that was the most important time for them in terms of indoctrination. And my birthday falls close enough to the satanic high holy days; all of October is like a nightmare for me."

"What about Halloween?"[22]

"Our clan didn't pay any attention to Halloween as far as I can remember. I have no bad memories associated with Halloween. But, you know, our clan saw themselves as the 'chosen ones,' so I wouldn't be surprised if they did some things differently from other satanists just to feel above them all."

Barbara was completely comfortable with me. It had taken a year, but our alliance seemed firm. She looked forward to coming for her appointments and, as she put it, "dumping the garbage." She had had such a hard time believing the satanic rituals had actually taken place that I urged her to get a small tape player so that she could listen to her descriptions of what had happened. Even though Barbara had very good

---

22. According to the satanic calendar, October 28, 29, 30, and 31 constitute the satanic high holy days. Sexual and blood orgies as well as animal or human sacrifices are a part of the ceremonies. Halloween itself began in ancient Britain and Ireland. It was a Celtic festival, called Sambain, celebrating the eve of the new year (November 1). It was an occasion for huge bonfires to frighten away evil spirits, as the souls of the dead were supposed to revisit their homes. This autumnal festival acquired sinister significance as the day when help might be invoked from the devil. Irish immigrants brought Halloween to America where the holiday gradually became a time for children's parties.

recall following her hypnosis sessions, it's natural to develop amnesia again for certain traumatic experiences.

She had begun to listen to the tapes in the evenings while preparing dinner.

"Bedtime is definitely out!" she'd said when we talked about when she could listen to tapes. "I'd never sleep."

So, her family learned to stay out of the kitchen, avoiding the occasional swearing and throwing of kitchen utensils. Once dinner was on the table, Barbara could leave her anger and disgust with the tapes and settle down into being a wife and mother.

It was during the month of October that Barbara discovered the most gruesome lesson she had learned from her grandmother.

"I'm looking out the window upstairs in the front room. I'm with Grandma and we're looking at the people down there in the street. There's a fight going on. Grandma says they're drunks. She says, 'They're drunks and they always act like heathens and that's why the whites treat us bad.' Now she says, 'Barbara, I have to share some important things with you. Because you have the gift and the power, you must learn the ways . . . the ways of the witching.' "

"How old are you?"

"I'm ten. I just had my tenth birthday. I don't want to learn things, but she says I have no choice, that I was born this way.

"Now we have to go downstairs to the church. I say I'm hungry and stop in the kitchen."

"Are you stalling for time?"

"Yes. She says to make a bologna sandwich, but I just make half a one. I hate it in the church. I hate it in there."

"How come?"

" 'Cause people die in there and bad things happen and it's scary in there. And people have babies."

161

"People have babies? What happens to the babies?"

"They die." Long pause. . . . "Grandma says I have to learn the ways . . . and if I don't, she'll be mad at me."

"So you go into the church."

"Yes. And it's just me and her. And the table's all fixed. And there's a little boy on it. Grandma says, 'You don't have to worry. This one's already dead, so you're gonna practice. You're not killing anybody, it's already dead. I didn't kill it, it was sick.' That's what she said."

"What does the little boy look like?"

"It's a black boy. Real black with kinky hair . . . real nappy. He has big eyes, but I don't know what color 'cause his eyes are closed. And he has a vest on and skinny arms and skinny legs and one of his toes is missing."

"Have you ever seen that before?"

"No. His big toe is missing on his right foot. Grandma says it must have been missing when he was born 'cause it doesn' look like it was just cut off.

"I have to be real quiet while Grandma says the stuff."

"What does she say?"

"I don't know. They're not real words. I don't listen. Now she sprinkles some smelly stuff around the room. Then she says, 'That was a special prayer for you to learn how to do this . . . to guide your hands."

"What is it you must learn to do?"

"I have to learn how to take out the heart. And the veins in the legs, the thing that makes the blood come out, without wasting any blood. I have to know how to get to them."

"What do you do first?"

"First, I have to name the parts. All the parts in the body and what they mean. I have to name them . . . the testicles and the penis and these are the signs of penetration. Now I have to cut them off. Grandma says, 'Don't jerk your hand 'cause you'll make it jagged. Go evenly, real slow.' And so I do.

"Then, I have to go down from there to the little part between where the testicles and the penis is to where they join at the limbs. 'Do not cut it yet. Wait till you get to the joint where the leg is. And then do not push on it real hard 'cause you'll make it bleed a whole lot, so you have to go real slow.' So I go real slow and she says I'm doing a good job.

"Then I hav'ta take my fingers and go in between the legs and there's white stuff and red stuff. Mostly red-looking . . . It's hard to find."

"What is it you're supposed to find?"

"A vein, or an artery. I found it, but you can't cut it, you have to wait and go further. If you cut it here, the blood will go inside the body. I'm feeling real funny. . . ."

"What kind of a feeling is that?"

"Like I've done something bad. Real bad. But there's nobody there sayin' not to do it. I just know it."

"You always know. But you have no choice. Grandmother's telling you what to do."

"I couldn't say no."

"What would happen if you said no?"

"She'd let them hurt me a lot."

"Who would hurt you?"

"The clan. She made me go to the Upper Room once. And there were four boys up there and she told them they could have me and she didn't care."

"She meant they could rape you?"

"Yes. But she won't say that."

"So if you make Grandma mad, she'll do something like that?"

"Yeah. And she lies. She said I have a way of bringing power over them and I can control any male. But that's a lie. I feel real bad."

"What do you do now?"

"I tell Grandma I won't do it anymore. I'm going to the

163

bathroom to be sick. But Grandma just says, 'Hurry up.' When I come back, she keeps telling me what to do. She says there's a line from the belly button down to the top of the penis, 'cept you don't cut there. You pretend the line goes all the way up to the neck and you cut where that line is up there. Then you open it up, but this body doesn't bleed like the ones Grand-daddy does. It doesn't hardly have any blood in it.''

''I wonder where it came from.''

''Grandma says he was already dead, but I don't know.''

''Could it have come from the hospital?''

''Yes. I don't like thinking about hospitals.''

''What happens now?''

''I have to go through these bones. You don't break 'em, you take your hand and go up underneath. Not really on the left, but not really on the right. And then you feel around for the heart and it feels different. It doesn't feel like the hearts on my paper. It's different from pictures. Grandma says to snatch it out with my hand. 'Squeeze it with your hand and pull it out and it will come out. You have the power to pull out a man's heart.' But it's kinda hard, but I do it.''

''And now what happens?''

''We don't eat it, 'cause Grandma says it's diseased. Grandma gets the cleaver and we chop up the legs and stuff, and then we have to wait to take it over to Reverend Conrad's in special bags.''

''What about the head?''

''The head is sacred, so you have to save it.''

Barbara and I were quietly horrified after the hypnosis session. I felt that I had to help her to integrate this new knowledge, not let it be set apart as something we couldn't touch.

''It's not really surprising, is it?'' I said casually. ''We've known all along that you were being groomed to take over the role of high priestess from your grandmother. You were her favorite and you were smart, unlike most of the others.''

164

"That's right," Barbara answered dully. "She never would have picked my mother. She had no self-control. She did whatever she wanted."

"Oh, no! This is too much!" Dan exclaimed when he heard about the lessons in human dissection. I described the details just as Barbara had said them to me.

"Does it sound anatomically correct, what her grandmother taught her?" I asked.

"It does. We didn't follow that sequence in gross anatomy, going straight for the heart and collecting the blood. We studied one organ system at a time. But that would be the way to do it. Good God! What is wrong with those people?"

"I feel like I'll never be able to understand them," I said weakly. "Also, I'll never understand how Barbara turned out to be so strong. She's one of the 'invulnerables,' children who grow up in harrowing family situations and somehow turn out to be healthy."

A group of psychologists and psychiatrists had been studying the invulnerables for years. The first book to come out on the topic describes studies of children from families where the parents were chaotically mentally ill and also families where the children were abused and neglected.[23] The studies found that among child victims, 6 to 12 percent become "outstanding" individuals. By "outstanding" the researchers are referring to excellent capacities for coping, competence, creativity, and confidence.

"And on the other hand," I said, "there are people who are destroyed by something that sounds rather minor. One rape crisis center did a study and found that of all their clients, the one who was most traumatized was a woman who as a girl

23. E. James Anthony and Bertram Cohler, eds., *The Invulnerable Child* (New York: The Guilford Press, 1987).

was fondled under the dining room table by the visiting minister. She hadn't been violently raped like some of the others in the study, and yet for some reason, she was having the most difficult time getting over the trauma."

"Sure sounds like constitution, doesn't it?" Dan said. "Some people are born stronger than others."

"Yeah. I have a very strong feeling that I couldn't have survived half of the torture that Barbara did. Puny constitution. I really did love human anatomy and physiology, though. If I had grown up in an educated family, I'm sure I would have gone to medical school. As it was, a two-year master's degree seemed just bearable. I couldn't imagine completing five to nine years of medical education after college."

"One physician in the house is enough," Dan said. "Our schedules are crazy as they are. We'd never hit home at the same time if we were both doctors. And there wouldn't be enough time for the girls."

The only time Barbara ever called me on an emergency basis was the day after that session. "I'm sorry to bother you, but I couldn't go to work this morning. I can't stand the thought of people seeing me. I feel so full of shame I don't know what to do. I really don't know what to do with myself."

I was alarmed because for Barbara to call me meant she was truly traumatized. I helped Barbara structure her day practically down to the minute in order to contain her anxiety. We included a movie (a comedy) and several hours of exercise, along with window-shopping, something she had come to enjoy. Then we arranged a time when I would call her that evening to see how she was getting along.

When she picked up the receiver, her voice sounded faint, barely audible. "I'll be all right until I see you. I feel real weak, though, real weak. I think it's just the depression. Thanks for calling me."

"You sure you'll be all right until tomorrow?"

"Yes. I'll be okay. Thanks."

That evening I made a fire in the kitchen fireplace after Dan went to his office to do his nightly paperwork. September was always a nice extension of summer, I thought. Still warm and balmy, but not hot. Somewhere in October, with the orange-yellow leaves going dry and crunchy, the cold snapped on and the nights became downright shivery. I hugged my knees and thought about Halloween and blood.

The good part of Halloween is that it helps children overcome their fears of physical helplessness, I thought. They take charge and turn into witches and warlocks, goblins and faeries, adopting magical powers. They may pretend to be physically mutilated and paint blood on their bodies, mastering the fear of someone else's doing that to them.

And the bad part, what is that? I wondered. Easy. The bad part is that some children and adults identify with the aggressive acts. They feel so insecure that they readily learn ways to feel more powerful than others. They learn to like scaring people, and then they may also learn to like hurting people.

I thought more about blood. Everyone knows that blood is supposed to stay inside the body. There is something innately upsetting about seeing blood outside the body. Unless you're a woman. Women get used to the sight of blood through menstruation and childbirth. Maybe that's why men faint more frequently than women when having their blood drawn, I thought. They haven't that experience.

I smiled to myself remembering the time I'd taken Julie to have her blood tested last year during an illness. I told her not to worry, women don't have trouble with blood tests, men do. When I began to expound on the psychological explanation, "castration anxiety," Julie said, "Mom, you'll use any excuse to talk about penises!"

"But it's true!" I continued. "Men have this extra external organ, which they unconsciously fear will be taken away from them. That's why some men spend most of their lives trying to prove that they fear nothing at all, engaging in all these 'counterphobic' behaviors.''[24]

"Mom, will you please leave before the nurse comes in? I can handle this myself. I don't have a penis, so I won't faint. Okay?''

Julie enjoyed teasing me about my outspoken monologues on sex. I wanted my daughters to learn about sex from me, and I wanted them to know they could ask me any question about human sexuality. If I didn't know the answer, I'd find it.

When Jasmine was in her early teens, she'd asked me one day, "Mom, is there such a thing as 'bad sex'?'' What she meant was, is there *unpleasant* sex? In her starry-eyed romantic notion of relationships, she thought all sex must be simple ecstasy. I explained that good sex usually stemmed from a mutual readiness and responsibility to share physical intimacy. If a partner was irresponsible and uncaring, sex could not only be hurtful, it could be a disaster.

Barbara, I thought, was certainly an expert on physical disaster.

---

24. "Counterphobic" behavior is embracing what most others are frightened of, thus "flying in the face of fear." Evel Knievel riding his motorcycle across the Grand Canyon is an extreme example. Young women who are sexually promiscuous are another example. Where most women choose their sex partners carefully, those who don't deny that they are in danger from indiscriminate sex or violence.

E L E V E N

As the holidays approached, many of my patients spoke of sadness related to missing a loved one, or of deep disappointment in their families of origin. Important time was spent on how to cope with dysfunctional family patterns and how to establish new, healthier ways of relating. Barbara, who had been working with me for thirteen months, seemed to be unaware of the time of year and of relationship patterns. She was immersed in her grief.

"I'm not sure which is worse, my anger or my crying. I'm not as angry all the time as I was, but it seems like now all I do is cry," she said.

Barbara did seem less agitated than in the past, but she looked overwhelmingly sad. Her eyes were puffy and her lower lip puckered as though she were fighting back tears. Her hair had grown out some and was beginning to look like a normal short hairstyle.

"We've learned that you have lots to cry about," I told her. "There's been so much hurt, so much abuse. That's worth a whole reservoir of tears. And you could never have your feelings when you were a girl."

"I know I can cry now. I go in my room and close the door at night and just lie on the bed and cry for hours. Sometimes I skip dinner and go to bed. Cal and the kids leave me alone and he never says anything. He just gets concerned in the mornings if I look like I may not be able to get to work. But I haven't missed another day since the time I called you. There's something else going on, too. I keep worrying about making a mistake. Every little thing I do, I worry that I'm not doing it right, like I'll make a mistake and it will mean a disaster."

"Let's see what we can discover about your crying and about making a mistake."

"I'm crying outside the church," Barbara said once in her trance.

"How old are you?"

"I'm eleven."

"How come you're crying?"

"I don't know. I cry all the time for no reason at all."

"For no reason?"

"Yes. That's what they say. I have no reason to cry." Barbara got a startled, frightened look on her face and then relaxed into a look of complete peace.

"Something really scared you, didn't it? Then you went away to the Light."

"Yes. Jesus came to help me. It's about the baby."

"The baby?"

"Everybody knows. They act like they don't, but everybody knows."

"What is it about a baby that everybody knows?"

"I'm fat now and I'm scared they're gonna kill me. In

church I said a prayer for Jesus to take the baby home and Grandma heard. She gave me that look, so I got up and ran for the door. The Fat Lady said, 'What's wrong with you?' and I said, 'Nothing.' Then one of the Keepers said, 'What's wrong with you?' and I said, 'Nothing.' But there's a lot wrong with me. Jesus didn't take the baby so it's still inside and I don't want it."

"What do you think will happen?"

"I won't ever get to go to school again. I'll never have friends again. That's what my mother says. She says I'll be a nothing. And I can't tell my friend Kathlene at school 'cause she's not part of the clan and they'd kill me if I told her. I go to her house, but I can't tell her."

"What have you been told by the clan about people finding out that you're pregnant?"

"Frannie, my friend in the clan, said that's why they killed Marie. I'd forgotten about that, but then I remembered when she told me. They killed Marie because she told people she was having a baby, and she gave her baby away and they didn't get to kill it. So they killed her. I had forgotten, so Frannie reminded me.

"Grandma said the white people would come and take me away. She said I'd never get to see any of them ever again. And my mother said something real mean. She said she'd tell everyone that the baby belonged to the fat, ugly man who lives downstairs. She'd say I was 'fast' and that she couldn't control me."

"They'd just make it all your fault."

"Yes. And I also think no one will ever like me."

"So, you cry a lot these days and there's a big worry that they might kill you?"

"I hope they do. Then I won't have that picture in my head all the time of the monster. Every time they do things to me I see the monster."

"When they do things to you? What things?"

"Screwing. They call it screwing."

"That must be scary."

"Not anymore. 'Cause I've turned into one of them."

"You think you've turned into one of them?"

"I am. You gotta be if you carry one of their seeds. That's what they said. And that's all I think about is that I have a devil in me. . . . And I hate it. I'd rather be dead than be a devil."

"So there's a part of you that wants to be dead and there's a part of you that's afraid they might kill you. Is that right?"

"Yes, 'cause I don't want it to hurt. But I know it hurts when they kill you 'cause they all scream, and I don't want to have to scream. I just want to die real quiet."

"Do you ever try to hurt yourself?"

"I tried to drown in the bathtub, but I couldn't do it. I tried to stick things up inside me, but that didn't do it. I cut myself once with a razor blade, but I didn't bleed enough. . . . And I climbed up a telephone pole once and jumped off the garage, but I didn't even break my leg. I even went down the street to where the drunks are and hoped they'd kill me, 'cause Grandma says that happens if you go down there. But they didn't."

"So, you're left with these feelings inside, wanting to be dead yet scared."

"That's 'cause the devil's waiting right there. I see his face all the time . . . waiting to come and get me. But if I die, he won't get me. That's what I think."[25]

"If you die, you could go be in the Light? Is that what you think?"

"Yes. I could be there all the time and I'd be rid of the pictures of the devil. But that's not gonna happen."

---

25. Barbara's struggle as a girl alternately believing and disbelieving in the devil is similar to children's ambivalence about Santa Claus. Children may try for years to believe consciously there is no person named Santa, but deep inside they still believe in him.

"It's not going to happen? How come?"

"Jesus told me I have something to do. He said I have to have the baby."

"So, Jesus has a purpose for you?"

"I guess so. But I don't like it. And the master says this is one of the burdens I have to carry."

"Who is the master?"

"Granddaddy. He says that when I give up the soul of the baby, it will lessen the burden. But I don't believe him."

"What does that mean?"

"It means I'm supposed to conquer souls in the world. It means I'm supposed to bring people to him to die, that's what it means really!"

"And you don't believe in that, do you?"

"No."

"Sometimes this all feels so sad and so hard for you that you want to be dead and you've tried to make yourself die, but it hasn't worked. And now, you know that Jesus has a purpose for you." I gave Barbara suggestions to rest and relax and to find that connection to the Light in order to strengthen her confidence and her faith that everything happened for a reason and that she would continue to heal, and then I brought her out of trance.

"How could I have had a baby at age eleven?" she asked after blinking her eyes and stretching her fingers.

"Do you mean, how could you have become pregnant? When did you begin menstruating?"

"I started early." Barbara gave a big sigh. "I know I was raped enough. All that shit about protecting me from penetration . . . everybody and his brother could rape me whenever they wanted. I still have trouble believing this stuff though! I guess I worked so hard to forget it. I don't want to remember and I don't want to believe it."

"Does getting pregnant feel like the big mistake?"

"No, I don't think so. That's something else."

I suggested we set aside a longer time for the next session. We had to find out what happened to the baby Barbara had apparently had at age eleven.

"I'm at school and Mrs. Oliver asked me to stay after so she could talk to me. She says, 'I know there's something wrong with you because you're very smart. Can you tell me what's the matter? How come you're not working where you need to be working?' I just looked at her and didn't say anything. If I tell her, I'll be in big trouble. She asks me if I'd like her to talk to my mother and I say no. She says I should stay after school with her for the next two weeks and she'll help me with my work.

"So I take the note home, and my mother's really mad. She's shaking me and screaming at me, 'What'd you tell her, you little bitch?' Then she makes me stay in my room and says I can't come out. Then she changes her mind and says I have to clean the middle room, and that's where they throw all the junk . . . all the clothes and trash. And I can't go downstairs to eat and I can't go downstairs to use the bathroom. And it takes all night, so I don't do my homework, so I'll be in trouble at school again."

"You have no choice, do you? You've got to do what Mother says."

"Then she comes back upstairs and looks at the room and says, 'Take your ass to bed. You and I are gonna have a talk come Saturday when Mama gets here.' "

"And what happens on Saturday?"

"Grandma comes to have her hair done, and when I come downstairs, she says, 'What's this I hear that you haven't had a visit from Mary Jane?' "

"What does that mean?"

"It means I didn't have my period. And I said, 'I don't know.' So Grandma asks my mother how long and Mother said, 'She hasn't asked for pads in two months.' And Grandma asks me, 'Who were you fooling around with?' So I told her Morton. But really, it was lots of boys. I didn't let none of them, but they do it anyway."

"How old are these boys?"

"Seventeen or eighteen."

"Tell me what they did to you."

"They take me to the Upper Room when nobody's there. Morton and I are supposed to clean the church for Sunday. It's not really for Sunday, even though they say that. It's for Saturday night when they do their devil things. And I'd be cleaning . . . they'd leave me by myself because I was a good cleaner, that's what Grandma said . . . and Morton and them were supposed to lift the heavy stuff. But then he'd make me go to the Upper Room and take off my clothes. Then he tied my hands like when they're being mean to me." Barbara got that tense and terrified look and then slumped into peacefulness.

"You just got real scared, didn't you?"

"I went to the Light."

"I want you to stay as comfortable as you are now, but look and see what happens in that room. Tell me what happens."

"After he ties my hands he says, 'I'm gonna pop your cherry. Not that you got one to pop. But I'll go real deep, that way I'll know.' "

"Do you know what he's talking about?"

"That means he wants to have sex with me . . . screw me, they call it. Then he opens the door and says, 'Okay, Tom, I go first. It'll cost you ten dollars and your friends, it'll cost twenty dollars.' He didn't say there'd be others," Barbara says in a tiny voice.

"And I didn't scream. And so they did it. Then Morton

175

said, 'You know you always get in trouble 'cause you always doin' somethin' wrong. So if you tell, I'm gonna get you more with that poker.' That's what he said."

"He'll get you more with the poker? What does he mean?"

"They use the poker on you in the Upper Room. They burn me on the stomach and on my legs."

"All right. Let that image fade away now. When I count to five, move back to the event with Grandma and your mother."

Barbara returned to Grandmother and Mother, but it was a little later. "I'm in trouble again," she said. "I slipped and told Mrs. Oliver I was going to have a baby. She was bein' real nice to me at school and I slipped and told her. She said I looked too skinny to be four months pregnant. I said I don't eat anymore and they make me wear a girdle, too. She just patted me on the head and said things would be okay. I don't think she believed me."

"What happens next?"

"Mrs. Oliver came to the house. And when she left, my mother was really mad. She screamed, 'What did I tell you about your fucking mouth? I told you to keep your goddamn mouth shut! Your mouth is going to be the death of you! Now we have to figure out what to do!' Then she goes downstairs to call Grandma. When Grandma comes, she takes us to her friend's house and they all talk. They decide they have to get rid of it and my mother says, 'I have me some quinine. That's the best medicine.'

"When we get home, she says, 'Come here. I have something for you, but it's not quinine.' "

"What is it?"

"I don't want to say. Because I seen her making it."

"You see her make it. What is it that she gives you?"

"She says only a teaspoon won't kill me. It'll just make me sick and make the baby come out."

176

"And what is that?"

"D-Con."

"That's poison, isn't it?"

"Rat poison. And it makes me really really sick. I throw up all the time and sometimes I throw up blood. So mother calls the school and says I'm real sick and I won't be back for a while."

"How long were you sick?"

"Two weeks. I missed school for two weeks, and when I went back, I thought Mrs. Oliver would be mad at me, but she wasn't. She was real nice."

"She likes you a lot, doesn't she?"

"Umm-hmm. She said I was really smart."

"Let that picture fade away. When I count to five, you'll move to the next important event. One . . . two . . . three . . . four . . . five . . . What comes to mind?"

"I'm in church with Frannie. And it's warm outside now, and I'm really really fat."

"Some time has passed, hasn't it? Are you aware that you're fat because of the baby, or do you not think about that?"

"I don't think about that. I'm just fat."

"And what's happening in the church?"

"It is time for me, they said. 'It is time to make the ultimate sacrifice. It is time to give of yourself and to give of your soul to the almighty and powerful one. . . . It is time . . . the time is now . . . we cannot wait any longer.' That is what they say."

"Who says those words?"

"Granddaddy. He's reading from his book . . . the book of spells. It gives him 'the power and the steady hand to do what I must do . . . to deliver not one, but two souls to the almighty, so that my hand will be steady as I reach in for the souls, and I will grab them both at the same time, and they will do my bidding . . . the souls will do my bidding.' That's what he says.

"Then Grandma comes to the door and says, 'Barbara, come here. I need you to help me get things ready,' and so I do. She tells me to get the special candles. She wants eleven and she wants seven. Eleven is for me and seven for the baby. That makes eighteen, three times six."

"So you help with the candles."

"That's my job. But I arrange them differently. And they bring in a different kind of table. The table that they kill people on."

"What does it look like?"

"It is metal and it's silver looking. And it has a thing on the bottom, like another table on the bottom, and they put things down there. It's long and they cover it with a cloth and the cloth has signs on it."

"What are the signs?"

"I can't tell you."

"You're not supposed to tell."

"If I tell you, I will surely die."

"No, you won't die. This is Gail and you can tell me. Remember, I'm here with you."

"It is the sign of the powerful one."

"Who is that?"

"The almighty. That's what they call him. But he's not. It's the devil."

"What does the sign look like?"

"It's the Star of David with eighteen circles around it."

"What do the circles mean?"

"Stands for eighteen candles. Three goes into eighteen six times. And the three forces . . . the three forces are darkness, evil, and lust." Barbara's voice lowers as she begins quoting words she has heard: " 'Lust is your desire that you get to have. All man has desires, but the weak and foolish ones deny that they have desires, and that's how their souls can be conquered.' That's what they say."

"And what about darkness and evil?"

"Darkness is when the time is strongest. Darkness can conquer the enemy. But that's not true."

"You know all this isn't true. Who is the enemy to them?"

"God and Jesus is the enemy. The Light is the enemy. And all the forces of the Light is the enemy."

"And what do they say about evil?"

"Evil is good. Evil is good. Evil is pleasure. Evil is when you fulfill your pleasures. And pleasure is winning and never losing. You win when you eat the heart. You win when you don't spill any blood. You have pleasure when you have pleased the almighty and powerful one. That's what they say."

"Are there any other signs on the cloth?"

"Yes. There is an animal's head . . . like a ram's head, but it's not a ram, but it has horns like a ram.[26] And on the front, the sign with the Star of David with the eighteen circles . . . the colors are purple and gold. The gold are the candles and the purple is the Star."

"What else do you see?"

"On the other side is a cross, and it's right-side up, too.[27] The cross right-side up means we have no fear. The enemy thinks that we are afraid of his symbols. His symbols mean shit! That's what they say. And on the back side is red dots."

"What do the red dots mean?"

"It is for the blood of those who suffered needlessly . . . those who suffered at the hands of the enemy. If you die and go to Him, that means you suffered. That means you know no pleasure, and it is those who were amongst us who had to suffer at the hands of the enemy . . . that is what the red dots

---

26. She is probably referring to the Baphomet, a demonic deity represented by a goat's head. It is often symbolized among satanists by the upside-down pentagram, the two points up representing the devil's horns, the three points down the denial of the Trinity, and the center pointing down to invoke satan.
27. Satanists usually invert the cross as a sacrilege.

are for. The less red dots you have, the stronger your clan, and we only have three red dots. . . . They will have four. Because I will be one.''

"What happens now?''

"They put the curtains up . . . these are special curtains. And they don't wait for it to get dark like they usually do. And then Grandma went next door and she told the lady that they were going to be doing a healing and so people will be screaming in pain, so to pay no mind. And I wondered who would be on the special table. I didn't think it was going to be me. But Grandma sent me upstairs to the bathtub to take a special bath, so now I know it's going to be me.''

"What is a special bath?''

"It is using the oils and richness of the earth. It is for purification. Grandma makes the oils that are specially scented.''

"And what happens after you bathe?''

"Miss Nonnie comes up and says, 'Let me look at you,' and she tells Grandma I don't have enough hair down there to be bothered about shaving it. That's what she says. And Grandma said to dry off and they give me a white robe to put on, and it's not like a church robe. It has no pleats, no zippers, no nothing. It goes on over your head. And I ask about putting on my underclothes and she says, 'You don't need any . . . not tonight.' And I ask her what she was going to do, and she said, 'The time has come.'

"And I said, 'You told me when the time comes, that my stomach would be hurting,' so she pulls my face to hers and says, 'Look! We can't wait until your stomach starts to hurt. You have to be very brave, because if you don't, they will kill you for sure this time!' That's what she said.''

"Oh, my . . . and now what happens?''

"I said, 'You promised not to let them hurt me if I be good again,' and she said she knows, and she's not going to let them hurt me, but if I'm bad, she can't help me. She said, 'I told you when they put you in the grave the last time, remember? I can't always help you. You have to be brave! Do you hear me?' And I feel really bad, so I ask her what they were going to do, and she says, 'The same thing they do with everybody else's baby,' and I wanted to die.

"So I sat upstairs in the kitchen and wait and Frannie comes up and she sits and looks at me and says, 'Girl, you sure are lucky . . . you're lucky you get to do this and be so special. Don't you know you're the most special person that they have here?' I said, 'No,' and she said I was real lucky and I said, 'I'm not.'

" 'But just think how close you'll be to the master,' she said. And that made me mad, so I called her a dumb-ass bitch, just like that, and she said, 'Now, why do you want to call me that?' I said, 'I can't believe how stupid you are!' And she said she's not stupid . . . that she's been around and she's been to real churches and that's stupid . . . this is the real thing. So I die a little more because she's one of them and I can't talk to her anymore.

"I have no friend now. So I told her to leave me and she does her stupid little bow that she always did. 'Yes, Your Highness. Yes, my great and worthy princess. I will follow your command.' I told her to kiss my ass, and she left."

"What happens to you now?"

"The Keepers come to get me. They take me down the stairs, and then they pick me up because my feet are not to touch the ground. They put me on the table and I'm not scared. I don't know why. I'm always scared of dying."

"Is it because of what happened with Frannie? Are you angry?"

"No, I'm hurt. I'm disappointed because she was my friend and she can't be my friend anymore."

"So, you're sad and disappointed, but you're not scared."

"I don't know why. It doesn't seem right for me not to be afraid of dying because I'm always afraid of dying. I'm always afraid of them hurting me, but I'm not. Grandma comes now and gives me some stuff to drink. It's real bitter and it's supposed to make me sleepy, but it doesn't. Everybody's dancin' around."

Suddenly Barbara stiffens in her chair and I can tell without asking that she's experiencing intense pain.

"It's bad . . . it's real bad . . . but I can't say anything to Grandma till she finishes her songs."

"What songs is she singing?" But Barbara has gone off to the Light. "You just went away to the Light, didn't you? You rest there for a moment knowing you're going to be all right, and then I need for you to come back and tell me what happens. You can do this."

"But if I come out of the Light, it will hurt."

"You don't need to hurt. You just need to look down and see what's happening."

"Grandma's doin' her three-four-six step. I don't know why she says four, but that's what she calls it. It is the special step when the seed of the master is to be born, and that's what she says I have. That's what's in me. And the singing . . . sounds like 'Come to Jesus,' but they don't say 'come to Jesus,' they say, 'Come to me, come to me, come to me, all ye faithful, you beautiful ones. Come to me for he is the one who will give you the gift of eternal life. Eternal life is yours . . . come to me . . .' And then they all lined up and they all come to Grandma and they . . . she doesn't have any clothes on . . . they each come and they kiss her on her breasts and they pour some blood on her, and I don't know where the blood came from . . . and Grandma says, 'And this is their entrance, as you come to me, you will enter into the circle of eternity and you will witness the coming of the master's seed. It shall bear the mark. It shall be the pure one. Come to me. . . .' And they all come, and it's lots of them, and that church isn't even big enough to hold a whole bunch of people."

"How many people, do you think?"

"Fifty. . . . And then Grandma turns around and she's looking at me and there's tears coming down my face. I'm not screaming, but I'm hurting real bad. My stomach hurts real bad. She comes over to me and she looks at me and I know that look. It says, I cannot cry or she will have to hurt me. Then she says, 'When the master's seed comes, there is no pain, but when the enemy has his hand on the seed, woman suffers and she suffers with great pain. When the master does, there is nothing.' So I have to act like I'm not hurting and I'm screaming inside. It's so loud in my head I can hear it."

"But you know how to be silent on the outside, so they won't hurt you?"

"Yes. The Light is with me, so I get to scream and scream in the Light. There's no one to hold my hand, and no one to help me, except for the Light."

"And what happens now?"

"Granddaddy comes with his special robe and he has the special knife, and he turns around and says, 'Hear ye, hear ye, hear ye . . . all who bear witness to this coming. It is now the time and we shall say 'Well done' when it is here. Hear ye once, hear ye twice, hear ye thrice. Hear ye two times thrice. Hear ye six times thrice.' That's what he said. And my stomach is like a tight tight knot . . . like it's trying to burst open by itself."

"And Grandfather is there with his special knife. What does he do?"

"I can't see right now."

"You can't see? But you know what happens, don't you?"

"I know what happens. And I see him. He has that shitty grin on his face."

"When does he get that grin on his face?"

"Whenever he's using the knife . . . whenever he's hurting someone. So now he's cutting my stomach. And it feels like he's pulling on it. And there isn't a whole lot of blood, because I'm still awake and I thought I would be asleep. I thought I'd be dead by now. I don't know . . . 'cept it hurts very bad. But I cannot scream."

"You know you cannot scream. What is he doing now?"

"I just feel what he's doing, but I'm looking at the people, trying not to think about it, so I won't scream out loud . . . so I'm looking to see who's there."

"Yes. Who do you see?"

"The closest ones . . . Sister Wilson and Sister Miller, and Morton, and Anthony is on the other side, and that bitch, and Sister Nonnie . . ."

"Who is 'that bitch'?"

"My mother."

"Your mother is there, too?"

"Yes. And she has the same grin. I hate her. Grandma is there and Grandma still doesn't have on any clothes."

"Do the others have clothes on?"

"The women have on white robes, and the men have on black robes. And Granddaddy has on a red robe. And now he has a mask on . . . the mask that he had when we went in the hospital. So now I know there's going to be a killing, but I still don't know who."

"Hmm. What does the mask look like?"

"It's made out of red, and it has horns on it, and it has a pointy-like chin and some ugliness, like a monster."

"So when he first came with the knife he didn't have the mask on and you could see that grin on his face. But now he has the mask on?"

"Yes. And feels like he's pulling on my stomach. And it hurts so much . . . hurts so much . . . hurts so much . . . I want Mommy to help me . . . but she won't help me."

184

"Do you call for her?"

"Hmm-mmm . . . 'Please help me . . . please help me' . . . but nothing happens, so I count."

"You count?"

"Yes. Lots of numbers . . . lots of numbers . . . but I can't stay with it because it hurts really bad."

"What are you aware of next?"

"They pull it out. Granddaddy does. And there's a thing hanging from her and it's on her neck . . . and he says, 'Oh, a she . . . we have us a she-devil,' and it looks like a double chin. It's ugly and has things on it and has blood on it. It doesn't look like the babies I've seen. . . ." With a big sigh: "So I had it."

"You had what?"

"A monster . . . the devil's seed . . . that's what they said."

"Oh, but you've never seen a newborn before. You don't know that they look funny like this at first. . . . They have blood and mucus on them and they don't look like babies that you see later on."

"And now I have to do it, and it's disgusting. I have to lick it clean."

"Who tells you to do that?"

"Granddaddy. He says, 'You must breathe the breath of life into her. You must make her whole. You must breathe the breath of life into her. You must clean her eyes, and you cannot touch her with your hands. Your hands are soiled because they have touched unholy things.' And it tastes horrible and it's gross."

"They put the baby up to your mouth? And you must lick her eyes and her mouth?"

"And blow into her mouth. That's what Granddaddy said."

"Does she begin to breathe?"

"She's crying. And they all start rushing around and they snatch her away and Grandma says to Granddaddy, 'You shouldn't have done that! You have made a bond now.' And she said that in front of all the other people. 'And now you know what must be done.' And so they take her away."

"And what about you? Granddaddy cut you open."

"He's still there . . . and it still hurts. They just throw a little towel over it, but it's not like a real big hole. It doesn't . . . I don't know . . . if it was a real big hole, I would be dead. And I'm not dead, so it must not be a real big hole. I don't know. . . ."

"How does Grandfather know how to do that? Deliver a baby that way?"

"He didn't do it. He only started to cut."

"Who did it?"

"Dr. Brady. He's the doctor from the hospital."

"Have you seen him before?"

"When I was six and in the hospital. And I saw him when I was eight, and when I was nine, and now. I don't know how he got there. I don't know where he came from."

"And what do they do with you?"

"They sing their songs and then they all leave. Then Grandma comes back, her and Sister Miller. Grandma's pulling my stomach. It feels like that . . . and she says, 'Be real still.' She says if I move, I'll make it come open again. So she puts tape on it . . . the kind you use in the hospital. And I have to stay there for three days and three nights. And I can't move. And I don't 'cause it hurts real bad."

"You have to stay there all by yourself?"

"Grandma comes and visits me and changes the bandage and she brings me something to eat, but I won't eat. She tries to get me to drink water, but I won't, so she gives me some juice. And she talks to me again. And I said, 'Grandma, what did they do with the baby?' And she says, 'They are preparing her for the feast.' And I said, 'You promised me they wouldn't hurt me, but they did.' She said, 'That is why I didn't let your grandfather do it. He would have killed you. I made sure the doctor was there. I told Brady if he didn't show up, I'd put a hex on him. His fingers would drop off one by one . . . and you know that's detrimental to a surgeon.' Then Grandma said, 'I have a way of taking care of my own.' "

"So Grandma made sure the doctor was there to take care of you?"

"Yes. Grandfather's done it before and not killed people, but she wasn't going to take any chances with me, she said."

"What happens to the baby?"

"In three days they bring her back. And I can get up now. And they bring in the other little table and the special cloth is folded on top . . . and they have special candles for when they do killings."

"What color are the special candles?"

"Kind of yellowish . . . they don't have color to them really. And they're cooking on the stove. They're cooking the brew. It smells like dead rats again. It has chicken feet and blood in it, but I don't know what else. They make the brew because it stinks and gives off a scent of death. That's what it's for . . . the scent of death."

"What happens now?"

"Not as many people this time . . . just our clan. Granddaddy made 'em stay, Grandma said. 'This is why this has to be . . . because once someone breathes the breath of life into her child, she will never give it up . . . never!' That's what Grandma said. And I said, 'What do you mean?' And she said, 'This has to be done. You cannot go on with your life if you have a baby, and you will not, do you hear me? You will not.' And I just looked at her and said, 'Can't you take me?' She said, 'No. That thing isn't worth living anyways, but you are.' And I said, 'Can't we give it to somebody? You don't have to kill it.' She said, 'I have already made the arrangements. I am not going to talk about this with you no more. Now, you're starting to get on my nerves. Sit your ass over there on that cross and don't move.'

"So I do. Then Grandma comes back with the baby and she's dressed in white and so is the baby. And my mother is singing and doing a dance, and she's twirling the baby around in the air sayin', 'Once, twice, and thrice. North, east, and south. North, east, and south.' And then she says, 'Once, twice, and thrice,' again. Then she puts the baby in the box with the special candles round it and she says, 'Once, twice, and thrice,' again. That's what my mother says.

"And then the Fat Lady, Miss Nonnie, comes in with her darling little babies. And she twirls the snakes in the air and says, 'Once, twice, and thrice. I have six darling ones to bring her to the master. Once, twice, and thrice.' So she goes over to put the snakes on the baby, and I get up and say, 'Don't!' Granddaddy tells me to sit down and I said, 'No.' And Grandma says, 'What do you want, Princess?' and that means that I can invoke my power, so I said, 'I will carry the snakes for her.' So they put them on me."

"But you're so scared of the snakes."

"It'd be worse for the baby."

"So you carry them for her."

"They put them on my arms and on my waist and I have to stand still while they are slithering. And they slither. And Miss Nonnie is laughing."

"That's so scary for you. Now what happens?"

"Miss Nonnie comes and gets her darlings and she says, 'Come, children, it is time.' She takes the snakes off me, and then my mother comes over and I bend down to touch the baby and my mother slaps me in the face. It really hurts. She said, 'Didn't I tell you that your hands are unholy? You're not to touch her.' So I just look. And my mother picks her up and goes, 'Once, twice, or thrice. Once, twice, or thrice. Once, twice, or thrice.' And she puts her on the table and they turn her once, twice, or thrice . . . north, east, or south. And it always ends in the south. And then Granddaddy does his special words.''

''What words are those?''

'' 'Hear us, O Master, as we commend this soul to you. This is the soul that was given . . . it was conceived by you and we will return the soul back to you. This is the soul that has been untouched by the enemy. This is the soul who has never experienced the enemy, who knows not . . . so now you have a pure soul, the most sacred and precious of all souls you have.' That's what Granddaddy says, and I don't believe him.

''Then he looks at me and says, 'We have to get ready.' I still have this white thing on, and he says, 'No. Put regular clothes on her.' And he said it really mean. My auntie goes and gets some clothes for me.''

''What does she bring?''

''It's a pink blouse and a plaid skirt with a jumper top. And I can't believe I can wear it even though I was really fat. . . . But I can wear it.''

''What does Grandfather do now?''

''He says, 'Stand on the cross, bitch, right now.' So I do. 'And stretch your hands out.' And I do. And they tie my hands. Then he says, 'And hold your head up or you will die.' And so I hold my head up. He wants me to look.''

''He wants you to see what he does?''

''Yes. And he didn't do it the regular way. He was real shitty about it. He just took the knife and stabbed her and the blood started squirting everywhere. And he carves it out . . . of her chest, and he has the heart on the end of the knife, and he says, 'Only the purest and worthy of us shall partake of this pure heart . . . not you, bitch,' is what he said. And so they do, and she bleeds all over the place, and they come and take my arms down and I sit on the cross and watch them.''

''And what are they doing?''

189

"They're eating her heart, and then they said, 'We have to save this . . . we cannot destroy the body. This is a special body.' And I know what they're going to do."

"What is that?"

"They'll cut it up and make it for special ceremonies. So I just sit there until they're finished and they all leave. And when they leave, I go get her off the table and I take off my blouse and put her in it, and I ask Jesus to help her, but He didn't. I asked Him to take her soul, but he didn't."

"How do you know?"

" 'Cause it was too late. I didn't ask in time."

"How do you know you didn't ask in time?"

"I just stood there and did nothing. They asked before me. Grandma and Granddaddy asked for her soul first. So they got it. Because I didn't do what I was supposed to do."

"Even though you know about the power of the Light . . . about Jesus. Why would you think that evil is more powerful?"

"I don't. I just think that first come, first served. So I really screwed up."

I asked Barbara to stay in her trance but come up to her present age, and then I asked, "Do you understand now that you felt you made a mistake in not asking for Jesus to take the baby's soul . . . that whenever you make a mistake or might make a mistake today you feel so terrible . . . you have that same feeling. When you were just eleven, you couldn't understand the power of Jesus . . . you felt responsible for that baby's soul, as though you had extra power and that just because you didn't make a request, you lost the baby's soul.

"It's important that you are clear about what you believe. We know that you believe in the Light, in Jesus, and in all the forces for good. You must not hold yourself responsible as though you had some other power. You were just a girl, and you could not change what the clan was doing. You did not have that power."

Just as Barbara had learned to scream inside, I was learning to cry inside. My heart wept through the entire session. I couldn't forget the image of an eleven-year-old girl wrapping her empty, broken baby in a pink blouse and sitting beneath the cross feeling hopelessly guilty. As for the medical and physical implications of giving birth in those circumstances, I was completely baffled. As always, I was more prepared than she was to accept her revelations as truth, but I was puzzled about the birth process she had described.

Barbara admitted she had a scar across her lower abdomen, but felt it was too tiny to be from a cesarean section. Although she didn't want any of her memories to be true, this one she hoped she could forget completely. The guilt and fear about the baby plagued her, however, and necessitated two more hypnosis sessions in which we returned to the gory details of the baby's birth and murder. During one of those sessions she recalled that the clan had called the baby Clarice. I could not find that name listed in the *Satanic Bible* as one of the "infernal names," or names of devils. In the baby-naming book I had used for possible names of my children, I found Clarice listed as a French name meaning "brilliant one." The other details of the birth experience remained consistent with the first session, and Barbara again used the word *pulling* to describe the sensation she kept having, in addition to the pain, when they were delivering the baby.

T W E L V E

I was beyond depressed. Every time I looked at Julie, my happy, exuberant teenager, I saw Barbara allowing the snakes to slither on her, or sitting alone beneath the cross holding a mutilated dead baby. Julie, for whom a big problem that year was whether her volleyball team would win their next game, my gorgeous Julie, I'd see being yanked into a van and taken off to be raped and tortured.

Another teenaged girl had just disappeared from a nearby town while on a long bicycle ride in the backcountry near her home. This can't be happening here in America, I thought. I stopped looking at the newspapers, let alone reading them. I wept constantly, but surreptitiously, explaining to Julie, if questioned, that it was only my allergies.

As Barbara described the horror of that birth process, I

couldn't help but remember that giving birth to my babies had been peak experiences in my life.

Jasmine was born in the sixties at St. John's Hospital, Santa Monica, California, the first Lamaze birth experienced by my jolly Armenian gynecologist. Julie's birth was similar to Jasmine's in that I felt in charge. I was the first woman to use the birthing room at Presbyterian Hospital here in Albuquerque; Julie was born in the same bed in which I had gone through labor. The room was like a living room with lamps and easy chairs. After I held Julie for a few minutes and welcomed her into the world, Dan gave her a warm bath right next to the bed. Then he returned her to me and she nursed for a solid hour, staring up at me as if to say, "I know exactly who you are and I know exactly who I am. I belong here."

That's the way childbirth should be, I thought, a celebration of the woman's body. Her finest achievement.

"How would you feel about seeing a gynecologist friend of mine?" I asked Barbara. She and I were still appalled about the childbirth disclosure and the infant murder. She was feeling overwhelmed by all of the images of horror. I had urged her to get a stack of white paper and crayons and at home in the evenings, draw the images that assaulted her. She dutifully brought her pictures in, and I held back my tears as I saw her drawings of the Keepers, the snakes, the special candles, her grandfather the high priest, the celebrants, and invariably, blood and dead bodies.

Her art therapy was helping her to process memories that kept appearing in her mind both day and night. Sometimes she would write the ritual words that came to her during the memories. The words, just like the behavior they accompanied, made little sense to me: "Evil, evil, yas esilro od tad ti yead tey yad yan em wen elur evil. The soul of the womb is yours, O Great Master of the land. Receive our sacrifice, Clarice, as our devotion to you. Give us all power as we drink the blood and eat the flesh for the master.''

While two sessions per week had seemed adequate for the first year of treatment, we had gone to three after Barbara remembered her lessons in human dissection. Now, three sessions per week were barely enough to enable Barbara to contain the vast amount of fear and guilt she experienced in reaction to the memories. I was grasping at anything to try to help her to finish putting the puzzle pieces of her life together and to release the feelings of terror that accompanied every new memory.

"Dr. Williams happens to be my gynecologist, but I know that she's seen a number of satanic abuse survivors. Cottonwood Hospital has been sending their sexual trauma inpatients to her. She's very gentle. What do you think?''

Barbara's eyes grew bigger and a smile began. "I'd love to see her. I force myself to go for a physical or a Pap smear every few years, or sometimes I just have to have a vaginal or kidney infection taken care of—I've had tons of those—but I always dissociate and get numb and I can't think or ask questions. And I've never felt comfortable with the physicians. One time I had to be in the hospital for a conization for an abnormal Pap smear and I freaked out.''

"Tell me about that.''

"After they rechecked and found that there was dysplasia, the doctor wanted to freeze the section, but decided not to because they couldn't see it clearly enough for all the scar tissue. So they decided to do the cervical cone biopsy. The doctor asked me if I'd had cryosurgery in the past! Of course I said no. After the procedure when I was in the room, they had to catheterize me and I started screaming and yelling. Poor Cal was so embarrassed. Now I know what that was about, though. It was what they did to me in the hospital when

I was six. Remember I told you I had to go to the bathroom and they wouldn't let me interrupt the ceremony . . . and they put clamps down there and catheterized me?"

"How could I forget? Let's get your medical records for Dr. Williams and I'll give her a call and set up a time for us to meet with her."

I met Barbara at Dr. Karen Williams's office one crisp November morning about ten A.M. Barbara had a sheaf of papers and handed them to me to look over as we sat in the waiting room.

"These are my medical records. Oh, and Sharon, my friend, is coming to take me to lunch when we're through. Remember, she's the one you made me give you as a backup person for when Cal's away."

"Of course I remember. I spoke with her on the phone once briefly. Great! Now I get to meet her." I had a sense that Sharon was as sensitive and caring a person as Barbara.

Barbara said to me, "Sharon really has become a friend. We can have fun together. She just teases me about my eccentricities, like never having any cash on me. It's a big deal if I get five dollars out of the money machine."

The nurse ushered us into Dr. Williams's examination room, and I could see Barbara begin to tense. Dr. Williams came in shortly, a large, friendly woman in her late thirties. She shook Barbara's hand and sat down. "Let's talk."

Barbara had made notes to refer to and began with her most pressing question: "Could I have had a baby when I was eleven years old?" Dr. Williams asked questions about her medical history, menstruation, and adult pregnancies. She asked about the process of Barbara's son's birth. Finally, she concluded that the history of Paul's delivery, born in five hours with no pushing, lent credence to the possibility she had given birth before. It would have been a vaginal delivery, however, so there was still doubt. Barbara told about the scar, the memory of her grandfather cutting her, the incredible pain of labor, which had been induced, and the forceps used in the delivery, the "pulling."

They talked for thirty minutes, then Dr. Williams asked Barbara if she wanted her to examine her physically. Barbara said yes, she was ready. Once she was on the examining table, Dr. Williams began from the head down. She looked at burn scars on Barbara's back and arms. "I know I have those all over my body," Barbara said. "Those are from them using a hot poker on me."

Dr. Williams inspected her hands. "Did you know you have a *W* or an *M* carved here between your thumb and forefinger on the right hand? I've seen this on a number of survivors."

Barbara said, "No, I never noticed that." She and I looked carefully at the letter. Barbara said, "It could be *M* for McKelly, the clan name." But I knew we were thinking the same thought: *W* for *witch*.

Dr. Williams then inspected the hairline scar across Barbara's lower abdomen. "This isn't a scar from a cesarean section," she said.

Barbara shook her head. "Yes. I think I know now that my grandfather cut me there to begin the ritual, but the doctor took over to deliver the baby."

Dr. Williams told Barbara that she was ready to do the pelvic exam and exactly what to expect. I turned to look at Barbara's face and was alarmed to see that she had dissociated and appeared not to be breathing. I gripped her hand. "Barbara! Where are you?"

"I'm very far away," she answered in her peaceful voice.

"That's okay. You can stay far away, but please keep breathing!" I added with some desperation.

Dr. Williams told us that the vaginal area and the perineum have great ability to heal. I expressed surprise. Because it feels so fragile and sensitive, I'd always thought it would scar and mutilate easily. No, she said, maybe for survival reasons it is one of the areas of the body that has great healing potential. She wasn't sure if she'd find any evidence of scarring. But she did. "It does feel like what appears to be scarring along the inner vaginal area next to the cervix."

"Could that be from the cone biopsy, though?" I asked.

"It's possible, but it would be unusual for there to have been stitches made here. This is not the usual place to find scarring."

So, now there was some possible medical evidence that the childbirth Barbara had described and the vaginal tortures in the Upper Room she had alluded to had actually taken place. Dr. Williams told Barbara to be sure to tell her physicians, prior to an examination, that she has trouble coping with any kind of physical procedure. "Just say, 'I have trouble with this,' and most of them will know what you mean without going into the abuse. But be sure to tell them."

When we left, Barbara turned to me. "She's so nice! That's the best experience I've ever had with a medical doctor!"

"Do you think you'll be able to handle doctor's visits a little better from now on?"

"Oh, yes. I'll just use my self-hypnosis and go away when I need to and be comfortable."

"And remember to breathe," I added, and we both laughed.

"There's Sharon!" Barbara said.

Sharon came over and gave Barbara a hug, then put her hand out to greet me. We both said, "I've heard so much about you," laughed, and shook hands. Sharon's round, sunny, freckled face was framed with light, curly hair.

I said, "I'm so glad you came here." Then, to both: "You two, have a nice lunch."

While denial and repression were the defenses that protected Barbara from emotional breakdown, intellectualization continued to save me, at least until near the end of her treatment when something much more mystical happened. In the meantime, her stories of infanticide and human sacrifice were so shocking that I had to read about the phenomena, try to understand whether such things could happen.

I discovered that throughout history, infanticide was a fundamental part of numerous cultures. Roman law not only gave the father the power of life and death over his children in infancy and childhood, but throughout life. Plato, Seneca, and Aristotle all endorsed the custom of killing defective children.

In ancient times it was believed in some societies that a building structure would only survive if a child was sacrificed and placed under the foundation. "Archaeological finds have revealed many jars among the Canaanites with bones of newborn infants. The jars had been buried under house corners, thresholds, and floors."[28]

"There is evidence that hell was originally the place where children were burned. The New Testament word for hell is Gehenna, a corruption of Ge-Hinnom. Hinnom is a valley near Jerusalem which the prophets railed against as the place where the children were destroyed. Jeremiah called it the 'valley of slaughter' (Jeremiah 7:32). It was in such valleys that children were killed at least in the eras of Solomon, Ahaz, and Manasseh, in biblical history."[29]

I found that in Old Testament times it was common prac-

---

28. David Bakan, *Slaughter of the Innocents* (Boston: Beacon Press, 1971), 29.
29. Ibid., 28–29. The author also describes the stories of Jesus and Moses being saved from holocausts of infant slaughter and references to other folk stories about massacres of thousands of children during that time.

tice to sacrifice the firstborn son as a burnt offering to God. This practice was reportedly stopped by the first Jew, Abraham, when God interceded as Abraham was about to sacrifice his son Isaac on the altar of Mt. Moriah. In A.D. 70, the Hebrews stopped the practice of animal sacrifice as well and instituted prayer as the main religious ritual.

Among some cultures, child sacrifice was committed for population control and economic well-being. Among the Hawaiians and Tahitians, it was customary to kill all children after the third or fourth. The Australian aborigines would kill the younger of even two children if a woman was forced to march for food or water and she could not carry both. Infanticide and human sacrifice was a regular feature of cultures such as Scandinavian, African, Eskimo, Polynesian, Egyptian, Greek, American Indian, Middle Eastern, and Mexican.

The concept of killing babies out of economic necessity, for family survival, made some sense to me. The idea of killing babies and other human beings out of superstitious beliefs was detestable.

In reading further about human sacrifice, I learned that anthropologists link the beginning of blood sacrifice not with the cultures of the hunter-gatherers, but with those of the cultivators.[30] These people believed in the myth of Dema, which suggested to them that crop plants originated from the body of a slain deity. Ritual killing of animals or humans is seen as a reenactment of the myth of life feeding life. The destruction of the offering, regardless of the means of killing, "liberates" the life force and makes it available to the deity. The primary purpose of the sacrifice is to gain favor from the sacred power.

Sacrificial offerings fall into three categories: (1) blood

---

30. Albert Jensen, *Myth and Cult Among Primitive Peoples* (Chicago & London: University of Chicago Press, 1963).

offerings, both animal and human; (2) bloodless offerings, such as vegetation and libations; and (3) divine offerings, where the victim, object, or plant is consecrated and thus seen to be a part of the god. In many rituals, participants consume remains of the offering in order to commune with the deity and to share the power liberated from the offering. This tradition is reflected in the Christian Eucharist, the bloodless reenactment of the crucifixion.

Humans have always searched for communion with the sacred. We long for association with ideas and values that transform the mundane into meaning and give us hope for a spiritual life beyond the physical. We wish for greater power to control the natural forces in life that render us powerless. Therefore, humans have always sought the mysterious connection to a powerful god. I understood the concept more than ever while treating Barbara. There had to be more than the death and destruction that Barbara and I found ourselves immersed in. There just had to be.

Sometimes during my personal meditation and relaxation exercises, I would experience a sense of awe, a brief glimpse of timelessness that puzzled me. Was this a connection with a higher power, with God? I didn't know.

Curiosity and the wish for access to a higher power explain the ever-present existence of magic. Magical thinking and practices are still a part of all cultures and are especially prominent in preliterate cultures. Magical rituals were initially used in paganism, the practice of seeking power and spirituality through nature. Human and animal sacrifices were practiced by the druids, for example, to ensure fertile crops.

Magical thinking corresponds to what we call "concrete thinking" in psychology. When Barbara's family tried to "suffocate Jesus" by literally plugging up her bodily cavities, they were using concrete thinking instead of the abstract thought necessary to realize that beliefs or even spiritual entities cannot be controlled by physical means.

Magical concrete thinking is part of the prejudicial thinking behind every act of destruction. When groups are involved, murderous violence on a grand scale often results. For example, during the fifteenth and sixteenth centuries, between half a million and nine million were murdered during the witch trials. The men in power blamed women for every sort of societal calamity.[31] Seen as morally inferior, women were believed vulnerable to consorting with the devil. A witch was a woman who had intercourse with the devil and was the devil's sexual slave. In fact, during the 1600s the term *witch* or *whore* referred to a woman who indulged in sex for pleasure, not for money. We had come back to the biblical days of the repression of the goddess religions and all things feminine.

Magical or concrete thinking also explains accounts of human sacrifice. James Michener tells us about the Carib Indians, around the 1300s, who killed and ate the most powerful of their enemies, thinking that they would thus inherit their prowess.[32]

The warrior culture of the Aztecs, in what is today Mexico and Guatemala, committed ritual human sacrifice on a grand scale. While some victims were drowned and some burned to death, the preferable method was the ritual knife. The victim was held down by four priests while the fifth priest slashed open the chest and tore out the heart. Since there were eigh-

---

31. My favorite historical text on the witch trials is Joseph Klaits, *Servants of Satan: The Age of the Witch Hunts* (Indiana University Press, 1985).
32. Michener's book, *Caribbean* (New York: Random House, 1989), presents an engrossing account, not only of the Mayan and island cultures of the Caribbean, but also of the sugar plantations' importation of slaves. I found it to be an important and shocking history of slavery. In the late 1700s *on one island alone*, St. Dominguc (now Hispaniola), the death rate of black slaves was so high due to mistreatment that forty thousand replacement slaves were imported from Africa each year!

teen monthly feasts, all requiring sacrifices, accounts vary from an estimated twenty thousand murders each year to over eighty thousand during one four-day period to inaugurate the Great Temple in 1487. Over one hundred thousand heads were displayed on the skull rack of Xocotlan alone.[33] Children were especially favored by the Aztecs for blood offerings to the rain gods. Children!

33. Reuben Fine, *The Meaning of Love in Human Experience* (New York: John Wiley & Sons, 1985), 16.

T H I R T E E N

My reading was making me frightened. To learn that baby girls were still being murdered in China, that East Indian women could still be burned to death if their dowry ran out, that Egyptian eight-year-old girls could still have their clitorises cut off to ensure that they couldn't enjoy sex, and that an American woman is raped every six minutes—all made me want to scream!

When I became the most frightened, I couldn't scream at all. My youngest daughter, Julie, and her good friend had decided they would do some early Christmas shopping together in Old Town. At fifteen, Julie was not yet driving, so I agreed to drop her off on my way to work. She and Stephanie would catch the Molly Trolly, a tourist ride between Old Town and all of the major hotels in Albuquerque, at the end of the day. Stephanie's father would retrieve them from the Pyramid Hotel on the other side of town, and Julie would then spend the night at Stephanie's.

Julie was a capable, independent child. She had to be. Six years behind her older sister, with two busy professional parents, she lived with our expectation that she develop interests and use her mind. *Bored* was the only taboo word in our household. One might be sad, lazy, anxious, or a myriad of other conditions, but boredom was not allowed. After Jasmine went off to college, Julie worked hard to develop friendships, hobbies, and sports interests to keep herself busy. She was a great kid. Dan and I felt lucky to have two bright, popular, intelligent daughters.

When I got home that day, I kicked off my shoes, fixed my diet 7-Up with a splash of bourbon, and sat down on the sofa to read a novel. After a while, I thought I'd call Stephanie's to see how the shopping trip had been. Lee, Stephanie's mother, answered the phone and told me they hadn't heard from the girls. I could tell she was controlling her voice so she wouldn't sound upset. "I'll call you just as soon as we hear from them," she said, and then hung up.

It was dark outside. The girls should have arrived at the hotel over an hour ago. Dan was away at medical meetings; he wouldn't be back for another day. I didn't even think of calling Jasmine. She had returned to Boulder, Colorado, months ago for her fourth year of college.

I had a sick feeling in the pit of my stomach. The thought of someone's having kidnapped Julie took over completely. I thought of every story of torture I had ever heard. I couldn't think clearly, I couldn't speak, I didn't know what to do except move. I found myself pacing around in circles. First slow circles and then larger circles, moaning, making strange guttural sounds. I felt if I didn't keep walking and making sounds, I would fly apart in a hundred pieces. I now knew exactly what my patients meant when they spoke of fears that they were "falling apart." I don't know how long I paced, my body feeling like a fragile container for confusion. I was definitely "beside myself." When the phone rang later, I moved toward it like an automaton, picked up the receiver, and heard Lee's voice, full of relief.

"They called. Tony's gone to pick them up. I'll have Julie give you a ring when they get here."

And just like that, life started flowing into my body again. The confusion and fear melted away, and I began to think rationally about what had happened to me, and how vulnerable I'd become to fear. I laughed out loud at myself, and then I broke into tears.

The following weekend Molly Goldman called. Molly and her husband, Jon, were old friends from Dan's UCLA days. When we had left for New Mexico, they had stayed in Los Angeles so Jon could finish his training. He was enjoying a successful career, and Molly had given up trying to get him to move to New Mexico. She had turned her attention to the New Age movement.

"Gail, the Whole-Life Expo is taking place here in a couple of weeks. Why don't you come out for a three-day weekend and go with us. I know it's short notice, but I thought you might be interested. I've actually talked Jon into going!" I groaned inside. A convention of California flakes, I thought.

"Well, now you'll have to talk me into going. I'm incredibly busy. What's this thing all about?"

Molly read off the list of programs and presenters. "The program I think we'll be the most interested in is Brian Weiss's past-life workshop." Now I knew why she had had to talk Jon into going. I felt I could talk to Dan until I was blue and he'd either laugh or just roll his eyes and say, "I'd rather go fishing." Past lives, psychics, and channelers didn't interest him. I had only thought about paranormal phenomena as entertainment.

My curiosity was piqued. "You've been into this stuff for years. How am I going to understand it? I'm having a hard enough time with the real world."

"That's why you need to come. I just feel that it's right for you now, that it might be helpful. Tell you what, pick up Brian Weiss's book, *Many Lives, Many Masters*.[34] If you like the book, call me back."

Jan found the book for me the next day and I read it in one evening. The next evening I called Molly.

"Count me in. The book was amazing, even though I can't say I really understand what happened. And I need a break right now. Even if the Expo is a bust, it'll be great to spend a few days with you two."

I would fly out Friday morning and come back Sunday afternoon, so I would not miss a session with Barbara.

Dr. Brian Weiss, then chief of psychiatry at Sinai Hospital in Miami, Florida, had been using hypnosis to treat a young woman with anxiety and panic attacks. When they could find no explanations for her symptoms in this lifetime, she began describing trauma that had occurred to her in previous lifetimes. While Dr. Weiss was skeptical, as a good scientist he began recording the sessions and researching the topic of reincarnation. The book documented his work with this patient and his own changing views about the psychic powers of the mind.

Los Angeles was warm and balmy in November, feeling much more like summer to me than fall. As we drove to the

---

34. Brian Weiss, *Many Lives, Many Masters* (New York: Simon & Schuster, 1988).

convention center, we caught up on kids and family activities. Parking turned out to be much less of a hassle than we'd expected, and we had time to wander among the hundreds of booths lining the entire ground floor of the center. Unusual jewelry, crystals, books on self-help and personal and spiritual development, various new health foods, relaxation aids, meditative music, and ecological-awareness materials were everywhere.

We lined up early to get into the room where Dr. Weiss would be presenting. We wanted to be able to sit up front and we were successful. Several hundred people crowded into the room, many of them forced to sit on the floor in front and along the sides. I remember no introduction, just an attractive young man of medium build striding purposefully up the middle aisle to the podium, introducing himself, describing his impressive academic background, and his book, *Many Lives, Many Masters*.

Many in the audience had come in order to actually experience a past-life regression for themselves. He asked that we get as comfortable as possible in our seats, close our eyes, and concentrate on his voice. He facilitated a progressive relaxation of all parts of the body, then suggested that we imagine ourselves walking through a dark tunnel, seeing the light at the end coming closer and closer until we stepped out into it. In that place, we were told to look down at our clothing and our feet. I remembered nothing else about Dr. Weiss's instructions after that. I was in a different world.

I was wearing moccasins. Alone in a forest of beautiful big trees, I didn't feel alone. I was a girl of twelve or thirteen and I had a small black dog. I felt indescribable comfort and peace in that forest, and I moved slowly around, gathering nuts. An immediate recognition of being "one with nature" came over me. I was simply another living being on the earth, and the trees were my friends.

I eventually walked back to our village, and I saw a young

man fashioning a bow. He was handsome and looked up at me briefly as he worked. There was no verbal communication, but our eyes seemed to exchange a great knowledge about one another. I realized that I was to become his wife and bear his children. I didn't want to leave my tranquil childhood and become a woman. The women worked hard and sometimes died in childbirth. I was afraid of having children. I liked the young man and felt attracted to him, but I didn't want to assume the role of a grown-up.

As soon as Dr. Weiss brought us out of trance, I realized that the young man in that lifetime was Dan. But the overwhelming realization for me was the sense of eternity I'd just experienced. I'd had a clear feeling that my self, my soul, lived on and on and on.

It was late when we finally left the convention center. Jon took us out for dinner.

"Well, I tried," Jon said, "but I couldn't get into a past life. I don't know what that means about me. I had a really nice meditative experience, but no visual images."

I told them about my experience as an Indian girl. I guessed the time to be in the early 1700s. "I don't know what it means, period, except maybe I'm more suggestible than you. I use hypnosis so much. Could it be a phenomenon of tapping into the collective unconscious, whatever that is?"

"That's one explanation," Molly said. "But I've been able to go into such incredible detail about some of my past lives that it doesn't feel like tapping into a piece of collective thought or experience. It feels like that was me. By the way, I was there in the same Indian village with you today."

My mouth fell open.

"I had the feeling that we were sisters," Molly said. "My teacher, Betty, tells me that I have great psychic ability, but I don't know about that. I just believe that the past-life images are one way my unconscious facilitates learning. I don't know, of course, whether they were real experiences. Some of my past-life recall feels more real than others.''

"What kind of learning are you referring to?" I asked.

"Lessons for the soul. I do believe in reincarnation and the soul. And I think we have many lessons to learn along the way as we evolve."

"Do you think we might have guardian angels helping us along the way?" I asked.

"Yes, I do. I think that guardian angels are separate souls who are more evolved and choose to stay around guiding other souls through their lifetimes."

"Instead of going off to nirvana, you mean?" I said.

"No, Disneyland," Jon added. We both laughed nervously, but Molly sat back and picked up her drink, assuming a look of great patience.

"I'm sorry, but this is so far-out I'm having trouble handling it," I said. "It reminds me of hypnosis meetings I attended where a highly respected physician age-regressed several of the physician attendees back to the womb and had them experience their births. Here were these grown men and women wiggling around and then stating as infants how each parent felt about their birth and whether they were welcomed or unwanted. Some of the therapists walked out in disgust. I stayed, but it felt like this reincarnation business . . . like I was having trouble fitting it into my mind. There's been no previous programming or preparation."

"It'll take time," Molly said. "You asked about guardian angels. I think of my guardian angel as being my 'higher self.' Some people believe that the 'higher self' is a part of them and is that part that is connected to God. But I think my higher self is a visiting angel."

"Could it be different for different people?" I said. "Maybe less evolved people need angels—no offense, Molly—and highly evolved people have a more direct connection to God."

"Could be. I sure don't have the answers. Just some beliefs about myself."

"I don't know what to make of any of this," Jon said. "But I must say I was impressed when Brian Weiss talked about the research he's doing with children who have clear past-life memories. Some of them are able to speak ancient languages, ones they couldn't possibly have learned today."

I slept like a well-fed baby that night. The next morning while drying my hair I had further insights. I turned off the drier and went to find Molly and Jon to tell them.

"This is really weird, but I just had another flash about that lifetime as an Indian girl. I died in childbirth, and for some reason I was furious at Dan. But I just realized Dan isn't to blame. He's just another soul trying to learn the lessons of living."

Molly and Jon looked at me, respectfully attentive, yet knowing there's not really anything to say to someone who has had a profound insight that doesn't sound profound. Jon nodded his head as if to say, "That's good, Gail." I felt completely foolish.

Molly made more of an effort. "Of course," she said, "the anger toward him is just a cover for your own fears about male domination and death."

"Right," I said, and headed back to the guest bathroom. A great sense of freedom resulted from that past-life regression. I felt lighter and giddy. For two days, I felt like laughing about how earthbound I'd been. My ability to get stuck in feelings of fear and anxiety, hostility and anger, seemed silly, I thought.

But insights pass. Although I never forgot the past-life experience, I quickly relegated it to the sidelines of my thinking. Back home, I had more pressing thoughts. I never shared the experience with colleagues. I did tell Dan about it, but I certainly didn't consider reincarnation an appropriate topic for the consulting room.

PART FIVE

WINTER 1989–90

F O U R T E E N

Barbara was talking about how hard the Christmas holidays were for her.

"Is it because of satanic rituals?" I asked.

"I don't think so. I don't remember any ceremonies associated with Christmas. They would have ignored the birth of their 'enemy.' Any kind of ceremony would have been an acknowledgment of Him. I think Christmas just reminds me of how deprived I felt of any emotional connections. That's probably why I pay so much attention to my kids," she said, sighing.

"I work so hard to make the holidays perfect, but I always feel terrible. I'm dissociated most of the time and I spend too much money."

"What do you spend on?"

"Presents for the kids. I know it has to do with wanting

not to be like my mother. She was so hateful, almost bragging about not getting us presents. But I go overboard, and then we're in debt and Cal's mad at me.''

"I want you to sit down with Cal and make a budget for Christmas. How much you can afford to spend on each child and on each other. Then, stick to the budget. Some parents tell the kids, when they're old enough, what the dollar amount is so the child can choose whether he wants gifts purchased or whether he wants the money. Last year the daughter of friends of ours chose the money, and she donated it to her favorite charity. She'd decided she was ready to get into the real spirit of Christmas!''

"I like that idea. I'll make a budget.''

"That's the easy part,'' I went on. "The harder part has to do with the memories and longings the holidays evoke. We're all supposed to have perfect families during the holidays. Since no one does, the celebrations become sad reminders of all that's been missing in our lives.''

"Everything was missing in my family,'' Barbara said, lost in thought. "Everything.''

"So for most of us, the holidays are a time for mourning. All the losses . . .'' I thought about the mourning I was engaged in for Robert, for Kait, for Gilda, and for all my patients, including Barbara, who'd lost their innocence, joy, self-esteem, sense of safety and of being lovable. All were robbed of their past, and of a belief in their future. The holidays would be hard for me, too, this year.

Just before Christmas, Barbara and I were talking about friendships and how, so often, as grown-ups, we must create families out of our friends.

"It does feel nice to have a friend for the first time, in Sharon, but it just feels hopeless, like it won't last. . . . Nothing good ever lasts for me. I can't trust that good feelings will continue. I just wait for the next awful thing to happen."

"Is Sharon really your first friend?"

"I know lots of people who think I'm their friend. But I never let myself get close to them or share myself. I've just been there to listen to them. And then we've moved away, and I forget them and never write or maintain contact. Cal has always questioned why I do that. With Sharon, I can't help myself. . . . I'm beginning to share and enjoy being with her. But it scares me. I don't trust that it'll be okay."

"Let's see what your mind has for you to work on today about that," I said.

Barbara went through the induction easily and automatically. When I suggested she let her hand float up to her forehead, her hand drifted back and forth on its ascent, like a feather.

"I'm in the church just sitting there . . . and it's empty. I'm thinking how empty it is . . . and how cold. I have clothes on, and it's hot outside and the door's open . . . but it feels so cold. . . ."

"How old are you?"

"I'm fourteen."

"What happens?"

"I'm real scared. And I'm scared to tell you. I don't want anybody to know. . . . I'm fat again."

"Fat. Do you mean pregnant?"

"Yes. And I'm so scared I think I've shriveled up and died. There's a knot in my chest and that's all that's left. If I could just stay little, I don't have to remember what happens . . . but I can't. So I came to the church for comfort . . . but there's no comfort here . . . just coldness. Frannie comes and sits next to me . . . and we just sit. I won't talk about it. No one knows yet. When they do, I'll never have any friends . . . not at school . . . not at home."

"What about Frannie? Isn't she your friend?"

"I only see her on weekends, but she's one of them. She likes it and I don't."

"What do you mean, 'she likes it'?"

"She's fat, too, but she likes it 'cause they give her things and they're nice to her, so she feels special."

"But you don't like it and you know you're not one of them."

"I just want to die. And I don't know if I can hide it this time as much."

"How far along are you?"

"I missed my period about four months."

"What happens next?"

"I won't tell my mother. But I tell Grandma. I went to her house and she and I are in the kitchen and I told her and she didn't say anything. She just kept peeling apples. And then we went to the dining room to talk at the table. I told her I didn't want to do this again and she went over to the china cabinet and got the Bible and she told me to pray, and I said, 'I don't want to pray to your devil.' "

"What Bible did she have?"

"It's a regular Bible, but they never read it right. They always put in their words. And I feel so sad . . . really sad. I told her I don't know what to do. And I beg her to make me not do this again, and then I start crying. Then June, a neighbor of Grandma's, comes in and she asks who the father is . . . and I say I don't know. And she says only whores don't know. So I cry more, but Grandma holds my hand and she says, 'She's not a whore.'

"June says she knows a doctor at University Hospital who will take care of it for me. She works there as a lab technician. Grandma says she'll pay for it. So June calls him and we go there to the hospital. And when he gets there, he tells the people that I was having a miscarriage and was bleeding. And two of the nurses were June's friends. So I stayed in the hospital for five days."

"Five days! What was that like for you?"

"I feel really good. I feel much better. But I can never, ever tell anybody. Grandma and June made me promise 'cause they said this is a nice doctor and he would be in big trouble if I ever told."

"And do you ever tell?"

"No. I don't tell my mother or anybody. They'd be really mad."

"Would they hurt June?"

"No. She's not one of them. She's real nice. They don't mess with her. They said ' 'cause she's an evil nigger from Alabama,' but she's not. She's nice and they don't mess with her."

"She must be a strong person."

"Yes, she is. And I could never tell anyone."

"Do you try to forget yourself?"

"Yes. It was very sad. And I didn't want anyone to do anything to me again. They just always did even if I didn't want them to touch me."

"You couldn't stop them, could you?"

"No. There were too many of them."

"Too many of them?"

"All the time . . . in the church, in the Upper Room, in the bathroom, anywhere. I told Grandma, and she said it had to stop, too. She told me to go to the church my mother goes to and not to come back. And so I go to the First Baptist Church with my mother. The people are nice there, but I still hate my mother."

"She hasn't been able to be a loving mother to you, has she?"

"No. She's mean, but I have to stay with her if I don't want it to happen again. B.J. lives with her now, so I'm safe there. He's pretty nice to me."

"So it's a good decision to stay there?"

"Yes, even though I hate her guts. Nobody messes with me anymore."

"Do you ever see Frannie again?"

Barbara is quiet for a long time. She looks increasingly uncomfortable. "Did something happen to Frannie?" I asked.

"Yes," Barbara answered in a small voice. "She died. I didn't want to remember. I never went back to the church except once. Frannie came and begged me to be there when they took her baby. . . . She was real scared, so I went and I sat in the back of the church. And Granddaddy delivered her baby, but he couldn't stop her bleeding . . . and she died. They didn't care . . . but I did. It was the only time someone died when they didn't mean for them to die. I never went back after that."

"And Frannie had been your friend since you were little."

"Yes. Even though she was one of them, she was my only friend. She was the only friend they let me have. I even thought maybe Granddaddy let her die so I wouldn't have any friends at all."

"Okay. I want you to let that image fade away now, and as I count from ten backward to zero, I want you to stay deeply in trance, but come up to your present age. Ten, nine, eight, seven, six, five, four, three, two, one, zero. . . . Do you remember all that you've just talked about?"

"Yes."

"Then you remember how, when you were a girl and you felt so very scared and bad, you would do something that you described as making yourself very very little, until there was just a tiny black ball inside your chest?"

"Yes."

"It was true that you needed to do that when you were a girl because you did it to try to lock out all the bad things that were happening to you. Now that you're a grown woman, it's important that you let that ball loosen up, that you let your body loosen up so that everything inside can work more comfortably. You no longer need to have that tension inside or the fears, or the feeling of being bad that would cause you to want to hurt yourself or to be dead. Do you understand?"

"Yes."

"Good. I want you to take your left hand now and reach up to the tiny cross around your neck. The gold cross you bought for yourself.[35] That's right. Feel that cross, and as you feel it beneath your fingers, that's going to be a signal for you to relax. You'll begin to feel the cross many times during the day, and that will be a signal to you to release that little ball inside that no longer needs to be there . . . that little ball of smallness, tension, fear, and guilt. Can you feel it going?"

"Yes."

"Good. That's very good. And remember what Jesus told you when you were little . . . you will have friends and you will be loved."

When Barbara opened her eyes, she just looked at me.

"You couldn't let yourself get too close to anyone, could you?" I asked. "You learned to fear that if you did, the clan would kill them."

"That's right."

"So now you're free to enjoy friendships for the first time. Let this be your Christmas gift to yourself."

Barbara stared at me, one of her penetrating looks. She wasn't ready to leave yet.

"I want to thank you for being my link to sanity," she said, a little unevenly. "I feel like you're saving my life. Maybe someday you could be my friend, too."

"I'd like that very much," I told her.[36]

---

35. After Barbara began meeting with the priest, I suggested she buy herself a gold cross. The only cross she had was given to her by her grandmother and reminded her of the satanic church. She brought it into my office one day and handed it to me with two fingers, as though she were getting rid of one of the snakes the Fat Lady used to put on her.

36. While socializing with patients is considered unethical, once treatment is concluded, friendship becomes a possibility.

The holidays were strange. Julie missed her friend Polly, and we all missed the entire Hemmings family. Ellen had planned to meet us at Steamboat Springs for skiing after Christmas, but she backed out at the last minute. I felt relieved. I knew that if Ellen and I were together, we wouldn't be able to function. All we would do is cry. I still cried every time I thought about Robert. Ellen told me during one of our long telephone conversations that she kept an ice bag in the refrigerator to use every morning so that she could begin to see out of her swollen eyes. She wasn't sleeping and had so much trouble handling her anger toward Robert that she'd begun seeing a psychologist.

Our compromise was that she'd meet us in Denver after our ski trip and take Julie home with her for a few days' visit with Polly. Our older daughter, Jasmine, would stay in Denver to get ready for school to resume.

The solitary peacefulness I felt while skiing infused me with good feelings. I loved the cold air, the beauty of the snowy mountains, and the feeling of being in control of my body. Although it sounded trite, I thought, it was true that in the ocean or in the mountains, I felt one with nature.

Dan and I would be making the long drive from Denver to Albuquerque alone. By the time we'd spent a few hours getting Jasmine back to her apartment and another few hours visiting with Ellen and the girls, it was late afternoon, a crazy time to begin an eight-to-ten-hour drive. It was snowing and warnings were issued over the radio to stay off the highways. Nevertheless, we started out.

Dan grew up in Michigan, driving constantly in snowy conditions. He felt perfectly comfortable. After the first few hours, it became apparent that the predictions of the Highway Patrol were accurate. It was snowing harder and harder and becoming increasingly difficult to see beyond several feet outside the car. We had listened to books on tape, then music, but finally I felt too tense to listen to anything. I tried to nibble on the sandwiches we had bought for dinner, but I couldn't eat. As we drove, I felt we were in one of those little glass balls you turn upside down, surrounded with nothing but snow. I strained to look straight ahead, as if my seeing might aid Dan's ability to navigate.

Going over Raton Pass, just inside the New Mexico border, was frightening. When icy, it can be difficult to cross. We did it in about twenty minutes, but I had to work to stay calm. Suddenly, we noticed we were not on the main road. Dan had steered us onto an off-ramp.

"Damn it!" exclaimed Dan. "I've never done this before! We're on our way into Raton. This is ridiculous!"

"Don't worry," I said. "Where there's an off-ramp, somewhere nearby there has to be an on-ramp."

We found it. As we inched our way back down onto the highway, we both looked to the left at the same time. We gasped. There was a massive pileup of cars, surrounded by blinking red lights and rescue vehicles. A terrible accident. Somehow, we had avoided becoming a part of all that wrecked metal.

"That's too weird," Dan said. "I've never taken the wrong road in a snowstorm. I felt as if the steering wheel were being pulled when we went on that off-ramp."

"Maybe it was," I said. "Maybe it was."

F I F T E E N

C al's company is transferring him in June and I'll have to leave you."

Barbara's words hit me like a bombshell. In our focus on surviving the holidays and understanding Barbara's growing attachment to Sharon and to me, I had repressed the awareness that she might be forced to end her therapy prematurely.

"I don't know if I'll be ready," Barbara said. "I guess it's silly to jump six months ahead, but I can't help it. I'm trying to stay relaxed, but my blood pressure has gone sky-high and I still feel real guilty, like I did something really bad."

"You and I have to have faith that if you're going to have to move, you'll be ready," I told Barbara. As usual, I was operating on two levels: my inner reaction of worry and sadness, and the outward offering of support and confidence in her ability to handle the separation.

"We're being guided in our work," I suggested, "and you will have the help you need. And you'll never lose me. Once there's a loving attachment between two people, it's always there. Now, let's find out what it is you're feeling bad about."

"I have to pick again," she said in trance, her voice sounding resigned and disgusted.

"You have to pick again?"

"I have to pick the king . . . the one who serves me well. And I'm not picking any of those assholes. And I'm mad."

"You look sad, too."

"Yes. I'm mad and sad . . . what they do . . . how they kill people. . . . I'm just sitting there waiting . . . with no clothes on . . . on the stupid table."

"How old are you?"

"I'm nine."

"And you're waiting. And what happens when the men come to serve you?"

"I don't want to talk about it."

"You don't even want to think about it. Of course not. But it's all right to tell me."

"They come down the aisle," Barbara cries now, like a sad little girl. "The aisle's like a keyhole. And this time I have to get on my knees 'cause I'm bigger. And they all march around me and I'm supposed to pick."

"How many are there?"

"Eight men and one boy. One for each year. So I have to pick, but I don't wanna pick. So I close my eyes. And Grandma says, 'Open your eyes. How you gonna choose without seeing?' And Miss Nonnie, the Fat Lady, gets mad and says, 'It is not fitting that we have gone without a king for the clan for this many years. The time is right, we must choose tonight.' But she can't put her snakes on me tonight."

"Why is that?"

" 'Cause I have to choose of free will. I cannot be coerced.

I cannot be choosing out of fear. I have to choose out of pure love for the almighty master."

"Who says those words?"

"Grandma says that. So I have to pick one, but I don't. Then she says, 'Well, since you can't pick from what they look like, then they all must serve you and then you say which one served you well . . . which one fills your mouth with the most fluid. But do not swallow until he's finished, so you can tell how much is in you.' That's what she said, and that's what I had to do."

"So, each one takes a turn?"

"Yes. And they're sick and disgusting, and I hate them all. And Jesus didn't come get me this time either. I'm mad at Him, too."

"You're full of feelings, aren't you?"

"I'm real mad. He didn't come get me and He made me sit there by myself this time. That wasn't right. I had nobody, and that wasn't fair!"

"What happens when it's all over?"

"I say none of them served me well. And Jesus didn't even come and tell me to say that. I knew to say that by myself! And He left me there by myself and that wasn't right. He never left me before. And He didn't come and get me." Barbara sounded exactly like a despairing nine-year-old.

"What happens now?"

"Nothing. They just get mad."

"They get mad at you?"

"No. They get mad at the men and said they musta been screwing around before they came. 'Cause if they weren't screwing around, they'd have enough to fill my mouth. That's what the womens says. But the Fat Lady's lookin' at me. I can tell she hates me."

"And is the ceremony over now?"

"Yes. But I have to stay there for purification. 'You must sit in the circle for two days and two nights, until the coming of the master. You will have nothing to drink and nothing to eat. This way your soul will be cleansed and ready. Then you will see the light of the darkness.' There's no such thing as the 'light of the darkness,' '' little Barbara says with disgust.

"So you stay in the circle of the key for two days and two nights?"

"Yes. Jesus doesn't come back either. And I cannot move out of the circle, or they'd kill me."

"What happens when you have to go to the bathroom?"

"I don't go. I just hold it."

"Let that picture fade away now."

When Barbara came out of trance, we talked some about the concept of "purification." Most religious groups use purification rites as part of their most sacred ceremonies. Fasting and isolation are two of the most common, but some groups use extreme methods of suffering to make celebrants "pure" enough to be acceptable to their god. When these acts are forced upon children, it's nothing less than child abuse.

Barbara continued to feel horribly guilty and anxious to the point where she had to work hard to control thoughts about killing herself. During her next session, we began to learn why.

"And when I count to five, I want you to move to an important event that will help you to understand more about your feelings of guilt. One, two, three, four, and five. . . . What comes to mind?"

"Jesus is mad at me."

"How do you know that?"

"I just know. He's mad 'cause I got mean."

"You learned how to harden yourself and not to feel hurt, so now you feel like you're mean?"

"Sometimes. And I think that He doesn't love me anymore."

"When did you first think that?"

"When I was nine. I thought He didn't love me, so I did bad things."

"You were made to do lots of bad things."

"Not this time they didn't make me. Grandma always said when I was twelve, I could use my powers to decide who should die. Grandma said since I didn't pick anybody to help me rule, I had to rule by myself. Since I didn't pick a grown-up man to help decide who lives and who dies, I had to decide. So I did."

"So you chose someone to die?"

"Yes, I did."

"Who did you choose?"

"Miss Nonnie, the Fat Lady . . . I picked her. I knew it was not right, but I did it anyway. Grandma said that I had the power and I could kill anybody, and I could eat the heart of anybody I wanted to. So I said, 'Anybody's heart?' and Grandma said, 'Anybody's except mine, 'cause I still have the power.' So I said, 'Miss Nonnie,' and she said, 'Okay.' So I got her." I could barely hear Barbara's voice, it was so tiny and sad.

"The Fat Lady scared you and laughed at you from the time you were small. She put her snakes on you and watched while the Keepers raped you and poked at you. She participated in your torture."

"But I wasn't supposed to kill. That's what Jesus said. But I did it anyway because I got mean. I got real mean after they took the baby. But everything got black when we killed Miss Nonnie. I knew Jesus was mad and disappointed in me, and I said I'd never do that again."

"And did you ever do it again?"

"No. We're not supposed to have those kinds of feelings."

"That was the only time you let your hatred take over?"

"Yes. And that's when people die. Jesus said that to me. It's why all the children died, and all the people died . . . when there're hate feelings in the heart and it consumes them and they kill. He said He'd help me to not hate people. So He did.''

"So that was the end of your hate. It died along with the Fat Lady?"

"Yes."

I gave Barbara positive posthypnotic suggestions to release the guilt and self-hate she felt as a result of Miss Nonnie's murder, but I didn't know what to say to myself. During the session, when Barbara told about using her power to order the Fat Lady's killing, I was elated and then embarrassed at my reaction. I felt like I did in movies I'd seen when the bad guy gets "what he deserves."

But this was reality. Barbara was struggling with a real murder, the death of a human being. I was trying to solve my anger by doing away with the outside cause of it. If we could just get rid of evil people, I reasoned, the world would be a better place. And yet I knew that placing evil outside of oneself is irresponsible and therefore evil. An old saying came to me: "If you're not part of the solution, you're part of the problem." Easy solutions to difficult problems don't work. I also doubted my ability to help Barbara come to terms with torture, killing, and "soul murder." Her sense of morality seemed more developed than mine.

Movies helped reduce stress for Dan and me. After a long day at work, bleary-eyed, with our briefcases bulging, I would look across the dinner table and say, "It's time for a movie," and Dan would answer, "The work will still be there in the morning. I'll just get up earlier."

Occasionally a friend would say, "How do you have time for movies?" We couldn't answer the question. You simply

227

make time for activities that keep you going. It was on one of those nights that we went to see *Batman*.

I had expected an old-fashioned good-guys-versus-bad-guys movie. Instead, what I saw was sadism and technology glorified over human relationships. In a movie house half-filled with children, we were first treated to the murder of Batman's parents by the Joker. Most of the movie chronicles the Joker's sadistic delight in maiming and killing.

If there had been a male hero for children to identify with, I wouldn't have been so upset. Batman, however, is only made a hero by his technological playthings. He can't relate to women. The night the heroine stays over, Batman hangs up-side down, bat-style, unaware of her presence. His butler has to remind him that the woman is attractive.

Batman doesn't have friends in this movie. His comic-book sidekick, Robin, is left out of the film altogether. So, the children of America were treated to two male models, one who kills in hideous ways and the other who's a social isolate and views women as inconsequential. I raved about all this as we left the theater.

"I agree with you," said Dan, "but I can't get excited about it. It's just a movie."

"But it reflects the disease of violence that's plaguing this country. Men are perpetuating it with these movies and teaching it now to little boys!"

"I don't think it's all that powerful as social learning. Kids learn much more from their parents about behavior than they do from movies. Besides, what good does it do for you to get all worked up over it?"

"Obviously, none. Why don't you get worked up? You men just sit back and let all the violence happen. Why don't you get together and do something about it. I'm sick of it!"

"Well, I'm sick of you attacking me about this stuff every other day! I don't have the time or the interest to form some organization to monitor violence just to please you. Get off my back!''

"Fine! Be irresponsible!''

The fighting escalated until, finally, we stopped talking altogether and just fumed separately the rest of the night. All the insight about my anger's stemming from a past life went right out the window. At this point, I didn't care where the anger came from.

Maybe I was simply burned-out, I thought. Maybe after Barbara's therapy was finished, I'd be finished, too, unable to go on working as a clinical psychologist. The way things were going, maybe I wouldn't have a husband any longer to heap my anger on.

But then we went skiing. Julie was on the Sandia Peak Ski Team, so every weekend during the winter we felt required to ski wherever the team was competing. In February, we drove to Purgatory for four days. Located just outside Durango, Colorado, Purgatory had become our family's favorite ski area.

Dan had been more receptive than I'd expected to my relating of the past-life experience at the Brian Weiss workshop. He'd been intrigued that he was a part of those images and pleased that I realized I had to work on my anger. Of course, after blowups such as the one after the Batman movie, I'm sure he felt hopeless about my ability to work on anything.

When we went skiing, however, all was forgotten. I could update Dan on the latest of Barbara's horror stories and he could emote for both of us.

"That is unbelievable! I can't stand it! It's disgusting!'' Dan shouted after I'd described the ceremony Barbara was put through of "choosing the king.'' I went on to tell him about the killing of the Fat Lady and ended with the scene I couldn't get out of my mind: eleven-year-old Barbara holding the remains of her dead baby.

"Where do these mutants come from? And are they still doing this crap?" For a moment I became alarmed that in his agitation he might toss himself off the chair and onto the ski slope below.

"I don't know. I haven't asked her if she thinks it's still going on. I'm afraid of the answer."

Dan's outbursts always helped relieve my own pent-up feelings. We agreed not to talk about sadistic abuse any more that weekend, and I accompanied Dan down Lower Hades, one of the most difficult runs on the mountain.

I felt wonderful that Monday. Exercising amid the grandeur of nature is all I need to stay on track, I'd thought as I drove to work. But I became worried when Barbara came in. She looked weak and tired.

"I just want to be dead. I don't know if I could actually kill myself, but I have this feeling of just wanting all of this to be over. If I could only have some peace!"

"What do you suppose is getting in the way of you having peace?" I asked her.

"I don't know."

"Let's get to work, then."

Once in trance, Barbara said there was nothing to look at. I persisted. "No problem, nothing's wrong," she said. I had read enough by then to know that all survivors of sadistic cults have been programmed to kill themselves, and I had a hunch that Barbara was feeling the effects of that programming and was also reacting to the strong indoctrination against revealing cult secrets. I became more direct in my questioning.

"Do those in the clan ever tell you anything about killing yourself or hurting yourself?"

"No. They never tell me to do that."

"Remember who I am. I'm Gail and I've been chosen to help you. Please open your mind and let me know if you've been told to kill yourself."

After a long pause: "Yes, I have. But I'm not supposed to tell you."

"Barbara, it's very important for you to know that your inner mind, your higher self, will allow you to look at the information that is important for you to know about this. Let me check with 'mind,' that part that holds all of you. Answer me with your fingers now. Is it all right for Barbara to look at what she's been told about killing herself?" Barbara's yes finger lifted. "Let that information come into your mind now."

Barbara began to speak, quoting an adult. " 'If you find yourself weakening and you cannot bear the pressure of the foolish ones, we will always be around to help you and keep you from destroying yourself and us. There are many many of us who will fall into the pit of the master and all our labors will be futile. If you find yourself weakening, you must do away with yourself, you must!' "

"Who says these words to you?"

"Grandma says them every time she teaches me something, every time I get in trouble, every time there's something new. And she says them over and over again for a long long time."

"Take a deep breath and let yourself relax. Good. Know that the light of Jesus is here with you as you allow yourself to look at these things you were told that are harmful and hurtful to you. I ask 'mind' again, is there any other information you were told that is important for you to know about now?"

"Yes. If I am to kill myself, I have to do it before all is forgiven."

"What does that mean?"

"I have to do it before Easter Sunday. I have to do it the

week before Easter. That's what Grandma said. 'That's when the enemy is most angry. That's when the enemy won't be protecting, and you can go to the master.' So that's when I have to do it and so I will.''

''You say you will? But you don't believe in the master.''

''Then I have weakened. I have no heart and no soul. I have weakened.''

''What makes you think you have no heart and no soul?''

''Because I'm never happy. That means I have no heart and no soul.''

''You're never happy because you've been forced to do so many things and you've been hurt so many times, all in the name of the master!''

''They never hurt me. I deserve it.''

''Who says that?''

''They do. They never hurt me. There's no reason for me to cry. They never cause me any pain. They only teach me lessons.''

At this point, I had the strongest urge to shout ''Bullshit!'' but I restrained myself.

''They only teach you lessons, that's what they say?''

''Yes. And now I have weakened.''

I felt I wouldn't get anywhere by arguing with her, so I decided to bring her up to her current age. ''Let that image fade away now. I'm going to count from ten to zero, and I want you to stay in your trance, but come up to your present age . . . ten, nine, eight, seven, six, five, four, three, two, one, zero. Barbara, are you aware of all that you just told me about?''

''Yes.''

''Do you believe in your grown-up self that you deserve the things that they did to you?''

''Sometimes.''

''Sometimes. Do you remember that you have always,

from the time you were very small, talked about how you know your soul is with Jesus?"

"It isn't anymore."

"How come?"

" 'Cause I saw it. It's just a black hole."

I felt an intense sadness for her.

"Listen to me carefully," I urged. "I believe that the black hole is that part of you that has suffered, feels so despairing and so sad. With so much sadness, it is hard to comprehend and it's hard to live with. So much fear and so much sadness. And you've also talked about so much pain and meanness, that's what blackness is. Is it possible for you to believe that?"

"I'm sad, very very sad."

"You have many reasons to be sad, but I want you to remember what you've always told me, and that is that you belong to Jesus."

"Not anymore."

"Has He said that to you, or do you say it to yourself?"

"I said it to myself because I am just as evil as they are."

"I don't believe that and I know Jesus doesn't either. Jesus wants you to live. And I want you to call upon the higher powers of your mind, that part of your inner mind that holds you and is connected with the Light, that is connected to Jesus, so that you can come to know that you are to live. There are still important things for you to do on the earth."

"There's nothing left for me to do. I have gone against the Way."

"The Way is the way of the devil! You've never claimed that for your soul! Never! But your grandmother gave you careful instructions, didn't she? She taught you over and over and over again that if you 'weakened,' as she called it, that if you were to ever share secrets of the clan, that if you were to turn away from them, that they want you to kill

233

yourself. That's what she told you over and over again until you learned it.''

''But she said I'd have peace if I do that,'' Barbara said.

''You've longed for peace since you were a little girl, haven't you?''

''Yes. I really want it now.''

''Killing yourself won't bring you peace. I don't believe that's even what you want to do. We'll be talking more about this, but I'm concerned for you now. I want you to find one place of comfort inside of yourself, and let that comfort spread as I count to ten. And I want you to attach a light to that comfort, and let the light spread, too, illuminating the inside of your self. That light represents my confidence in your will to live and to care for yourself. One, two, three, four, five, six, seven, eight, nine, ten. . . .''

''I can't believe this,'' Barbara said in a dull voice when she was out of trance. ''I never knew. . . . I still feel so sad. And being sad, to them, was like being mentally ill.''

''Yes. Any warm, good feelings would go against the satanism and would be perceived as weakness.'' After a long silence I said, ''Now, I'm glad you're seeing the priest. We need all the help we can get. Easter's only two months away.''

''That's right,'' Barbara said in a faraway voice, obviously recalling the instructions. Then she looked directly at me. ''You know I'll do my best to work with you.''

During the next two sessions for that week, Barbara and I discussed her feelings about her grandmother. We often used the Monday session for hypnosis and the next two sessions to try to deal with the effects of the memories. We both had trouble comprehending how Barbara's grandmother could have loved her and periodically saved her life, then given her constant instructions on how and when to kill herself should she ever come close to divulging the clan secrets.

The following Monday, Barbara wouldn't look at me when I came into the waiting room. I noticed she had a huge bandage on her lower leg, and once she was seated in my office, I asked what had happened.

"I burned myself," she answered.

"Intentionally?" I asked.

She gave her long, low "Yessss." And then: "I hope you won't put me away."

"Tell me what happened."

"I was in one of my moods . . . where I couldn't talk to anybody or read or watch TV. So I went into my corner and started smoking, and then I just began to push the cigarette into the skin on my leg. I felt no pain at all . . . until later.[37] I made up a story when I went to the doctor. He said they were second-degree burns and dressed them and put me on an antibiotic. I'm so embarrassed. That's what other people do . . . self-mutilate, not me."

"Well, it tells us that you really are a survivor of extreme sadistic abuse. The 'others' who do this kind of thing do it for the same unconscious reasons . . . to mitigate emotional pain, follow orders to self-destruct, and as proof of being alive. Most survivors, like you, have been through many near-death experiences. Feeling pain forces the realization that you didn't die."

Barbara's eyes opened wider. "Yes. I think on some level I always believed they succeeded in killing me."

"My only worry is whether you might hurt yourself again."

---

37. Many survivors of extreme sadistic abuse self-mutilate in various ways, usually by cutting or burning themselves. In addition to the "programming" to self-destruct, child victims have always been told that the abuse is their fault. Their guilt is so intense, so painful, that inflicting physical hurt relieves some of the suffering. Another woman survivor of incest and torture actually shot herself in the leg to stop the memories of her father's abuse. "I'd rather have ongoing physical pain that I created than have to think about all the things he did to me," she said.

"I don't think so," Barbara said earnestly. "I can't stand the fact that I did this! And you're right, it was unconscious. It's like I didn't even know I was doing it until I was doing it."

"If you can promise me you won't do anything else to hurt yourself, I won't push for you to go to the hospital. Most self-mutilators are addicted to the behavior. It's even thought now that they get an endorphin release each time they do it. But I don't think you're addicted to any behaviors that are self-destructive! I believe that you are on a path toward recovery, not only from all the pain of your past, but from all the ways that you learned to hurt yourself because of low self-esteem."

Barbara's eyes were teary as she looked into mine. "You're the first person who's ever really believed in me."

"What about Cal?"

"He believes in me in some ways, but he worries that I'll always be angry and have problems. I don't know how to describe what feels so good about you. I think it goes back to the first time I was in the grave and you stayed there with me. It doesn't matter that it was hypnosis because I was really back there reliving it all again. And you stayed with me and you touched me when I needed to know I wasn't all alone. And it meant so much to me."

"This is a very special relationship for both of us. Our lessons are simply reversed. You're learning to trust in a person, and I'm learning to believe in God and the forces of Divine Goodness."

"You'll need divine help to deal with Cal. He's insisting I go to the hospital. He just thinks I have too much to deal with right now."

"I'll give him a call. Can you promise me that you won't hurt yourself again?"

"Yes. I'll even put it in writing."

"Good. And I'll ask that you visit two hospitals anyway as

a kind of compromise. Just have a look and talk to the admissions people so you get a feeling for which hospital you'd choose if, for some reason, we decided you needed a lot of extra-intensive help."

Barbara frowned, suddenly sheepish.

"Stop looking like that," I said. "This isn't a punishment. It's just good planning."

"Okay. I'll do it," Barbara said, allowing a grin to show.

"Let's just keep working hard enough to get you through most of the garbage before Easter."

"What happened to me was garbage all right, that's for sure!"

I called Cal at his office and said I'd been told that he was insisting on hospitalization. "What?" he answered. "I just told Barbara that I wanted her to check into hospitals that specialize in posttraumatic stress syndrome. I want her to know what's available in case she needs to work faster."

"I thought what she was saying sounded a little pushier than I take you to be," I said. "She must be responding to her guilt feelings. I did ask her to look at two hospitals here in town."

"My big concern is that we'll probably have to move this summer or fall. I really hope she'll be ready to do that."

"I do, too. What I can tell you is that she's working very hard."

PART
SIX

SPRING
1990

S I X T E E N

For all my confidence on the phone with Cal, my self-doubt often overwhelmed me. Maybe Barbara should be in the hospital. What if she kills herself between now and Easter? I'd never forgive myself. I talked about it with my colleague Marcia.

"It's a judgment call," she said. "So much of what we do is based on clinical intuition and our knowledge of the therapeutic relationship. If you think she can get through this without hospitalization, she probably can."

Although I usually felt reassured by Marcia's clinical opinions, this time I felt uncertain. Between Barbara's sessions and late at night I'd ruminate about her safety. I wondered how less than two years of therapy could overcome at least fifteen years of satanic programming by her family.

One of those nights, finally despairing that sleep would never come, I asked the Light to be with Barbara and protect her. I realized the next morning that I had drifted off to sleep immediately afterward. If that was a prayer, it had certainly worked. Maybe I, too, would come to believe in the Light. I had no other advisers to turn to. And soon I would be desperate.

On March 20, Dan's mother had a stroke. She had some right-side paralysis and slurred speech, but the stroke was considered to be a minor one. The doctors thought she could recover most of her physical functioning with several months in the rehabilitation wing of the hospital. A complicating factor was her chronic asthma and lung disease. Daily visits to the hospital became a part of our routine.

In that state of mind, I was completely stunned when Barbara stormed into my office on Monday, two weeks before Easter.

"What on earth has happened?" I asked.

"I'm so angry with Michelle I can't stand it!" she said. "I feel like killing her I'm so mad!"

I went cold. I'd never seen Barbara act like this. She'd talk about how angry she was toward the clan or about Michelle's behavior, but she'd never erupted with dangerous hostility.

"This isn't like you," I said. "What happened to set off this anger?"

"She is so impossible! She stands in front of the refrigerator and pours juice and gets it on the floor, and then I get home and the floor is a sticky mess! And she just stares at me when I get mad. Those penetrating eyes! She's had them since she was a baby." Barbara's eyes gleamed.

"I don't know what to say. You're an expert on children. In your last session you described killing someone who victimized you when you were a child. You were programmed to kill yourself Easter week, only one week away, and now you're talking about killing your daughter. I'm completely baffled."

Barbara sank into her chair and covered her face with her hands. "I don't know what's happening to me. I just feel so much anger. I guess the hate never went away. I'm just afraid it never will. I'm afraid if I don't hurt myself, I'll hurt Michelle."

My mind was racing trying to think of what to do. Most of the survivors I had consulted with, or knew of through our therapist networking, had all made serious suicide attempts or at the least, had mutilated themselves on many occasions. I desperately wanted to help Barbara avoid committing destructive acts toward herself or her daughter. We were both silent for a long while.

I suddenly had a thought and gathered my courage to ask a question I never imagined I would ask any patient. "Would you be willing to explore a past-life experience to see if we can learn something that will help you understand more about these feelings, something that may help you to get through the next week?"

Barbara's eyes widened. She looked at me, questioning, "I didn't know you did that type of thing."

"I don't. I mean, I haven't. I've never done it before. I've been reading a lot about past-life regression therapy, though, and if it might help you, I'm willing to try if you're willing to be my first case."[38]

I went on to tell Barbara about Brian Weiss's book, *Many Lives, Many Masters,* and of his solid reputation as chief of psychiatry at Sinai Hospital in Miami. I explained that Dr. Weiss had written a documentation of his use of past-life therapy to help a young woman with anxiety and phobia.

"He wasn't pushing the concept of reincarnation, but writing about the phenomenon of how it worked in order to

---

38. One of the books I had read was by a psychologist, Edith Fiore. In *You Have Been Here Before* (Ballantine Books, 1986), she documents her use of past-life regression hypnosis to help patients in extreme crises, often those for whom no other treatment has been successful.

help his patient. I have to tell you that most of my colleagues who use hypnosis would only use past-life regression to come to some understanding of symptoms that can't seem to be explained by experiences in this lifetime. In your case, we know exactly why you have symptoms and even why you have urges to kill yourself. Maybe it would tell us something, though," I added weakly.

"I'll try anything at this point," Barbara said.

This time, after Barbara was in her usual deep hypnotic trance, I suggested she float up onto a cloud and begin to drift back through time until she could look down on some part of the world and enter a lifetime. After several minutes Barbara began to stiffen and shake just the way she did whenever she was experiencing torture as a child.

Oh, no! I thought to myself. What have I done? There's just more suffering here. I was certain I'd made a mistake dabbling in an unorthodox area I knew so little about. This horrible feeling continued as the session went on.

"Where are you?" I asked.

"Underneath a porch," she answered.

"What are you doing underneath a porch?"

"I live here."

"How old are you?"

"I'm six or seven."

"Who lives with you?"

"No one. I live by myself. They do not know that I'm here."

"Who doesn't know?"

"The people who live in the big house."

"Tell me about the house."

"It's white with big poles in front. There are six of them. They're on each side. There's a big porch that goes around the front and the back. There are three steps up to the cement porch. There is a crawl space underneath there. That's where I live."

"What is the name of this place?"

Barbara was quiet for a few seconds. "Jamaica."

"How does it happen that you're living under the porch?"

"I ran away from that bad house."

"How come?"

Barbara began shaking in fright again. "My father was hurting me. He did things that were not common for fathers to do, so I ran away and I live under the porch."

"Where is your mother?"

"She is dead. She died two years ago after he beat her."

"And what happened that caused you to decide to run away?"

"I spilled broth on the floor of our hut. He became very angry and began beating me on the head. I had to run away."

"And what do you do during the day?"

"I mostly stay under there so no one will see me, and then I crawl out at night to look for something to eat."

"Where do you find food?"

"In the little house nearby."

"Who lives in the little house?"

"No one. That's where they do their cooking."

"Are you black?"

"Very black, and so was my evil father. Black, like a coal. That's what the older people said."

"Listen and see if you can hear any of the people talking now. Maybe someone would call your name."

"I don't hear. I used to before he hit me in the ears, but I can't hear anymore."

I got a painful knot in my stomach. "So, your father destroyed your hearing?"

"He was a very evil man."

"Move ahead in that lifetime now to when you're a little older."

"I don't get any older."

"You don't get any older?" The knot in my stomach melted into sadness. I knew I had to help her to look at her death in that lifetime.

"Move to the time when you die then, but take a nice deep breath and experience no discomfort. Simply observe to see what happened. . . . That's right. Let yourself relax and feel no discomfort."

"I'm still under the porch and I'm very very cold. It is too cold to be outside, but I can't go anyplace, so I'm very cold and my ears are bleeding. I'm so very very cold."

Barbara had often been cold and shivering in my office when she was remembering abuse. We had traced it to the several times when she had been left in the graveyard overnight with no clothing. Here was another possible explanation.

"So cold," I soothed. "It's too cold to be outside, but you have no place to go . . . and how do you die?"

"I'm so cold, and very scared, and very very tired. Somebody was calling me. She says, 'It's time to go.' She calls me Denise."

"Who is it?"

"It's a lady's voice. She came and got me so I wouldn't suffer, she said. And I see the dogs go in and drag her out. But I was gone before the dogs came. That little girl, Denise, died."

"And what happened to your spirit?"

"It is very angry. Very very very angry. It's a young one, so it doesn't know. I am a very young soul. And I have lots of pain and lots of anger. And the voice says I have to learn about anger."

"Are there other voices?"

"Yes. But I don't see any people. There's no one with me."

246

"And where are you now?"

"In nothingness. I'm just floating in a white space. There's no ending and no beginning. It's just a space. And it's just me."

"Does this space have a name?"

Barbara cocked her head as if listening. "It is the Place of Many Lessons. And I have to learn about my anger. I have to learn about that. That's what they said."

"Stay in that white space until the next time you take human form . . . until another time . . . and then look down from your white space and emerge into that next lifetime."

"I have no other times other than this. I only have two times."

"So, you've come into this lifetime now?"

"Yes. I was away a very very long time."

"What did it feel like when you were in that white space with no beginning and no end?"

"Like I was sleeping. Sleeping and listening. I was so mad I wouldn't listen to them because I was wronged, I said. I spent so much time fussing with them because I was little and it wasn't fair. So I wasted much time. They said I wasted much time to have peace and joy. I wasted time to enjoy the flesh all because I wouldn't listen about anger. So I have to learn about anger, they said."

Barbara, at least, had good reason to be angry, I thought. I certainly must have my own lessons to learn about anger.

"All right. Let that image fade away now, and I want you to imagine a rosebud right in the center of yourself. It's all closed up, and now see a ball of golden light way out in space coming closer, into our atmosphere, and as it comes and touches you, let the rosebud begin to open up. As the light and warmth touch it, the bud opens into a beautiful rose.

"And you can see the beauty of that flower that is within you, the beauty that is possible within you. You can feel it, and let that feeling remain with you, and let the joy of that feeling spread now as I count to ten and you become more and more comfortable and ready to be back here in the room with me. One, two, three, four, five, six, seven, eight, nine, ten.''

"I don't know how to describe what I feel,'' Barbara said when she opened her eyes. She had a radiant smile. "I feel peace for the first time in my life. It's amazing.''

"What did you think about the reason your father beat you?''

"Yes,'' Barbara said in her low, resonant voice. "I got that. My father beat me because I'd spilled broth. I felt like beating Michelle because she spilled juice. This is just too amazing!'' With a deep sigh, she added, "I feel so much better. Thank you. I'll see you next time.''

I was touched by the "thank you.'' Following most of our hypnosis sessions, I felt like apologizing to Barbara for opening her up to such pain, like a surgeon operating on a patient and leaving the wound open. This time, Barbara was left with no pain, only a feeling of comfort and well-being.

I did not feel comfortable at all. I felt amazed and confused. Instead of relief or a sense of accomplishment, I had only questions. Was it really a true past life she had experienced, or do we pull these thoughts from our creative imagination? If so, how can we create and participate in a situation with which, in this lifetime, we've been completely unfamiliar? Barbara had never been to Jamaica. And whether the experience is real or not, why did it work for Barbara when the traditional approach of remembering and working through trauma had not?

The questions coursed through my mind that night and I couldn't fall asleep. Too, I was wary of quick change. In my training I'd learned that when patients suddenly claim that they're better, it is often a defensive maneuver . . . a "flight into health." The flight into health is simply an attempt to delude oneself (and one's therapist) that the problems are completely resolved. There is no need for further work.

I was also wary about a therapist—me—doing something clever to take away a patient's symptoms. That felt too much like grandiosity. Maybe I was indulging my own wish to save Barbara. Maybe, in pursuing past-life regression, I was getting caught up in narcissism, my need to appear wonderful to my patient.

That night in bed, I went through my relaxation exercises and imagined a white light pouring over me and surrounding me. It didn't work. I kept thinking about Barbara's being beaten to death in that lifetime. I was also curious about her statement that she was a young soul and this was only her second lifetime. The past-life "gurus" all insisted that we'd been through hundreds of lifetimes! How could they know?

I finally decided to turn to Barbara's spirit guide, the feminine voice who called to "Denise" when she was dying, telling her it was time to go. If spirituality was helping Barbara, maybe it could help me.

"If you're there, please help me now. Let me know if this is the right kind of work for Barbara." As I sank deeper into trance, words began to come to me. "There is no need to worry. Barbara has much work to do. You have helped her to be able to do this work." I felt a sense of great joy and calmness as I fell easily into a deep, restful sleep.

The next morning, I didn't know what to make of that voice. Maybe I had just reassured myself. After all, that's what I wanted. Maybe it was my own higher self or my spirit guide, or both. Whatever it was, I felt relaxed and peaceful. I also had a sense of clarity that Barbara and I both would be helped when we were in great need.

When Barbara appeared for her next appointment, she continued to look radiant. "I still feel peaceful. It amazes me. I'm calm at home and with the kids. I have no impulses to anger at all. And my blood pressure is down to normal. I feel warm inside for the first time, too," she said with a laugh.

"I'm so pleased for you."

"This next part is really weird, though. I had a dream that was related to the past life. In the dream, I saw that my father from that lifetime died. He killed himself. Then I realized that he reincarnated as Michelle."

"Whew." I gripped the sides of my chair. "That is really something. I guess it's similar to accessing current lifetime memories under hypnosis. Once the door is open, you begin to remember more and more. So, after you left here, you continued to have further revelations. Does it seem right to you?"

"Yes. It explains so much about the way I've always felt about her. I told you her eyes always intimidated me from the time she was a baby. Now I can understand the intensity of the relationship. I'm very easy with Paul, but Michelle was always a trial for me. Now I know why."

"Well, according to the reincarnationists, the same souls tend to incarnate together in order to work out their problems. It is an interesting thought that you have to relive a life with your father in order to learn to control your anger and to forgive. And he has to relive a life with you in order to learn to love and to trust that he'll be cared for."

We spent the rest of that session, as well as the next two, discussing the lessons Barbara seemed to be learning. The topics of forgiveness and life after death seemed to be very appropriate for the time just before Easter Sunday.

I felt relieved to see Barbara unburdened from the suicidal depression she had been in. She not only felt good emotionally, her mind was actively engaged in understanding her relationship with her daughter. I not only felt that Barbara was no longer suicidal, I hoped that her therapy had turned the corner. If Cal was transferred, I wanted Barbara to be ready to accompany him and begin a new life.

While I had found my own past-life experience intriguing but little more, I could not dismiss Barbara's experience so easily. I became consumed by curiosity. I began reading every book I could find on the topic and also books on the out-of-body experiences reported by those who have come close to death. These near-death experiences have been written about extensively by Dr. Raymond Moody.[39]

I was most impressed by *Reliving Past Lives: The Evidence Under Hypnosis* by a psychologist named Helen Wambach.[40] Dr. Wambach spent most of her professional life researching past lives until her death in 1985. She used hypnosis to help over one thousand subjects look at one or two past lives. Each participant was given the same suggestions in hypnosis, to enter one of five time periods, and to examine the clothing, eating utensils, food, money used to buy food or supplies, etc., during his or her brief sojourn back to that lifetime. Participants were also asked to observe their death and what happened to their spirit after death.

The participants filled out extensive questionnaires following the past-life regression. When Dr. Wambach compared the data to archaeological and anthropological findings about life in each time period, she discovered that the descriptions her subjects gave matched correctly the historical findings. Subjects, for example, could describe the coins used in the marketplace of China in 1200 B.C., or the food and eating utensils used

39. Raymond Moody, Jr., *Life After Life* (New York: Bantam Books, 1975); and *Reflections on Life After Life* (Bantam Books, 1977).
40. Helen Wambach, *Reliving Past Lives: The Evidence Under Hypnosis* (New York: Harper & Row, 1978).

in Scandinavia in A.D. 800. And none of these subjects were students of history.

Dr. Weiss reported that he is currently working with a large group of children who have past-life recall. Some of their descriptions of places they lived, cemeteries, and other landmarks in centuries-ago Europe have been corroborated. And these are children who have never even been to Europe in this lifetime! Most amazing to me are the children in Dr. Weiss's subject pool who are able to speak ancient, foreign languages during their past-life trances.

While every new account I read excited my interest, I continued to be puzzled, confused. I am a scientist. A psychologist. Everything in my training pointed away from what I was learning. What I had to accept was that Barbara had seemed to benefit from the experience in a way that seemed hard for her to put into words. I could see the changes in her mood and in her face, especially her eyes.

SEVENTEEN

Barbara was beaming when she came into my office. "Easter was really nice," she said. "For the first time in church, I didn't have any of my crazy urges to grab a wooden cross and hit people over the head with it. It was just a nice weekend. I still feel that peace."

"What would you like to work on today?"

"I feel like I have to continue to learn about everything that happened to me, so I'll be ready to leave you when Cal gets transferred. He's pleased about my progress, but the way he watches me, I just know he's thinking he'll get his request to relocate any day and will I be ready to move."

"What do you think about that?"

"I know I'll be ready now, but I've grown so attached to you. . . . You're the first person apart from Cal that I've ever felt really close to. And I don't want to leave that. I know I can get along without you. I've always been on my own. But I don't want to be without you now." Barbara looked terribly sad.

"Being able to say good-bye is one of the hardest things human beings have to learn. It's about coping with separation. Having the sad feelings means that you've made an attachment to me. You've learned that it's safe now to be in a loving relationship."

"Yes. And I don't want to be without it!"

"You'll never be without it again. Once you know love, no one can ever take it away from you. Like your connection to the Light. The clan could never take that from you. When you choose love, it's yours forever."

"I know. But it doesn't seem fair that I never had anyone until you, and now I have to lose you."

"Are you going to forget me?"

"No! I could never forget you!"

"That's what happens with love. You never really lose it. It stays inside and warms your heart and constantly teaches you how to love yourself and others. It's a gift and you received that gift from the Light when you were very little."

"I guess that's right."

"What do you think is left from your childhood that you might need to know about?"

"I've been telling myself that nothing more happened to me after I was fourteen because I didn't want to know about anything after the time I met Cal when I was seventeen. It's hard enough to share the stuff that happened when I was little. I don't want him to know about anything after we met." Barbara looked down and was silent.

"You're thinking that maybe something did happen though, aren't you?"

"Yes."

"Okay. Let's see what it is," I said gently.

Barbara's body relaxed into a deep trance. When I asked her to tell me where she was, she answered, "Calvin's driving me home from school. He got to drive his parents' car and he's driving me home."

"And how old are you?"

"I'm seventeen." Barbara's voice sounded like a happy teenager's, not the usual depressed and frightened little girl's.

"Do you like Calvin?"

"Oh, yes. A lot. I have to pretend I'm from a normal family, so I tell him my mother doesn't allow me to ride with boys in cars. I tell him to drop me off down the street and I walk home. I did that for a couple of months . . . making up rules so I'd seem like the rest of my friends."

"You want him to see you as being normal."

"Yes. And I take him to meet Grandma and she said she liked him. He was really nice to me. He never did anything. He never tried to get over me."

"What does that mean?"

"He never tried to have sex with me. He just talked to me and I talked to him and we'd go for walks and for drives . . . stuff like that."

"So you fell in love with him."

"Yes, but I didn't want to. I thought if he found out about the clan, he'd call me names . . . he'd call me a creep and a whore. So I told him I was a virgin and I didn't believe in having sex until you were married. So that kept him away for a while. Then I went to talk to Grandma about what to do. She said before I could have a boyfriend, I had to wait and get out of the clan. So I wait."

"What does that mean, 'wait and get out of the clan'?"

"It means I have to wait till next fall at my fake birthday. And I'm in college then. It's October and it's called the Coming Out Ceremony."

255

"Tell me what happens at that ceremony."

"The men form a line up the stairs to the Upper Room, the torture chamber I call it. Grandma comes by and unlocks the door, and they fix it up. They put dark curtains and dark shades on the windows, and they put the dresser and the wardrobe in front of them. They put chains on the bed. Not ropes, chains. Then Grandma says I have to get a bath in the hot oils to soften up my skin."

Barbara's body began to stiffen and her face contorted so much that I knew the torture had begun. "Barbara," I said, "you're being hurt so much. Why don't you float out of your body and look down so that you don't have to feel so uncomfortable and scared. That's right. Just float up above and look down and tell me what's happening to you."

"They're beating her, and she's chained to the bed and they're beating her on the back. And she has no clothes on and they're beating her."

"Who is it, beating her?"

"Grandaddy and Ben. They beat her with switches and a razor strap. And she doesn't cry. She just lays there. Then each man gets on her and says, 'You're gonna pay, you fucking bitch.' I can tell who they are by their smell and their voice. Then they heat up the propane stove." Barbara begins to pant and twist her body. "It's hurting too much. It feels like he's trying to push my insides out. And now they put a rag in my mouth so I won't scream or bite off my tongue."

"Drift away again. You need to float away from your body and not hurt so much. Just look down and watch."

"Granddaddy says, 'This does not deserve my manhood. It is filthy and she is filthy. She is nothing but a cunt and cunts don't deserve me. Is the sign ready?' I have to do something 'cause it's going to hurt really bad. I go away to the Light so I won't die."

"You're shaking all over. What are you aware of?"

"The burning . . . the burning inside me." Barbara goes limp and then says with fatigue in her voice, "It's over and they're laughing. I'm still alive."

"Why do they laugh?"

" 'Cause Granddaddy says, 'I've never seen a strong bitch like this one before. She can handle anything.' "

"So now it's over?"

"For now. Later on, they bring the snakes in. Granddaddy says, 'Just as you came into the room, as you came to be our princess, in order not to be, you have to go out the same way."

"What does that mean, 'going out the same way'?"

"I have to be with the snakes for five days and five nights. And I have to see the jaws of hell. It starts on Sunday, the day the enemy rests. That's what they call Sunday. And there're lots of snakes. But I feel I've had worse. There's nothing else they can do to me."

But Barbara begins to look uncomfortable again.

"What's happening now?" I ask.

"Granddaddy's over in the corner. He's putting some kind of grease on him . . . on his whole body . . . including his penis. Now he's having intercourse with me. And I don't care," Barbara says, crying.

"You do care. Why do you say you don't?"

"There's nothing to care about with them. It's just something else I have to endure in order to get away from them."

"What happens when he's finished?"

"He ejaculates on me and rubs it all over me, and then he leaves. I'm cold and I don't sleep. I can stay awake for long periods of time and I do. I know now that most people die during this ceremony. They usually kill other people. The only reason I didn't die is because I had lived through the snakes many times before, so I didn't die of fright. And I had lived through the poker before, too. So I didn't die. And I certainly had lived through my grandfather and the others raping me

257

before. And they could not cut my heart out because it was sacred, and that is why I got to live. That is what they said.

"And so I survived the five days and five nights, and then they let me go. And I had to not remember what happened. So I forgot."

Barbara and I were always shocked by a new revelation of the torture she had been subjected to. This time was no different. She was silent, but I was moaning, "Oh, my God." I asked, "Are you surprised by this memory?"

"No, I'm not surprised. It fits. I knew they didn't just forget about me when I met Cal and began spending time with him."

At the next meeting of the therapist support group, I shared the fact that Barbara had come through the suicidal depression without requiring hospitalization.[41] I was hoping she had entered the last stage of treatment where the task was to wind up the memory work and integrate her insights into an understanding of herself. The others felt pleased to hear that treatment could actually lead to a conclusion, since most of the survivors had been working in therapy for many years with repeated hospitalizations.

Although I wanted to give the other therapists encouragement, I wasn't courageous enough to mention the past-life regression. I didn't know how to talk about it. What we all continued to do was to compare notes as to the types of abuses being reported. It was interesting to note the similarities. It was also comforting to know we could describe gory details with each other because we couldn't really discuss them with anyone else. It was continually upsetting to realize that Bar-

41. By this time, there were over thirty members signed up to meet and discuss multiple personality disorder, dissociation, and the sadistic abuse that leads to these symptoms.

bara's experience was not unique but was shared with other women who were in treatment right here in Albuquerque.[42]

We discussed the fact that all of our patients were "refugees" in that they had left the areas where they had grown up, breaking most, if not all, family ties. Many were frightened that members of their cults would find them. All had been told they would be killed for divulging cult secrets, just as Barbara had been told.[43]

We took time to talk about the torture scenes we had the most trouble with personally. One woman said the "snakes inserted up the vagina was too much for me." We all agreed that infant sacrifice was overwhelming in its emotional impact on us. Another therapist described one of her patients, as a child, being forced to remain overnight in the opened-up abdomen of a corpse.[44] This therapist was having a difficult time working with survivors of sadistic abuse because she was the mother of small children. We all agreed that mothering was enough of a task without coming to work and hearing horror stories about child victimization. We suggested that if there

---

42. The great majority of survivors are women. As one of my later satanic abuse patients said, "Most of the murders committed by the cult my father was in were murders of men. Women were killed, too, but they were primarily used for sex and childbirth. That's one reason more women eventually escape. The men who survive are the cult leaders. They're smart and often upstanding members of the community. They're great psychopaths, and since most of us have been hospitalized at one time or another, we have no credibility when we try to report their crimes." This woman's father was a high-ranking law enforcement officer in California.

43. Periodically I had asked Barbara whether she feared members of the cult would try to find her. She said, no, she had been away for too long. When I asked once how she would feel if we were doing this work on the East Coast, she stiffened, got a look of terror, and said, "We would both be in great danger."

44. Another survivor who came to work with me later on told of the same ritual. As a small child, she had been placed nude inside the corpse of a man the cult had murdered in a ceremony that had taken place in the woods. The men sat around the child in the corpse drinking all night, and whenever she would move to get out, a gun would be fired into the ground near her so she wouldn't dare to move.

was any way to screen out these patients, she should refer them to others.

I was curious as to whether my colleagues knew of any African American survivors of satanic abuse. They didn't. Nor did any of the therapists running the dissociative-disorders clinics around the country. My colleagues' patients had described large, well-organized satanic clans and cults in areas across the entire country. On the surface, it looked as though satanism was a white, middle-class practice.

I was concerned that reliving the "coming out" ceremony might throw Barbara back into depression. I observed her carefully when she came for her next appointment.

She smiled at me and said, "I'm okay. I really am. Cal did get his transfer, so I just have to keep working."

"What work remains, do you think?"[45]

"I have to somehow come to terms with my mother. I keep thinking she just couldn't have hated me the way she seemed to. Mothers aren't supposed to hate their children. So I have to understand more about that."

Once Barbara was in her trance, she said, "I'm here."

"Where are you?"

"I'm upstairs in my room."

"How old are you?"

"Six. It's my birthday, my 'for real' birthday. And my mother's coming up the stairs. I had a real birthday party. It's before I went to the hospital. It was a nice birthday. I got lots of stuff, a coloring book and crayons, and I got a dress

---

45. I've learned from the survivors of sadistic abuse that they themselves, more than any other class of patients, know exactly what they need to work on. Patients in the "normal neurotic" category are usually looking to the therapist to tell them what they need to do or what phase of treatment they're in—even to tell them when they're ready to stop treatment. Survivors such as Barbara seem to know in what direction to move, when to take a break, and when to end treatment.

from Auntie. Grandma gave me a doll and I got jacks, and we had cake and ice cream. And my mother gave me six pennies, pretty new pennies. . . . But she had a mean look in her eyes when she gave them to me.

"After the party, me and Vaughn went upstairs to go to bed. Mother came up the stairs, she said, to 'tuck me in,' but that's not what she does."

"What does she do?"

"She's mad at me 'cause she wanted me to come live with her and I said no. So she's mad. She comes and takes back her pennies. She calls me an 'ungrateful little bitch' and gives me six hits with her fist. And she takes away the money."

"What does that feel like?"

"Nothing. I liked the money. It was pretty. It was the only nice thing she ever did, so I thought maybe she liked me. But she hates me. She said it wasn't worth the fourteen dollars it cost her to have me. That's what she said."

I asked Barbara to stay in her trance, but counted as she came back to her current age. "How do you make sense out of your mother's meanness towards you?"

"She says I ruined her life because she got pregnant with me and everybody was mean to her. She had to quit school and Granddaddy was real mean. She said he locked her in her room and didn't feed her for days. Grandma started sneaking her food when he'd go to work at night."

"Would your grandfather have been capable of letting her starve to death?"

"Grandma wouldn't let that happen."

"But he was real mean to her?"

"Yes. And she said she lost all her friends. Except one . . . Miss Mona. That's the one who had the bar and prostitutes. My mother sold me to her once for fifty dollars, but she just kept me there for the weekend and didn't make me do anything."

We spent the next few months looking at the many ways

Barbara's mother abused her and tried to kill her. One time, when Barbara was ten, her mother starved her for over a week. Barbara finally took money from her mother's purse and wandered into the nearest bakery. She bought two cherry pies and ate both of them, making herself ill. Her stepfather intervened at that time, saving her from her mother's homicidal wrath.

Another time, her mother locked Barbara in her room for days, saying she could not come out even to use the bathroom. Barbara found a jar in the room and urinated into it when she couldn't hold on any longer. Her mother found the jar and forced her to drink the urine. That memory was one of the most painful for Barbara. For her, it was more upsetting than the repeated physical abuses.

Following a talk I gave on treating satanic ritual abuse,[46] a psychoanalyst, Dr. Theodora Abel, commented on Barbara's experience: "It's not surprising that she was so upset by having to drink the urine. After all, what is a mother supposed to give us to drink? Milk. The urine symbolizes the mother's hatred for her and all of the other degrading, life-threatening experiences she exposed the daughter to."

46. "The Aftermath of Ritual Abuse: Diagnosis and Treatment." Presented at the Department of Psychiatry, University of New Mexico Medical School, February 1, 1990.

PART
SEVEN

SUMMER
1990

E I G H T E E N

ust as the spring winds had subsided, the turmoil that had marked Barbara's emotional life now seemed to abate. Summer felt warm and peaceful. Even though Barbara's memories of her mother were awful, she was content, pleased that she had "done" therapy. It was only fitting, I thought, that she had finally earned some peace.

We both felt that something special had occurred with the past-life hypnosis experience. We talked periodically about that and about the spiritual Mother who had called to her to leave her body after she had died as the seven-year-old girl in Jamaica. During one session, where Barbara was remembering other times when her biological mother tried to kill her, a spiritual Mother returned.

"I see me in the crib, but I see me standing at the window

sick. I'm a baby in the crib, but I'm four or five at the window."

"In what way is the little girl at the window sick?"

"I throw up all the time. I can't go outside 'cause I'm sick. But everybody's outside playin'. Grandma says I'll get everybody else sick if I go outside."

"So what are you thinking standing there by the window?"

"I was sick like this before."

"When was that?"

"As a baby in the crib. I was remembering."

"What happened at that time?"

"I just threw up all the time."

"Do you have some idea about why you got sick like this again?"

" 'Cause she makes me eat things. It's some kind of soup of onions, but it stinks really bad and it makes me really, really sick. She says it's the soup that Grandma made, but it's not. Grandma's soup is sweet, and this has a bitter, bitter taste. And mother said I had to eat all of it. So when I did, I got sick. And she gave it to me before when I was little. I almost died then."

"You know that. You almost died. What do you suppose your mother put into the soup?"

"Rat poison. I know she did. And Grandma thinks I have whooping cough or something . . . scarlet fever . . . but I don't have that. I just throw up all the time and sometimes blood comes up. And then I remembered being in the crib. I still can see me over there, but no one guessed then."

"Nobody guessed what your mother was doing. But now you know."

"I remembered the taste. But I don't know why she'd want to kill me." The four-year-old Barbara seemed to be thinking very hard. "She's hardly ever home. Only bad mommies do that," she concluded. Then with a brighter voice: "I have another mommy!"

"Tell me about her."

"She's different. I remember her from the crib. She just came and rubbed my stomach and rubbed my back and . . . sometimes I don't think I rolled over by myself. She turned me over, but it wasn't a person who did that. It wasn't!"

"Your spirit Mother, did She keep you warm?"

"Uh-huh. And She told me she [the real mother] didn't give me enough to kill me, that I'd be all right. And She told me to be a quiet baby. And then that way, she won't try it again while I'm a baby."

"She reassured you, didn't She?"

"Uh-huh. So then I was a quiet baby. She only came when it was really bad."

"What was another time when it was really bad?"

"When Granddaddy put me in with all those snakes. When I was three. Feels like a long time ago." (For a four-year-old, one year earlier is a long time.)

"What did She tell you then?"

"She told me I'd be okay and to practice counting the walls so I knew where to walk. I could count. And She told me I wouldn't be hungry and I didn't get hungry. And She'd let me know how long I had left. She'd say, 'Well, this is going to be a long time, but I'll stay with you. Then She'd say, 'We're halfway there and you're doing okay.' Then She said, 'It's almost over. You'll see, you can make it.' Then he lowered the chair down, but there was no Light when She was there."

"You felt Her presence with you, though?"

"Yes, I was alone and very very cold, but She taught me to stay alive. She taught me to be a quiet baby, and then She taught me to be a quiet little girl so I would live. I'm gonna go find Her now."

I was startled to hear Barbara say that. She had only looked for spiritual helpers in the past when she was suffering torture. I watched her look of concentration. "Tell me when you see Her, or when you feel Her."

"I am nothing now. She is standing with me. She is the one who came to get me from under the porch. She's always there, all the time. I call her Mother."

"Is She like God?"

"Yes. She is part of the Light. She has always been there. She comes when I get scared and when I think nobody loves me."

"What does it feel like when you're with Her?"

"Like nothing. Just calm."

"Does She say anything to you?"

" 'We've come very far, and we've learned a lot, and your time is short. I'll be with you.' "

"And how do you feel now?"

"Kind of nervous because I don't know what the words mean. They're not scary, but I don't know what they mean. I'll have to think about it."

"Before the past-life experience, I would have been frightened by hearing that my time was short," Barbara said later. "But since then, my entire sense of time has changed. I'm not afraid of death and I'm not worried about not having enough time."[47]

"Isn't it amazing how your outlook changes when you've experienced eternity?" I asked. We chuckled together. I had

47. Carl Jung wrote, in *Memories, Dreams and Reflections* (New York: Random House, 1961), "We must not forget that for most people it means a great deal to assume that their lives will have an indefinite continuity beyond their present existence. They live more sensibly, feel better, and are more at peace. One has centuries, one has an inconceivable period of time at one's disposal." Page 301.

changed in much the same way following the past-life work-shop I had taken. Everyday reasons (excuses) for becoming anxious and tense had simply fallen away. Even freeway driving didn't produce stress any longer, and as a transplant from Los Angeles, I thought of that as a minor miracle.

"Oh, I wanted to tell you . . . Cal and I have had sex every day for five days now!" Barbara wore a pleased smile.

"Wow! I'm impressed. And how does that feel for you?"

"It feels great! I no longer have those feelings of being bad or like a whore if I initiate sex. Needless to say, Cal is happy."

"What about the smoking and drinking?"

"I didn't tell you? I never smoked another cigarette after I burned myself. And after Easter, I stopped drinking. Cal and I have a glass of wine together occasionally, but I don't drink to contain my anxiety anymore. I don't have any anxiety since the past-life work!"

"That's wonderful! What do you think you have left to do here now?"

"I think there's still something left about my mother and my grandmother."

At our next session, I decided to structure the hypnosis by using a technique I learned from Helen Watkins called the Door of Forgiveness.[48] After Barbara was in trance, I suggested she see herself in a long hallway with doors on either side. I suggested she open one of the doors and see what was inside. She did, and saw a mirror.

"I look in the mirror and my eyeballs hurt. Grandma used to say I had monsters in my eyes, that I could kill the world with my eyes. But I don't see that. I just feel that they hurt a lot."

"Your eyeballs hurt. Why do they hurt?"

---

48. Helen taught at the University of Montana for twenty-five years. She and her husband, Jack Watkins, have developed many useful techniques to facilitate hypnotherapy.

"Because I see a lot. I see that my mother hurt me and my grandmother hurt me. And I hurt me. I tried to kill myself sometimes."

"Is it the anger and hate that's so hurtful?"

"Yes. And hating myself."

"Look closely into that mirror. Look at your eyes."

"They're hurt and they're sad, very very sad. And I don't want them to be hurt and sad anymore."

"Tell me what you need to do in order to feel better."

"Tears wash away hurt and water washes away dirt. So that is what I have to do. I know how to cry now. I don't have to do it in this room. I know how to cry."

"Is there anything else you need to do in this room?"

"No."

"As we go out into the hallway, can you see the door at the end of the hall, the Door of Forgiveness?"

"Yes, I see it."

"Are you ready to go there now?"

"Yes."

"Open the door and go in."

"I feel scared. I was always so scared . . . about being hurt. And I thought it would always happen. Sometimes I thought it was because I was bad and Mother didn't like me, and Granddaddy didn't like me either."

"You thought you were hurt because you were bad?"

"I did then. When Grandma hurt me it was because I did bad things. When I would tell people things and look in places I wasn't supposed to. Whenever I would break the rules."

"Can you begin to understand that you weren't being bad, you were being a normal, curious girl?"

"She told me not to do those things and I did them anyway, so I didn't listen. I was hardheaded."

"Your being hardheaded was one of your strengths. You tried not to listen when they told you to do bad things to other people. Do you remember that?"

"Yes, and then I got hurt."

"You suffered for that. It's important that you recognize that your being 'hardheaded,' as you call it, has a lot to do with your strengths, being smart and curious, with your ability to be defiant of the clan when they wanted you to participate in evil, and with your ability to survive all the hurts."

"They hurt me a lot, though, and they said it was because I was hardheaded."

"That's what they said, but those were lies, those were excuses to hurt you. Can you begin to forgive yourself for being a normal, smart little girl?"

"Yes. I did bad things though. I lied and I stole, so that makes me a liar and a thief. I lied to my mother all the time, and I stole her money."

"Yes. Why did you steal her money?"

"Because she wouldn't give me any food. But it hurts me to know that I was a liar."

"Lying and stealing in order to eat makes you a survivor. The kind of lies that the clan told were much more serious, because they told lies in order to hurt people. It's time to forgive yourself for all those hurts, to forgive your part in all that, and to let the tears wash it away . . . wash away all the hurts. Especially since you had no choice about anything. No choices at all. Do you understand that?"

"Yes. I will throw it away. Throw away the lies and all that I did. And the hurting myself."

"What are you thinking about?"

"How I burned myself with an iron when I was little. And then I burned myself with the cigarettes because I was mad."

"Can you forgive yourself?"

"I don't know what to do instead of hurting myself when I get mad."

"Maybe you're learning to not get mad at yourself anymore. You learned from the clan and from your mother to get real mad at yourself, didn't you?"

"Yes. I was supposed to hurt. When I did anything wrong, I was supposed to hurt. That's what they said. My mother said I would pay for every wicked deed, and I've done many. I didn't do anything to people though. Not by myself."

"Can you throw that idea away, too? Those words of your mother's . . . those punishing, hurtful words?"

"Yes. But I can't be a new person until I forgive her. It's a sad, sorry child who can't love her mother."

"Who says those words?"

"My mother and my grandmother."

"And you believed them, didn't you?"

"Yes. There's something wrong with me because I don't love her. I never did and I never will."

"How could you love a mother who never loved you? Do you know that children learn to love their mothers from the mother's love? And if the mother's love isn't there, it's not possible to love them back. Your mother didn't love you, did she?"

"No, she hated me. She tried to kill me many times. In the real Bible it says I'm supposed to honor my mother and my father. I don't know my father, but I hate my mother. I hate the ground she walks on."

"It's a normal feeling when you've been so very very hurt. As you begin to forgive yourself, that hatred toward your mother will begin to dissolve as well. It will begin to float away, just float away. Because the two are related. And forgiveness is related to love. And these feelings are much more powerful than hate."

"Does that mean I'm not a bad child?"

"It means you're not a bad child. It means that as you begin to like yourself more, feel better about yourself, those hateful feelings will fall away. You won't be able to have love for your mother because she never had love for you. But you'll be able to feel neutral, even compassion, for her. Do you know those words?"

"Yes."

"So let the hurt feelings be washed away, the hateful feelings washed away. Can you feel it?"

"Yes. I feel different inside. There's no more knot. I feel calm."

"Can you feel the Light?"

"Yes, and there's a peace now."

"Good. Let the Light come in and fill your entire body. Let it heal your hurt, both emotional and physical. Let it heal you completely, and know that this work has begun and will continue, so that you can go on feeling this peace and this forgiveness."

In the beginning of the story, I wrote about the importance of the psychological defenses as part of our ego organization. I described how essential the defenses are to children. The defenses of denial, repression, rationalization, projection, and others enable us to get grown-up. And once we're grown, they protect us from overwhelming emotional trauma. The problem is that we come to feel safe and secure with the old patterns of thinking, believing, and behaving.

Barbara's powerful anger, hate, and rage probably saved her life as a child. Then it was appropriate for her to hate those who oppressed her, to let her rage seethe in order to stay focused on survival. At certain times, she felt she only lived in order to get big enough to kill her grandfather. Revenge was a motivating force. All her defenses helped her.

Once we're grown, however, the defenses become obstacles. Most of us can see how hanging on to childhood fear, anger, sadness, envy, or greed obstructs the way to healthy feelings of openness, joy, and love.

From the psychological view, the defenses form the resistance to committing to change in psychotherapy. From a religious view, the defenses are the work of the devil. They keep us stuck in childhood patterns of anger, stubbornness, and depression, and prevent us from maturing into a greater capacity for inner peace and closer interpersonal relations.

Barbara had released her anger, rage, and hate, all of the defensive emotions she had focused on her abusive family, as well as on her own insides. Those feelings had caused her to feel worthless, "no bigger than an ant." One look at Barbara now and the change was remarkable. She no longer scanned the environment cautiously, holding back to see what others would expect. Confidence surrounded her like a halo. "For the first time in my life, I feel comfortable within myself," she said one day.

N I N E T E E N

There were more hypnosis sessions during the summer, primarily going over the same material regarding her mother and her grandmother. Barbara wanted to have a sense of closure with these two most important figures in her life.

During one of these sessions, she reviewed the time of her grandmother's death eight years previously. She had gone to the hospital to visit her grandmother, and "at some point, Grandma asked me to help her to the bathroom. As she began to lower herself to the toilet, she reached down between her legs and took some vaginal liquid and put her fingers to my lips like a kiss. She said, 'This is the beginning of the joining of the souls. This is from my soul to yours.' Those were the last words she spoke to me."

"They were true believers, weren't they?"

"Yes. The upsetting thing is that Granddaddy's still alive."

"Do you think the church is still operating?"

"Oh, yes. Granddaddy's too old to participate much, but one of my mother's brothers, Eddie, is running it." Barbara laughed. "I can't help it. He calls himself a reverend and I don't think he finished the tenth grade! Plus, he's done time in prison."

Barbara had talked of reporting the clan from the very beginning. Now that she was strong enough emotionally, and completing her therapy, we decided on a plan of action. Unfortunately, our plan coincided with family tragedy. The day Barbara came in to say she was ready to return to the East Coast to photograph the places where the satanic activities took place, she looked awful. "Poor Cal," she said. "Last night his younger brother was murdered."

"Oh, no! What happened?"

"We're not sure. We don't have any details, except that he was shot down right in front of their mother. I suspect it was drug involved. So, we'll be going back sooner than we planned."

"I'm worried about you. You won't visit any of those cult places by yourself, will you?"

"No. Cal will be with me. I won't go near any of my family, but we'll be with his, and we can leave the kids with his sister. He and I will take a few days after the funeral to do our photographing."

"I feel so bad for him," I said. "I suspect this kind of violence isn't so shocking to you."

"No. One of my uncles is walking around today with six bullet holes in his chest. When he was shot years ago, he told the police he didn't know who did it, because when he got out of the hospital, he wanted to know he could get to the guy. And of course he did. The worst thing is I think the clan killed my little brother, Vaughn."

"What? Why would they do that?"

"Because he was a junkie. In '82 he stole a lot of stuff from my mother's house. He was never seen or heard from after that. And you know my mother! She could kill anybody without a second thought."

I shook my head. "Well, I'm planning to go to San Francisco for a meeting, and while I'm there, I'll meet with Sandi Gallant of the San Francisco Police. She specializes in investigating cults and hate groups. She can tell us whom in the police and the FBI we should contact here."

Barbara returned from her trip with an excellent set of photographs. She showed me a picture of the family "church" first. "I was hoping the crawl space in the utility closet would still be there. You know, where they kept the heads?"

"You didn't go inside, did you?" I asked her anxiously.

"No, but that space was open and just screened off along the alley. And you can see in this picture that it's all been filled with concrete. So, I guess they've cleaned up their act."

Barbara showed me pictures of the cemetery where she was buried alive several times and left with the body parts on her during the Princess of Darkness ceremony. She showed me pictures of the apartment building that used to be the hospital where the little boys were killed. She also had a picture of the Jewish temple where the regional Princess of Darkness ceremony took place. The temple is now a Masonic hall.

"Unfortunately, the funeral home isn't there anymore. You know, where they burned the body parts? It's gone. Oh, and listen to this! I went to the police and asked to talk to whoever's in charge of ritual abuse investigations. They said, 'No one. We don't have any of that.' I couldn't believe it! And the guy looked at me as if I were just another crazy. So I asked for directions to Missing Persons. I knew they had to have that!

So, at least I reported that Vaughn's been missing since 1982. Not that anyone will care."

My meeting with Detective Gallant was informative. I had found her in a tiny office in downtown San Francisco's Hall of Justice. She told me the police and FBI don't believe there is a national conspiracy or nationwide organization working to proselytize for satanism. They believe that most groups are acting on their own, with many who use the satanic organization primarily for child pornography purposes.

"I think there are also a lot of sex rings that get into satanic rituals for more excitement. The normal sex activities get boring after a while, so these folks have to find more intense ways of stimulation," the detective said. That made me think of addictions generally, and how one has to use more and more of the addictive substance in order to achieve the desired state of euphoria.

Detective Gallant said that one of the biggest problems for survivors is credibility. "I suspect that of the thousands reporting, only ten percent are describing a true religious belief system, like Barbara came from. Also, most of the survivors are in and out of the hospital. They don't do well under the pressure of repeated tellings of their story. Your patient sounds unusually strong. I only know of one other survivor who is that strong. She teaches about ritual abuse, is absolutely clear about what happened to her, and there's no secondary gain."[49]

I agreed with Detective Gallant that Barbara was incredibly strong. I felt her to be one of the most stable people I had ever known. I told her that Barbara was curious to know if she had heard of other black survivors. She hadn't. Her response fit with those of my colleagues around the country.

"What about fear of reprisal for talking and breaking the cult secrets?" I asked.

---

49. Secondary gain occurs when people find that their symptoms bring them extra benefits, such as special care in the hospital or ongoing income from an injury. Not surprisingly, the symptoms don't go away.

"I would play down the fear," Gallant answered. "I feel that if the cults wanted to kill these people, they would have done it long ago." Later on, I heard the belief expressed by many people that once a survivor has gone public, she's actually safer. It made sense to me that the more names law enforcement personnel had of these satanist criminals, the less likely they would be to hurt one of their past victims.

"I'm both surprised and not surprised," Barbara said after I had related Detective Gallant's points at our next visit, "that she didn't know of other black survivors. There have to be others around, but I guess it's true that they probably wouldn't turn to white therapists or agencies for help."

Barbara and I progressed through our meetings with law enforcement officers. We gave them facts . . . dates, places, names, exact descriptions of rituals. But the therapy sessions were spent discussing our relationship. Barbara was overjoyed about having warm feelings for me and for her family. She felt she was appreciating Cal's dedication to her for the first time. "He's always been my best friend! I can tell him anything. I was so afraid in the past he'd judge me, I couldn't enjoy him. Now, I can really enjoy him."

"Even sexually, right?"

"Even that. Yes. And I like spending time with Michelle. She's so smart. She's interested in so many things." Barbara seemed to think for a minute. "Let's face it, I'm not afraid people will hurt me anymore!"

"That must feel good."

"It really does. There is something, though. I'm worried I won't be able to handle law school." Back in the fall, Barbara had applied to a law school in the city where they expected to be transferred. Right after Easter she had learned of her acceptance.

I burst out laughing and I couldn't stop. "I'm sorry," I

sputtered. "I can't help it. After all you've been through, you're not sure you can survive law school!"

"All right," Barbara said. "I get it," and she, too, began to laugh.

Our last meeting came and passed so quickly neither of us could believe it. We discussed our relationship and how wonderful it felt for Barbara to be close and accepted by another human being. At the end, she stood awkwardly for a moment and then asked, "Could I give you a hug?"

"Of course! I'd love to hug you," I said. We embraced warmly. "I'll never forget you," she said.

"I'll never forget you, either. I've learned so much, but it feels like just a small beginning. I have a tiny start on my understanding of evil and of the human spirit. I'll have to keep working on it. And I want to keep in touch with you."

"For the first time, I want to keep in touch with you, too, and Sharon. I'm not going to move and leave my friends behind anymore. I'll write to you."

She did. We also kept in touch with phone calls. We took turns calling each other about every two weeks. When I learned I would be attending meetings several months later in the same city to which Barbara had moved, I called her immediately.

"Guess what? I'm going to be there for a meeting this fall! We can plan to spend an entire day together."

"Oh, I'm so happy, I can't wait!" Barbara exclaimed. But then there was an awkward silence.

"Is something wrong?" I asked.

"Well, it's just that I don't know how to spend a whole day with a friend. What would we do?"

"One thing we'd do for sure is to have lunch at the fanciest restaurant in town. What else can you think of?"

"I know!" Barbara said exuberantly. "Let's go shopping!"

E P I L O G U E

One year later Barbara returned to Albuquerque to visit me and Sharon. We spent a day together in my office catching up. "So how is law school?" I asked.

Barbara laughed, remembering how I'd teased her about her fears. "It's not as bad as I thought it would be. Some of the professors are good teachers, and some are downright awful. But I figured out the last time I was in graduate school that you learn in spite of the professors. What always amazes me is that I measure up to the other students. I'm really doing well."

"Doesn't surprise me in the least. I'll bet the hardest part is the balancing act of school, mothering, and wifeing."

"Yes! That's really hard."

"What would you say was the most important thing that came from your therapy?"

"I left here knowing who I was. I accepted me. I felt like a whole person who could take care of herself. And I talk about my feelings now. Especially to Cal. I know how to get my needs met, where in the past, if I was upset, I'd stop talking and stop eating. Basically, I think I learned that I'm loved."

"You had to work hard to get to that, didn't you?"

"Oh, yes."

"Are there any remaining symptoms of posttraumatic stress that you're having to deal with? Any fears?"

"Old men. I don't like old men. I still don't like to be touched. But I'm more open and I'll give people hugs. I'll never be comfortable with someone standing behind me."

"What about the real posttraumatic stress symptoms . . . nightmares, sleep disturbance?"

"I've decided that's something you live with. I have nightmares all the time. The difference is I know what it's about. When I was coming here during therapy, I was flipping out because I didn't know what was happening. Now, I wake up, realize I had a nightmare, and just snuggle closer to Cal and go back to sleep."

"That's fascinating. I've read that survivors of extreme trauma like the Holocaust or prisoners of war never stop having sleep disturbance. It doesn't bother you so much though?"

"No. The nightmares don't stay in my mind. They're not about the satanic stuff. They're just about being physically hurt. I think they're more related to my mother." Barbara paused. "That's the one area I still don't feel resolved about. I still feel hate for my mother and I don't want to. I feel blocked in any kind of understanding of her."

"Would you like to do some work on that today?"

"Yes."

I put a tape in the recorder as Barbara got comfortable in the chair. Then I began the relaxation induction we had used so many times before. As soon as I asked Barbara to go to an important experience that would help her to learn something about her mother, she became tense and began to shake.

"Where are you?"

"In the kitchen."

"How old are you?"

"I don't know."

Barbara's voice made me think she was very small.

"Are you real little?"

"Um-hum."

"Something must be scary. What's happening that's so scary for you?"

"She's yelling."

"Who's that? Your mother? Why is she yelling?"

"They're hurting her."

"Who's hurting her?"

"Granddaddy."

"Granddaddy. Can you see them? . . . No? Where are they doing this to her?"

"In the dining room."

"And you're in the kitchen so you can't see, but you can hear. Tell me what you hear."

"He said, 'You nasty little whore. I'll give you something.' And she's crying."

"Who said those words, Granddaddy? . . . Yes. Now what happens?"

"My mommy was crying. I go to the door and he's hitting her. I don't know what he's doing, but he's hurting her."

"What do you think to yourself?"

"Mommy back."

"You want your mommy back. What happens next?"

"Granddaddy gets up and my mommy is crying."

"What do you do?"

"I go to her and I kiss her on the cheek."

"You want her to feel better, don't you?"

"My mommy just sits there and cries . . . and she holds me."

"And then what happens?"

"She takes me upstairs. She's leaving me. That's what she says. And she's never coming back."

"Why is she leaving?"

"Because I was bad."

"Because you were bad? Does Mommy say that?"

"No, but I was 'cause I looked, an' she tol' me to stay in the kitchen."

"So you think that because you looked, you were bad and now Mommy is leaving. Do you know the real reason Mommy is leaving? The real reason is because Granddaddy hurts her and she can't stop him from hurting her."

"Nuh-huh." Little Barbara shakes her head no.

"I want you to let that picture fade away now, and as I count back from ten to zero, you stay comfortably in your trance, but come up to your present age. Ten, nine, eight, seven, six, five, four, three, two, one, zero. Do you remember what you were just telling me about?"

"Yes."

"How old were you?"

"Two."

"Can you understand that when you were two and you disobeyed your mother by looking, you couldn't think of any other way to explain why your mother left? The only way you could explain it to yourself then was to say you were bad and it was your fault."

Barbara nodded yes and said, "Um-hum."

"Now, it's very important that you recognize the true reason why your mother left you and that that has to do with the way she was treated by Granddaddy. What do you think now that he was doing to her?"

"He raped her."

"He was raping her. Yes. So, it's important that you recognize with the complete powers of your mind now that you're grown, that the true reason your mother left was that she could not accept the abuse any longer. She didn't want to be raped by Granddaddy. Can you see that now?"

"Yes."

"Let that picture fade away and answer me with your fingers. Are there any other experiences with your mother that would be helpful for you to look at today? . . . Yes. When I count to five, move to that experience or event. One, two, three, four, and five. What comes to mind?"

"I'm in the kitchen."

"How old are you?"

"Nine."

"And what's happening there?"

"They're fighting again."

"Who's fighting?"

"My mother and Granddaddy. They're fighting about me."

"What do you hear them say?"

"She said she loves me, and he said she didn't and that I belong to him."

"He doesn't care what she says?"

"No, and she's scared of him. This time she wasn't mad at me, she just had to take me there. She doesn't have a choice."

"So there is a part of your mother that loved you, isn't there?"

"Yes."

"And she fights with Granddaddy, but she can't win the arguments with him, can she?"

"Um-hum. He's mean."

"Does anybody ever win against him?"

"Sometimes Grandma. But nobody else."

"How does it feel inside when you hear your mother saying that she loves you?"

"It feels good."

"Where do you feel that feeling?"

"In my heart."

"That's where love lives, right?"

"Yes."

"Okay. Answer me with your fingers. Is there any other experience with Mother that would be helpful for you to look at? . . . No. All right. What I'd like for you to do is to feel that feeling in your heart, feel that feeling of love that you've discovered is there and was there from the time you were very little. You didn't realize that your mother cared for you and loved you, but she couldn't win the battles with Granddaddy. So she had a harder and harder time being with you and expressing that love. But you know it's there so I want you to feel it right now . . . feel it in a deep, three-dimensional sense, because I want you to follow that feeling to another experience with another mother. A spiritual Mother who, from the time you were a baby, when you were very sick or in danger, would come and love you, too. Let me know when you're in touch with that mother."

"Yes. When I'm a baby, and when I'm four. She came and told me not to cry too much and to fight."

"What do you suppose She meant by that?"

"I didn't want to stay. I didn't want to live. And She said I had to stay in my body and live. She said I had many things to do."

"Do you believe She'll be there for you if you might need Her again?"

"Yes."

"That's so very important for you to know. That you not only have your mother's love, but you have your spiritual Mother's love as well. And what do you need to do about your mother?"

"Understand and forgive."

"What do you understand now?"

"She's not a monster."

"She's a real person who tried to love you. Only a girl of fourteen when you were born, she tried to love you but Granddaddy's abuse drove her away and drove her to hate."

"Yes. That's why she hurt me, to get at him. She thought he loved me, but he didn't love anybody."

"Hate never works, does it? Is that one of the lessons you learned from the Light?"

"Yes. A long time ago. That hate won't work. That is true."

"Do you feel you can forgive your mother now?"

"Yes."

"And an equally important question: Can you forgive yourself for the hateful feelings that you've felt toward her?"

"I don't know. I hurt her by not having anything to do with her all these years. I didn't want to hurt her."

"Do you think that now that you know that your mother did love you, that you can *begin* to do the work of being a little softer toward yourself?"

"Yes."

"Wonderful! All learning and growing is a process, so let this be the beginning of the process of forgiving. Find that place in your heart where you feel the love, where you feel the connection to your mother, to your other Mother, and to everyone in the family of mankind who's ever loved you, because there have been others as well . . . feel that love, feel that connection. It's a powerful connection . . . an attachment to these people that can never be broken. Once there's love, it can never be broken. Feel that love in your heart and let it spread throughout your whole body now as I count from one to ten. . . ."

Barbara opened her eyes, stretched, and beamed. "Do you know that just before I left to come here, my mother called? She somehow found out where I live and got hold of my number."

"What happened?"

"I was real neutral. Cold actually. But now I know that poor woman never had a clue."

"She didn't know how to care for you?"

"No. She must've felt like a jealous older sister. She really thought she could get back at Granddaddy by hurting me. And of course, that evil man never cared what happened to anyone."

"What will you do?"

"I'll write to her. Tell her I need some time. But I think I can make it work. I'm skilled enough and sensitive enough."

"And I'm totally amazed. I'm convinced that you're a much more evolved person than most of us."

Barbara laughed. "I sure don't feel evolved."

"I think your capacity for forgiveness is much greater than mine. Another concern I have is about the clan. Is it dangerous to be in touch with your mother?"

"I don't think so. I think she left before I did when I was seventeen. Remember, I said when I was fourteen, I began going to the Baptist church with her?"

"But isn't she right there in the old neighborhood?"

"No. In fact, the Baptist church we went to was white."

"Really!"

"Yes. I think she was trying to get away from the clan, too."

"Let me ask you something else about mothering. How are you doing with Michelle?"

Barbara showed a glorious smile. "I really love her. I have to work at expressing myself with her though. I was having a hard time after we moved, so I took her to filial therapy."

"I'm not familiar with that."

"It's where you play with your kids; learn to communicate through play. It was important for me because I never knew how to play. We went for about six times, and it helped.

"Michelle can be very strong-willed and difficult, but she's getting more sensitive toward me. Once I was washing my hair at the sink and I was just wearing a bra. She came in to tell me something and saw all the scars on my back. 'Oh, Mom!' she said. 'I knew your mother hurt you, but I didn't know how bad she hurt you.' So, she's sensitive and she also knows, both kids know, to never come up behind me without announcing they're coming. I guess they're more respectful of me."

"As well they should be," I said as I dabbed the tears away from my eyes. "I need to ask something else. For professional reasons . . . people are going to ask me why the past-life regression was important. Why did it work when the traditional therapy wasn't working to get you out of the suicidal thinking?"

"Because I was a lost soul. I really believed the clan had taken my soul. I thought Grandma had taken my heart and there was nothing left for me to do except die. I learned from the past-life work that my soul will never die. My soul is eternal. Also, I learned that I wasn't alone. I'm connected to all of the other souls. And they want to help me. Remember in the between lives state the others were trying to encourage me?"

"Yes. And what would you say are the important lessons from the Light?"

"The biggest one, that it's always there. The Light never left me. I would turn my back when I was angry or wanted to die, but the Light was with me all along. I believe it has been my guiding force."

"Do you think of the Place of Many Lessons as heaven? We use that word in our culture. You never used that word."

"I believe that *heaven* is a term that man made up to describe achieving peace. But to me, it's not tangible. It's a mass of knowledge. It's a mass . . . of lights. All souls have lights . . . eyes.''

"Do you think of eyes because of seeing or understanding knowledge?''

"Yes. Eyes are the 'windows to the soul.' When I look in someone's eyes, I can tell who they are. And I believe eyes never change. You can see if the Light is there. So, I believe that place is peaceful and helpful.''

"And would you term that heaven, or would you really call it, as you did in hypnosis, the Place of Many Lessons?''

"The Place of Many Lessons. I hope this doesn't sound anti-Christian, but I don't believe in heaven and hell. I believe there is a place where all souls ascend to regardless of how you live your life. Because people who do despicable, horrible things come back and maybe despicable, horrible things eventually happen to them. I don't know. But I believe they have to learn certain lessons. I believe there is . . . eternity.''

"Peaceful, helpful, but always more learning?''

"Yes.''

"What else should we talk about today?''

"I still wonder what will happen between you and me.''

"What would you like to happen?''

"I don't want to lose the relationship with you. I never felt I needed friends in the past. But you've taught me about integrating my head and my heart. It feels like a foundation that you're a part of. I don't want to lose that.''

"And my feeling is as I always said to you, that once there's a love bond between people, it never disappears. And it is a spiritual bond, because it doesn't matter how far away in the world you are from a friend, you're always friends.''

"Right. And it has to go both ways. I want to be there for you, too. I learned that from Sharon.''

"Sounds good to me,'' I said.

Barbara wanted this story told. She was pleased and wished to be as helpful as possible when she found I was willing to write the book.

About six months into the writing, I was feeling overwhelmed. I felt I hadn't the time or the experience to produce such a book. On a Wednesday morning, I had run home from my office, after learning of a cancellation, to work at the computer. I was feeling pressured and low when the phone rang.

Barbara was on the other end. "I've been thinking about you nonstop for three days. Are you all right?"

I collapsed into an easy chair. "No, I'm terrible! How did you know? Why would you think to call me at home on a Wednesday morning?"

That low, resonant voice answered, "I don't know. I just knew I had to call."

I complained and carried on about the enormity of the writing project for at least fifteen minutes and then caught myself. "I'm sorry to lay all this on you."

"Wait a minute," she said. "Remember how I told you that our friendship has to work both ways? You've helped me, now I intend to be there for you."

And of course, she kept her word.

As for my personal life, Dan and I continued our fighting until we realized we were placing our relationship and family at risk. We finally called a psychologist friend and convinced him to help us with marriage counseling. After several sessions, we felt as though we had collapsed into an easy chair together. We knew we would be helped. And I knew I would never forget Barbara's last words to me in the office: ". . . I believe [we all] have to learn certain lessons. I believe there is . . . eternity."

For information about hypnosis or past-life regression, contact:

The American Society of Clinical Hypnosis
2200 East Devon Avenue—Suite 291
Des Plaines, IL 60018

The Association for Past-Life Research and Therapies, Inc.
Post Office Box 20151
Riverside, CA 92516

For information regarding cults, contact:

Cult Awareness Network
2421 West Pratt Blvd.
Suite 1173
Chicago, IL 60645

A F T E R W O R D

BY CARL RASCHKE

ITEM. In Clifton, New Jersey, police and local authorities began an investigation into what could have motivated five suburban teenagers to plan the ritualistic death of seventeen-year-old Robert Solimine, Jr. According to press accounts, the five teens admitted to having plotted the murder of Solimine during a "prayer meeting" while a former altar boy strangled him.

ITEM. British police took into a custody a video that, according to the newspapers, "offers the first tangible evidence of satanic ritual abuse" and aired it as part of the television documentary *Dispatches*. The video purports to show the abuse of young adults in a context of "sex and blood rituals" occurring beneath a picture of occultist Aleister Crowley. In an article dated February 16, 1992, in *The Observer*, medical experts and Scotland Yard's Obscene Publications Branch reportedly validated the authenticity of the film. The film contains scenes in which satanic symbols are carved into the flesh of a hooded man, a nude female is bound and raped, and an apparent abortion is performed on another woman. There are also shots of the buggery of Hispanic children. Finally, the video displays the use of drug drips and catheters on a young girl with the same clinical precision that Barbara describes.

Scotland Yard said that the cult members who allegedly made the video had been convicted in the past of "publishing pornography," but that the claims of satanic ritualism had been ignored because "it is is not illegal and disbelief is so strong."

ITEM. A recent *New York Times* article quoted a number of psychiatrists and social theorists who deny that memories of sexual abuse in general, and satanic ritual abuse in particular, are accurate. These professionals have recently formed a not-for-profit organization called the False Memory Syndrome Foundation aimed at "aiding families victimized by [the syndrome], which foundation members describe as adults suddenly 'remembering' that they were sexually abused as children when in fact they never were." A large portion of these allegedly "false" memories, the critics claim, have been induced by the therapeutic process itself.

In a recently published book, however, Minnesota psychologist Dr. Renee Fredrickson has argued that the broad majority of claims concerning sexual abuse in the past are easily corroborated. A 1987 study by Dr. Judith Herman, a Maryland psychiatrist, concluded that about 75 percent of women who told stories of sexual abuse in childhood were able to confirm the facts behind the memory.

Although Gail Feldman, as any responsible professional would do, took Barbara's story to the police and the FBI, there was no response from law enforcement. Inaction in these cases is not uncommon. The problem has nothing to do with the credibility of the therapist, or even in most cases with the facts of the case itself. It has to do with the rules of evidence regarding crimes committed in the relatively distant past, particularly when multiple offenders are involved, and because of prosecutors' fears that the "satanist" factor may confuse, complicate, and possibly "contaminate" the case before it goes to a jury. After the outcome of the McMartin preschool trial in southern California, police may be even more gun-shy.

The anxiety of police and prosecutors over pursuing allegations of satanic ritual abuse, however, would probably not be as strong without the decided influence of a single individual—Kenneth V. Lanning, Supervisory Special Agent for the National Center for the Analysis of Violent Crime with the Federal Bureau of Investigation, Quantico, Virginia.

Lanning has gained a reputation in recent years as the FBI's "authority" on satanism, primarily because he has consistently denied its existence, while overseeing certain cases where the aforementioned types of activity have been alleged. Although the FBI supposedly does not have any "official" position on occult-related crime and violence, and certain other FBI agents with whom I am familiar do not take Lanning's side on the issue, a growing number of local police regard his extreme views as somehow representative of FBI thought and policy.

Proving in a courtroom that ritual abuse has actually occurred, especially when physical evidence is spotty and the events in question have happened in the distant past, can be a forensics nightmare for attorneys. Ironically, juries are often open to hearing, and believing, tales of satanic ritual abuse. If the theater of public opinion were the same as a court of law, prosecution would be much easier. But the American legal system—for good reasons, it turns out—favors the defense, and many technicalities of the rules of evidence militate against introduction of the "satanist factor" from the start. I myself have served as an expert witness and consultant in quite a few court cases, frequently on the side of the defense, and have found objections by the other legal team to the consideration of my testimony upheld by the judge. The reason has little to do with the quality of the testimony. It has to do with the fact that, unfortunately, "religious" motivation—particularly when it is part of the code of a secret society—is deemed irrelevant. Juries are told to concentrate on the external character and behavior of the criminal himself.

The difficulty of obtaining convictions with ritual crimes committed in secret is comparable to the problems that law enforcement officials encounter with organized crime. Small criminal cabals are difficult to monitor and detect. They are even more elusive when it comes to sustaining a criminal brief. Victims of ritual crime will never receive justice until the manipulation of the legal system and law enforcement procedures by clever advocates is braked. The task is arduous, the road ahead steep. But a mounting public awareness of the problem, and perhaps a growing legislative interest in championing the rights of victims, should eventually turn the tide.

It is often the case that the right book at the right time will place the issue in its proper focus, while spurring both the type of public disclosure and legislative initiative necessary to attack the problem. This book seems to have just the right timing.

E D I T O R ' S   N O T E

Lessons in Evil, Lessons
from the Light is para-
mountly a book about evil.
About the human capacity
to inflict evil, to endure it,
and to heal. The accounts
of murder, mutilations, unspeakable child abuse, and sheer
terror that Barbara Maddox witnessed and endured are as
horrifying as any that could be imagined. And yet today she
has come to terms with those memories. While the experiences of her childhood are worse than our worst nightmares,
the story of her personal triumph is a tribute to the strength of
the human soul.

But still, many questions remain unanswered. Why was
nothing done to bring the satanists to justice? Why have the
allegations never been investigated? Is this story of evil incarnate really true?

Dr. Feldman states that she and Barbara Maddox did in fact
pursue prosecution of the case. She claims to have contacted
Mr. Kenneth V. Lanning at the Behavioral Science unit of the

FBI school at Quantico, Virginia, who she reports gave no support or advice, and dismissed the notion of investigating the cult or its activities. We called Mr. Lanning to confirm that information. He did not specifically recall speaking with Dr. Feldman. He said that he receives hundreds of calls every year from therapists and their patients recounting similar experiences, and that he invariably refers them to the local branch office of the FBI, or to the local authorities. Dr. Feldman recalls no such advice or recommendation. We also read Dr. Raschke's afterword to Mr. Lanning. He stated that Dr. Raschke misrepresents his opinions, position, and influence. Mr. Lanning said that he does not deny the possible existence of satanism, or multigenerational satanic cults, but that in no individual case has he found conclusive proof that such cults in fact exist. Doctors Raschke and Feldman argue that reports from all over the country confirm that such cults do exist; Mr. Lanning points out the difference between logical and legal "proof."

Both sides are persuasive. Upon closer scrutiny of their statements it seems that what we have are not so much contradictory accounts as conflicting positions and vantage points. Mr. Lanning is arguing from the position of a law enforcement officer who must investigate and prove each individual case in the legal sense. Accumulated related circumstantial evidence may point to a probability, but does not constitute proof in a court of law; therefore, regardless of Mr. Lanning's personal opinions, his options are limited. Doctors Feldman and Raschke extrapolate the proof of their argument from the suffering of the survivors.

Satanic cults have existed since the Middle Ages. It is of course possible that they do not exist in this country, or to believe that in this century, the Holocaust notwithstanding, humans are no longer capable of such depravity. Yet we feel that to deny the existence of such cults is to deny both a social and human truth, and that in Barbara's case by accepting the reality of the worst, we can also see proof of the best.

REFERENCES

Adler, T. "Victims of Stress Suffer from Intense Thoughts." *APA Monitor* (October 1989): 16.

American Orthopsychiatric Association, Inc. "Human Rights Concern—The Medical Profession and the Prevention of Torture." *ORTHO Newsletter* (Spring 1986).

Anthony, E. J., and B. Cohler, eds. *The Invulnerable Child*. New York: Guilford Press, 1987.

Bak, F. "The Church of Satan in the United States." *Antonianum* (Italy) vol. 50, no. 1–2 (1975): 152–93.

Bakan, D. *Slaughter of the Innocents: A Study of the Battered Child Phenomenon*. Boston: Beacon Press, 1971.

Ben-Sasson, H. *A History of the Jewish People*. Cambridge, Mass.: Harvard University Press, 1976. Page 318.

Bernstein, M. *The Search for Bridey Murphy*. New York: Doubleday, 1956.

Bettelheim, B. *Surviving and Other Essays*. New York: Random House, Vintage Books, 1980.

Bliss, E. *Multiple Personality, Allied Disorders, and Hypnosis*. New York: Oxford University Press, 1986.

Braun, B. Letters to the Editor. *International Society for the*

Study of Multiple Personality and Dissociation Newsletter (March 1989): 11.

————. "Psychotherapy of the Survivor of Incest with a Dissociative Disorder." In *The Psychiatric Clinics of North America: Treatment of Victims of Sexual Abuse,* vol. 12, no. 2, ed. R. Kluft, 307–24. Philadelphia: W. B. Saunders Co., 1989.

Buie, J. "Age, Race, Gender, All Influence PTSD." *APA Monitor* (December 1989).

Caputi, J. *The Age of Sex Crime.* Bowling Green, Ohio: Bowling Green State University, 1987.

Carmen, E., and P. Rieker. "A Psychosocial Model of the Victim-to-Patient Process." In *The Psychiatric Clinics of North America: Treatment of Victims of Sexual Abuse,* vol. 12, no. 2, ed. R. Kluft, 431–43. Philadelphia: W. B. Saunders Co., 1989.

Carr, A. *The Reptiles.* New York: Time Incorporated, 1963.

Chandler, D. *Brothers in Blood: The Rise of the Criminal Brotherhoods.* New York: E. P. Dutton, 1975.

Coons, P., E. Bowman, T. Pellow, and P. Schneider. "Post-Traumatic Aspects of the Treatment of Victims of Sexual Abuse and Incest." In *The Psychiatric Clinics of North America: Treatment of Victims of Sexual Abuse,* vol. 12, no. 2, ed. R. Kluft, 325–36. Philadelphia: W. B. Saunders Co., 1989.

Cranston, S., and C. Williams. *Reincarnation: A New Horizon in Science, Religion, and Society.* New York: Julian Press (Crown Publishers), 1984.

Cressey, D. *Theft of a Nation.* New York: Harper and Row, 1969.

Deikman, A. *The Wrong Way Home.* Boston: Beacon Press, 1990.

Doore, G., ed. *What Survives? Contemporary Explorations of Life After Death.* Los Angeles: Jeremy Tarcher, 1990.

Fine, R. *The Meaning of Love in Human Experience.* New York: John Wiley & Sons, 1985.

Finkelhor, D. *Child Sexual Abuse.* New York: Macmillan, 1984.

Fiore, E. *You Have Been Here Before.* New York: Ballantine Books, 1986.

Firestone, R. *The Fantasy Bond.* New York: Human Services Press, 1985.

Firth, R. "Offering and Sacrifice: Problems of Organization." In *Reader in Comparative Religion,* ed. W. Lessa and E. Vogt. Evanston, Ill.: Row, Peterson, 1958.

Frank, J. Restoration of Morale and Behavior Change. In *What Makes Behavior Change Possible?* ed. A. Burton, 73–95. New York: Brunner/Mazel, 1976.

Freud, S. "Remembering, Repeating and Working Through." In *Complete Psychological Works,* standard ed., vol. 12. London: Hogarth Press, 1914.

Gallant, S. "Overview of the Occult"; "History of the Occult/ Satanism in the 1980s"; "Youth Culture and Satanism"; "Ritualistic Sexual Abuse of Children and Investigatory Problems"; "Ritualistic Homicides/Voodoo, Witchcraft, and Satanism." *Occult Activities and Satanism in America.* Five sixty-minute audiocassettes. Mill Valley, Calif.: William Shear Associates, 1990.

Ganaway, G. "Historical Versus Narrative Truth: Clarifying the Role of Exogenous Trauma in the Etiology of MPD and Its Variants." *Dissociation* 2, no. 4 (1989): 205–19.

Gimbutas, M. *The Goddesses and Gods of Old Europe.* Berkeley and Los Angeles: University of California Press, 1982.

Goodwin, J. *Sexual Abuse: Incest Victims and Their Families.* Boston, Bristol, London: John Wright, PSG, Inc., 1982.
    . "Sadistic Sexual Abuse: Illustrations from the Marquis de Sade." Paper presented at the Seventh International Conference on Multiple Personality/Dissociative States, Chicago, November 1990.

Goodwin, J., and N. Talwar. "Group Therapy for Victims of Incest." In *The Psychiatric Clinics of North America: Treatment of Victims of Sexual Abuse,* vol 12, no. 2, ed. R. Kluft, 279–93. Philadelphia: W. B. Saunders Co., 1989.

Harrower, M. "Rorschach Records of the Nazi War Criminals: An Experimental Study After 30 Years." *Journal of Personality Assessment* 40, no. 4 (August 1976): 341–51.

Hastings, J. "Sacrifice." In *Encyclopedia of Religion and Ethics,* vol. 11 (1928, reprinted 1955): 1–39.

Head, Joseph and Sylvia Cranston. *Reincarnation: The*

Phoenix Fire Mystery. San Diego: Point Loma Publications, 1991.

Hicks, R. "Police Pursuit of Satanic Crime." *Skeptical Inquirer* 14 (Spring 1990): 276–86.

Hill, S., and J. Goodwin. "Satanism: Similarities Between Patient Accounts and Pre-Inquisition Historical Sources." *Dissociation* 2, no. 1 (March 1989): 39–44.

Jensen, A. *Myth and Cult Among Primitive Peoples.* Chicago and London: University of Chicago Press, 1963.

Johnson, R. A. *We: Understanding the Psychology of Romantic Love.* San Francisco: Harper & Row, 1983.

Kahaner, L. *Cults That Kill.* New York: Warner Books, 1988.

Kaye, M., and L. Klein. "Clinical Indicators of Satanic Cult Victimization." Unpublished case notes, 1985–87.

Keith, A. *The Religion and Philosophy of the Veda and Upanishads,* vol. 2. Livingston, N.J.: Orient Book Distributors, 1925.

Kendrick, T. *The Druids: A Study in Keltic Prehistory.* London: Methuen & Co. Ltd., 1927.

Kerlinsky, D., and A. Costa. "Psychiatric Aspects of Childhood and Adolescent Involvement in Satanic Cult Practices." Unpublished paper, 1988.

Klaits, J. *Servants of Satan: The Age of the Witch Hunts.* Bloomington, Ind.: Indiana University Press, 1985.

Kluft, R. "Thoughts on Childhood Multiple Personality Disorder." *Dissociation* 3, no. 1 (March 1990): 1–2.

———, ed. *Childhood Antecedents of Multiple Personality.* Washington, D.C.: American Psychiatric Press, Inc., 1985.

Krickeberg, W. *Pre-Columbian American Religions.* New York: Holt, Rinehart & Winston, 1968, English translation.

La Vey, A. *The Satanic Bible.* New York: Avon Books, 1969.

Lewis, C. S. *The Screwtape Letters.* New York: Macmillan Publishing Company, 1961.

Lifton, R. *Thought Reform and the Psychology of Totalism.* Chapel Hill, N.C.: University of North Carolina Press, 1989.

Lifton, Robert Jay. *The Nazi Doctors.* New York: Basic Books, 1986.

Malinowski, B. *Magic, Science and Religion.* New York: Doubleday & Co., 1948.

Michener, J. *Caribbean.* New York: Random House, 1989.

Moody, Raymond, Jr. *Life After Life.* New York: Bantam Books, 1975.

———. *Reflections on Life After Life.* New York: Bantam Books, 1977.

Nathanson, D. "Understanding What Is Hidden: Shame in Sexual Abuse." In *The Psychiatric Clinics of North America: Treatment of Victims of Sexual Abuse,* vol. 12, no. 2, ed. R. Kluft, 381–88. Philadelphia: W. B. Saunders Co., 1989.

Olson, J., K. Mayton, and N. Kowal-Ellis. "Secondary Post-Traumatic Stress Disorder: Therapist Response to the Horror." Paper presented at the Fourth International Conference on Multiple Personality/Dissociative States, Chicago, November 1987.

Panos, P., A. Panos, and H. Allred. "The Need for Marriage Therapy in the Treatment of Multiple Personality Disorder." *Dissociation* 3, no. 1 (March 1990): 10–14.

Peck, M. S. *People of the Lie: The Hope of Healing Evil.* New York: Simon & Schuster, 1983.

Piggott, S. *The Druids.* New York: Praeger Publishers, 1975.

Pulling, P. *The Devil's Web.* Lafayette, La.: Huntington House, 1989.

Putnam, F. *Diagnosis and Treatment of Multiple Personality Disorder.* New York: Guilford Press, 1989.

Raschke, Carl. *Painted Black.* San Francisco: Harper & Row, 1990.

Russell, J. B. *The Prince of Darkness: Radical Evil and the Power of Good in History.* London: Thames and Hudson, 1988.

Schatzow, E., and J. Herman. "Breaking Secrecy: Adult Survivors Disclose to Their Families." In *The Psychiatric Clinics of North America: Treatment of Victims of Sexual Abuse,* vol. 12, no. 2, ed. R. Kluft, 337–50. Philadelphia: W. B. Saunders Co., 1989.

Scobie, A. *Murder for Magic: Witchcraft in Africa.* London: Cassell & Co., Ltd., 1965.

Sereny, G. "Children of the Reich." *Vanity Fair* (July 1990): 127–30.

Shengold, L. "The Effects of Overstimulation: Rat People." *The International Journal of Psycho-Analysis* 48, pt. 3 (1967): 403–15.

———. "Child Abuse and Deprivation: Soul Murder." *Journal of American Psychoanalytic Association* 27 (1979): 533–59.

———. *Soul Murder*. New York and London: Yale University Press, 1989.

Singer, I. *The Jewish Encyclopedia*. New York: KTAV Publishing, 1901.

Singer, M. "Consultation with Families of Cultists." In *Systems Consultation: A New Perspective for Family Therapy*, ed. L. Wynne, S. McDaniel, and T. Weber. New York: Guilford Press, 1986.

Sklar, D. *The Nazis and the Occult*. New York: Dorset Press, 1977.

Smith, M., and L. Pazder, *Michelle Remembers*. New York: Simon & Schuster, 1980.

Smith, R. C. *Edgar Cayce: You Can Remember Your Past Lives*. New York: Warner Books, 1989.

Sondern, F. *Brotherhood of Evil*. New York: Farrar, Straus & Cudahy, 1959.

Spence, L. *The History and Origins of Druidism*. New York, Melbourne, Sydney, Capetown: Rider and Co., 1949.

Spiegel, D. "Hypnosis in the Treatment of Victims of Sexual Abuse." In *The Psychiatric Clinics of North America: Treatment of Victims of Sexual Abuse*, vol. 12, no. 2, ed. R. Kluft, 295–306. Philadelphia: W. B. Saunders Co., 1989.

Spiegel, D., T. Hunt, and H. Dondershine. "Dissociation and Hypnotizability in Posttraumatic Stress Disorders." *American Journal of Psychiatry* 145, no. 3 (March 1988): 301–5.

Stearn, J. *The Search for the Girl with the Blue Eyes*. New York: Doubleday, 1968.

———. *The Search for a Soul: Taylor Caldwell's Psychic Lives*. New York: Doubleday, 1973.

Stephenson, J. *Women's Roots*. Rapu, Calif.: Diemer, Smith Publishing Co., 1984.

Stone, M. *When God Was a Woman*. New York: Dorset Press, 1976.

———. "Individual Psychotherapy with Victims of Incest." In *The Psychiatric Clinics of North America: Treatment of Victims of Sexual Abuse*, vol. 12, no. 2, ed. R. Kluft, 237–56. Philadelphia: W. B. Saunders Co., 1989.

Summit, R. "The Centrality of Victimization: Regaining the Focal Point of Recovery for Survivors of Child Sexual Abuse." In *The Psychiatric Clinics of North America: Treatment of Victims of Sexual Abuse*, vol. 12, no. 2, ed. R. Kluft, 413–40. Philadelphia: W. B. Saunders Co., 1989.

Talbot, Michael. *Your Past Lives: A Reincarnation Handbook*. New York: Crown Publishers, 1987.

van Berschoten, S. "Multiple Personality Disorder and Satanic Ritual Abuse: The Issue of Credibility." *Dissociation* 3, no. 1 (1990): 22–30.

van der Hart, O., P. Brown, and R. Turco. "Hypnotherapy for Traumatic Grief: Janetian and Modern Approaches Integrated." *American Journal of Clinical Hypnosis* 32, no. 4 (April 1990): 263–71.

van der Kolk, B., and O. van der Hart. "Pierre Janet and the Breakdown of Adaptation in Psychological Trauma." *American Journal of Psychiatry* 146, no. 12 (December 1989): 1530–40.

Van Dyke, A. "Feminist Curing Ceremonies: The Goddess in Contemporary Spiritual Traditions." Ph. D. diss., University of Minnesota, 1987.

Wambach, H. *Relieving Past Lives: The Evidence Under Hypnosis*. New York: Harper & Row, 1978.

Wedeck, H. *A Treasury of Witchcraft*. Secaucus, N.J.: Citadel Press, 1961.

Weiss, B. *Many Lives, Many Masters*. New York: Simon & Schuster, 1988.

Welwood, J. *Journey of the Heart: Intimate Relationship and the Path of Love*. New York: Harper Collins, 1990.

Wheeler, B., S. Wood, and R. Hatch. "Assessment and Intervention with Adolescents Involved in Satanism." *Social Work* 33, no. 6 (1988): 547–50.

Yang, C. *Religion in Chinese Society.* Berkeley, Calif.: University of California Press, 1961.

Young, W., R. Sachs, B. Braun, and R. Watkins. "Patients Reporting Ritual Abuse." *International Journal of Child Abuse and Neglect* (January 1991).

Zalantes, M. *Cults: Faith, Healing and Coercion.* Oxford and New York: Oxford University Press, 1989.